EXPERIENCE OF SPONTANEITY

Peter Slade

LONGMAN

LONGMAN GROUP LIMITED
London
Associated companies, branches and representatives throughout the world

© *Longman Group Ltd (formerly Longmans, Green and Co Ltd)*

First published 1968
Second impression 1969

SBN 582 31028 8

*Printed in Great Britain by
Lowe & Brydone (Printers) Ltd., London*

To my wife Xonia,
who helped me
sort out many descriptions
of past events

Acknowledgements

I wish to express my thanks to the Education Authorities of Staffordshire and Birmingham in whose areas so many opportunities came my way; to those H.M.I.s, University, College and Home Office staff, present and past, who perceived what I meant and stood by me; to those doctors, psychologists and Churchmen who first took my work on trust and then started to use it; to all actors, professional and amateur, who have worked under my direction and taught me more about believable education; to all those who have contributed to knowledge on spontaneity; to members of the Educational Drama Association and friends; and to many who, down the years, have sent messages from far corners of the Earth and have allowed me to share their enthusiasm and their loneliness.

PETER SLADE

The publishers and the author are grateful to the *Birmingham Post & Mail* and Cater's News Agency for permission to reproduce photographs.

Introduction

In an age that one fears may be growing rapidly more selfish, materialist and rude, I should like to draw attention again to some of the simple and gay things in life, for they are what make it worth living. Such matter must, of necessity, be somewhat subjective, for all of us have different views on what is amusing or interesting and as the material has been taken from my own close experience and covers quite a number of years, it cannot help but be partly biographical. It has something to do with drama, but is much more nearly a function of everyday life, where spontaneity, natural wit, courage in adversity, sympathy with sorrow or just sheer high spirits contribute to all that might be called the golden hour. People often ask me now, 'How did all this begin with you? What influenced you to start thinking the way you do?' My final decision to write was because of continual remarks such as 'but that's all very well in such and such a case, but it would never work with so and so'. In nearly every case the person just happened to be in another situation, that is all, and because the unnoticed or undeveloped power of improvisation is in all of us, I have chosen instances of as many different people and backgrounds as possible, including young people and adults, as so many requests came also for descriptions of activities with older age groups than those outlined in my first book *Child Drama*. So when anyone tends to say 'You can't do that' with any given group, my mind nearly always leaps to attention with the cry 'Oh surely—yes, you can', for I find I have often done it. Maybe it is really a question of having a belief and joy in poetic values, seeing beauty in everyday things, or perhaps just being young in heart.

I would like to encourage all who read this, at least for a spell, to be young in heart again.

PETER SLADE

Contents

Illustrations

I. The Nature of Spontaneity

Spontaneity at its best and most attractive is an expression of joy. But it can be a purge for sadness also. In the following pages examples of both are given, together with many intermediate stages and suggestions of ways in which we can make use of this dynamic phenomenon in human nature. Spontaneous expression is perhaps easier to notice in the child, yet it has its primitive and advanced forms amongst adults also. It can be in words, dance, music, affection or in everyday action, kind or unkind, generous or vindictive, in loyalty to a cause or in a sudden burst of reaction such as treachery. But generally it has come to be associated with something gay, constructive and attractive. The *Oxford English Dictionary* describes spontaneity as voluntary or unconstrained action or movement . . . arising from natural impulses. Certainly impulse is there in a spontaneous moment and always perhaps the feeling of impulsive and sudden, often unexpected, even to the person creating. 'It just slipped out', 'It sort of came to me' are common descriptions of spontaneous actions and remarks (also even of bits of 'business' in theatre). One person who was renowned for dropping bricks used to say 'It was out again before I could stop it'. Voluntary it must always be and unconstrained it may often be, but need not be, for spontaneous impulse can be guided. Indeed, if our instincts were not somewhat eased into a mould there could be no civilisation. So that it is the best of this quality which one wants to foster and preserve and attitudes and environment which will encourage and improve it.

Regular opportunity plays a great part in development of spontaneity, though unexpected opportunity may also provide release.

As to the inference that this quality must always be of the person alone, without outside instigation or inspiration, I doubt whether this is always true. Spontaneity only seems so, partly perhaps because it arises often quite suddenly from the unconscious; but what sparked it off? There is nearly always something from outside which causes the attitude or provokes the impulse. It is generally a situation in human terms and the apparent spontaneous action suddenly happens because of how the individual assesses or wishes to use the situation. He may be wrong about it but reacts swiftly one way or the other. This is nowhere more clear (apart from the more violent forms of 'unconstrained actions') than in daily conversation. For, after all, conversation is improvised dialogue and each word and thought follows from a lead given by someone or by something happening. It is good conversation either by natural talent and affected by environment or, much more so, by practice in communication. This practice must start when young, to establish Language Flow, preferably at home but certainly in the infant and junior school. If equal opportunity in education is to be anything more than lip service, the least we can do is to help young people to sort their ideas and be able to express them. After this may follow the refined art of conversation and discussion. Because of many pressures and inventions today, the art of conversation is dying. Television tends to put a brake on conversation at home but occasionally has programmes which include conversation as such. One is often struck, however, by the number of people who cannot speak a straight sentence nor wait for others to speak. The rudeness of interruption, particularly in political discussions, is often disappointing and could do with firmer chairmanship to civilise it. It lacks the art of timing which is the chariot of wit. Wit is a dying thing because, like conversation itself, it needs to be sharpened. It arises suddenly, is unexpected, spontaneous, but appears in flashes as mind duels with mind.

Practice in improvised dialogue can help us here, for it adds to the speed of reply. Do we not often feel too slow when in society of others? Someone else may jump in first and the conversation may turn another way, it is too late for our clever remark. Sometimes we think long afterwards of a devastating reply, 'But of course I couldn't think of it at the time'. This practice in improvised speech is important for some slow-minded people and children, for constant failure to establish your thoughts can lead to speed anxiety and thus even to stammering, though usually (one hopes) to not more than a mild inferiority. Spontaneous dialogue certainly aids the development of individuality, for voice—indeed any expression—is a very personal thing and has its own intimate flavour and style, which strengthens in purpose and flexibility and range as the mind uses the physical organ. Out of this ability for sudden creation arose the dialogues that in wit and thrust blossomed into the Commedia dell'Arte, littering Europe with characters, situations and conventions which were to last many years after, from Goldoni to the present day.

It is worth noting that much of this spontaneous speech seems to have arisen between characters that became rather set. I mention later on this rut of rôle playing, as it affects delinquency, but for the moment will confine myself to the fact that actually to assume another character or rôle often provides stimulus for new ideas, which form a Language Flow. Children often find this when providing the voice of their Teddy Bear or doll. One of my own forms of indulgence is to spout improvised Milton by the yard, but when I remember a certain master at school and become him, I spout much better. This may well have been part of the strength of the Commedia. The rôles were built so well that a person more or less became them and this itself produced a large part of the flood of invention. This again is what I mean, when saying that situation or circumstance can provide inspiration, which ultimately releases the inner creation; there is something which starts it off. Certainly a good start can often provoke good follow-on, though too much structuring or imposition will kill. Perhaps that is why I first invented the Ideas Game. This is where you ask for ideas, or select some, and out of several quite separate suggestions weave a story which can be acted. Often, the very incongruity of the ideas forces one, almost, to invent. It is extremely useful if you suddenly find you have no ideas at all (see page 120, a report on the Youth Club at Rugeley). We can all feel ourselves in this forsaken state at times and I hope the examples given later will help and encourage those using improvisation in clubs for young people, social groups and schools.

What is the value of spontaneity? Many people still think it unnecessary or a waste of time. Apart from developing the ability to speak (and incidentally to write with more imagination), other qualities become evident—a growing absorption in the task and a sincerity about the way of doing it, particularly in children, useful for all learning and general attitudes to life; also a mounting confidence and ultimately a mounting happiness. I count this as important for, in an age of materialism many of us are too consciously in pursuit of happiness and do not always achieve it. By allowing the unconscious to flow in a simple and natural way we achieve the golden hour or moment, sometimes in unforgettable companionship and joy.[1]

In schools, of course, spontaneous work can bring great happiness. I am not one who thinks school need be an unhappy place, and many are the 'unexpected' youngsters who have *wanted* to go to school because of this exercise. But there is skill in the guiding. Purpose must be envisaged and techniques worked out and known. These can vary from the simplest building of a story round a room, piece by piece with individual children, followed by work with partners and then groups, to helping patients to speak at all, through such things as letting them create poetry to gramophone music, or just sing in the bath. It is through purpose in this sense and its accompanying technique that the best group work emerges, either in education or theatre training. Not through dominated production but by vitalising a moment correctly, so that interplay of the highest quality can take place. During this process, forms of group sensitivity, group intuition and awareness of the needs of others, appropriate behaviour for a given situation and lessons in harmonious aesthetic achievement can be learnt, both in speech and movement, but better perhaps than in any other way.

In guiding spontaneity, teachers and youth club leaders often talk too much. We must be ready for the moments when those taking part seize upon an idea and make it their own. Time must

[1] Something of this can happen in the theatre too, but only when spontaneity is a quality of the acting. You know at once if it is there for it is electric (both actors and audience share something special) and I personally die yet another death if it is not. Michael MacOwen, former Director of the London Academy of Music and Dramatic Art also describes this as 'lit up'.

[4]

be allowed for *them* to create, although you may have worked pretty hard to build up an atmosphere (see the description of 'Flood and Mermaids to the Rescue', p. 129, and 'Currant Buns', p. 83). Give plenty of suggestions about what to do but don't show how to do it. That must normally be left to the group. It is easy to 'show how'. You get quicker results sometimes, but not necessarily of the right kind and in the end your group begins to depend too much upon you and gets lazy at just that emotional point which should be the climax of imaginative invention. Analyse yourself fearlessly. Why do you do it? An honest answer may well alter your habit.

Finally we see that spontaneity can lead to a religious experience by way of absorption and sincerity (see 'Unserious Leading to Serious', p. 126).

In my short introduction to this book I express the hope that readers will become young in heart again. I certainly want this, but more also. The book began because so many people asked me to follow up my first writing with descriptions of work with older groups, then they began to ask for histories of certain sides of the work and finally for autobiographical details. I tried therefore to weld these things together and only expected at first to offer a simple collection of the descriptions themselves. Indeed the book can still be read in that way only, if preferred. Or the descriptions can be read first, with reference to comments (which are printed in a distinctive type) as a follow up. Friends, readers and finally my publisher suggested that the detailed comments should be added, so that the full purpose of the work and the deeper philosophy might emerge. I am grateful to them for making me bring a number of ideas to consciousness and set them down.

In the first section of the reports it will be noticed how spontaneity flows out of a child, then out of older people as a natural thing. As we go along the reader may see how, down the years, I began to use this quality more consciously for constructive ends and began to find techniques for various purposes. The one which stands out is the Ideas Game. Although many other ways of starting have been used, the game more often sparked off the particular stories which seemed, out of hundreds, to be most worth the telling. After such experiences, groups may make up stories by themselves. In the autobiographical parts I have tried to be honest even where it did not necessarily show me in a very good light. I now see this all more objectively and include parts which might be of value (particularly the early years) for parents, nursery schools, psychologists and child guidance clinics, if only because it is so extremely difficult to obtain categoric descriptions of behaviour and material of this kind.

The descriptions themselves make a sort of history, but for the reasons stated, some more detailed history has been added. As more and more improvisation is used in education (for social reasons) and in professional theatre training, it is good to keep the record straight. I would like to pay tribute to the early work of Miss Mary Kelly in the 1920s, of A. S. Neill and Robert G. Newton in the 1930 depression and after, also of Miss Frances Mackenzie. Although many others have used improvisation, no doubt, before and after the 1930 period, it has been my great pleasure to have seen numbers of people, who have worked with me at one time or another since then, rise to important positions and use their influence in this field, both in creation and in training others. It would not be possible to record all their names (nor, of course, the many who have told me that some remark or writing of mine started them off) but my regard, in this country, goes to Brian Way, who worked with me for a number of years, my admiration to Caryl Jenner, an old friend, who was in one of my early companies and has striven so hard for Children's Theatre; to my wife for her work with women's groups; to Andrew Campbell for organising so many important events; also to Jack Beckett and Tom Fisher, to Barbara Mogford and John Hudson, Janet Goodridge (née Erridge) and Audrey Stanley, to Stanley Evernden and Margaret Faulkes, to John Hodgson and Leslie Williams, Rodney Wood, Ken Tucker, Derek Bowskill, to Tom Knowles and John Ball and very particularly to Phyl Lutley; lastly to Sylvia Demmery who has worked so closely with me and who, like Brian Way, has represented me and taken my methods to various parts of the world.

A special mention for Kenneth R. Scott and A. E. Thomas whose friendship often sustained me. To these and a number of young Drama Advisers, professional actors, some university staff,

[6]

psychologists, doctors, members of the Educational Drama Association, tutors in Colleges of Education, students, young people and many many children I am grateful for creating things with me, discussing important aspects, building wisdom together and discovering therefrom more about the nature of spontaneity.

Other important names entirely in their own right in the Creative Drama world, almost all of whom have come slightly into my orbit, but all of whom I would wish to count as allies are: Stephen Joseph,[1] E. J. Burton, Peter Clough, Pamela Chapman, Patsie Yardley, Alan Garrard, R. N. Pemberton-Billing, Marjorie Sigley, Richard Courtney, Patricia Yates, Dorothy Heathcote, Gavin Bolton, David Gordon, and David Lyttle and Vera Gray (of the B.B.C. Education Department, who kindly attended my Summer Schools and London Dance Groups). There is also a large army of people who may agree with me but whom I do not know.

[1] Whose death became known after this was written.

II. Descriptions of Spontaneous Experience

FROM KITCHEN TO CONFERENCE TABLE

Some years ago now I wrote 'The truth will no doubt have been guessed before now. The organic development of Child Drama does not stop. It goes on well into Youth-Club age and can have a strong influence even on the adult work that follows.' Spontaneous work can precede, go parallel with, or be associated with early script play trials to improve the acting and vitalise the scene in theatre work, though improvisation is an art in itself. Many people have asked me for descriptions of work after childhood, drama advisers, teachers, psychologists, professional actors, tutors at colleges and, again and again, students. Here they are, though it seemed ultimately that it would be better to try and show a whole development, from young to old and in places show the bridge between improvisation and theatre and other subjects; for although spontaneity is normally accepted as associated with a first creation, it is a quality and adaptation for good purpose may be tolerated. Repetition can be tolerated and approved if it contains an illusion of immediate spontaneity also, for this can only be present if a reenactment or reliving is there. It must have *life*. It is at this point that the first spontaneous outburst becomes a play and in many instances is the basis of theatre for children, particularly for juniors and of fascinating creations by older children and young adults. Here then are the descriptions that partly include, but generally follow, childhood.

Search for Joy

Earliest memories, smells, pain, war and peace under the kitchen table

Young children live fully like poets. To explore, discover prove and then rejoice should be their heritage. The rejoicing arises out of total expression, forms of flinging your whole self against the sky on mountain tops in innocent festivity. You are spiritual and animal all at once. A sound, a smell, a feel has a richness bathed in wonder, that in later years may soon be lost. Only the fortunate retain it. In the courage of the young, unhappiness is foiled, for most of us find ways through and the bursting of the bonds is the moment when a light turns on. Such golden moments should be held, in the memory if need be, but by the wise at all times, even now. For we can re-remember and can help others to remember by discovering again the simple experiences of life at depth, the beauty. So many people are afraid of beauty, even the word. They become hardened against it like belief in Father Christmas, or sickened by its over use. But by rediscovery we set off a chain of little memory explosions, which otherwise our anxious worldly minds had missed—wordly without knowing the world which lives. To savour a thing and recognise it, as it happens *now* is the pleasure of the wise. No book on spontaneity would be complete without reference to the child, indeed it would be an insult to deny the early years as part of growing man.

The immediately following reports are set down and offered then in the hope that a memory may be evoked in many minds and perhaps some ancient jewel restored. Out of the simplest thing is spontaneity itself released and the great overcoming is then set loose for the child to be a hero. It is not your childhood of which I write, it is of course my own. But even in essential difference, if you will not be bored or angered but objectively remember, I trust that some of it will suddenly be yours as well.

1. Overture and Beginners

Not 1812 but 1912 onwards

Of my birth at Chernocke House in the High Street of Fleet in Hampshire, there are naturally no memories; nor conscious ones of boots thrown at my head by big brother nor of being suffocated practically for good by a maid. And of London, in the beginning of the first World War, they are somewhat vague, tinged with such items as 'an ossifer on a friksy horse', prayers such as 'God bless the appelins (Zeppelins) and make 'em good boys', the smell of balloons round the old woman at Kensington Gardens, and the match seller with big feet at Holland Park; also the drone of voices across a square like gongs and bees, when you are hidden as one small tear under a huge weeping summer willow and the slush-slush of leaves in Autumn, which incense the mind as you snow-plough through them, chanting as you go. Later in London, things become a little clearer; hotel gongs, family meals; meringues on Sunday; chocolate elephants with string in their legs. You wait and hope for it, biting through, then suck the foot off, before the neck turns to hot mud. Boys running in rows like birds, roller-skating noises— older children tromboning along with rhythmic clicks; me dancing along between the pavement cracks and jumping 'doyng' on the manholes; a horse on its bottom on Notting Hill; unable to rise on the ice, it sat there comfortably, almost as if reading the paper, in its armchair of shafts. Red generals, National steam buses and 'pirates'. A haunted house and a man singing 'Once in Royal David's city' with slanting stripes of snow behind him. Yachts on the round pond and hungry ducks. And the children's bands. These were wonderful. Throngs of children using paper on combs and home-made drums and other instruments not hitherto known much to man. We always hoped to see one marching about. Some of them were so good that they stopped the traffic; they stopped everybody. Once I saw a policeman stop traffic *for* them as they wheeled smartly across a main road (Bayswater Road and into what is now Queensway).

Then my father went to Egypt suddenly, by telephone, I told people, in a funny yellow suit with straps called Sam Brown. Later the funny suit came back and I played cricket with a moustache and braces in the garden.

From then events begin to focus, like marks on walls of flooded basement flats and my first school belt with an 'S' snake clasp. Tight and hot. Tight, tighter, in case they fall down. 'What are you doing with your clay? You are just smoothing it flat. Naughty boy, you've done nothing.'

'Have. It's a tennis court.'

Followed fearful raffia napkin rings and threading thongs through leather holes. Gold star for good work. Pride. Hours of play with toy soldiers. Loving one stuffed monkey, beating another —the new one. Better, much better—beating my French governess till she left. Being left to be attacked by a swan at Hampstead, being left behind corners on every walk, to make me scream. Putting sand in a suspect German boy's eye, till he died of closed-up-throat-in-the-night (grown-ups told us this in hushed voices after he had disappeared for ages), having my wrists tied up in a Spanish girl's long black hair, who was fellow prisoner over the bars of a drain. The oozing slime beneath had bubbles that burst like poached eggs at breakfast. Rows with big brother, angry eyes and twisting of wrists; trying out twisting smaller children's wrists when not being twisted oneself: nicer. Pinched by a fat girl in school, often. Can't do it back. Gentlemen don't. So, one day, I kicked her in the dark and no one knew who. My first Indian suit, but my brother had one too. I cut my hand and could wear a bandage and be different. It hurt, making the cut last longer. Then my soldier suit. Red tabs at last and a staff officer's cap. My brother didn't have one.

I was a person.

But my first strong memories are of our return to Chernocke House, in recent years a bridge club, a library, then an old ladies home, I am told. My brother had gone to school, to our mutual satisfaction poor lad, for who can tolerate a chap born three years after you. I played the Dormouse in the Mad Hatter's tea party, wearing large cardboard ears on my officer's hat. Some early events are in misty order, but this must have been when four or five years of age, in my mother's honour, whom I only saw, it seemed, for about an hour after tea each day. My brother, home again for the holidays, was Mad Hatter. He talked very loud and said the Dormouse was stupid. Why couldn't it talk instead of going to sleep? Luckily he went away to school again and I could get on with the serious business of the War. The programme was: out before breakfast, if you didn't get caught, to see the grown-up soldiers march off, and standing to attention while your face was slapped by a Nurse, if you were. During the morning, some schooling and the making of mud cannon balls. Apple bombs were good too, because they burst and burned a broken brown patch like gunpowder on new white walls, but the gardener didn't like it. Learning 'poyms' in the afternoon, frantic, ghastly, sentimental rhyming slosh, and forced resting. But after tea, that was the time. Seeing mother for a short while, then 'Battle' with the cook. The cook was Nellie and she was my friend. She was deaf, so she put up with my noise and I always hoped she would save me from the slapping. Sometimes she did, when she heard it. Years later, I dedicated the last section of my first book to her, in memory of the marvellous moments she allowed me. 'Battle' was an intense, violent and prolonged private game. Nellie was just there, she didn't take part but she was 'with' me all the time, living almost every moment. (Young teachers of young children could have learnt a lot from her.) I fought, I threw cushion bombs, I shot German after German, thousands and thousands of them. I died and died with terrible wounds and grinding groans but always rose again, for Child Drama is full of the symbol of resurrection. Down the years, each evening after tea, I fought my War, sometimes with hats suggested by Nellie, sometimes as a ghost after being blown to bits. One of the first major disappointments of my life was when the Armistice was signed and it was explained by grown-ups that you couldn't go on shooting now. I dutifully and gravely entered the railway carriage and signed the peace of Europe, on savage terms, under the kitchen table. All one can say is that the outbursts must have had great cathartic effect, for I have less inclination for war now and the changed situation led to more peaceful play *upon* the kitchen table, 'shooting the rabbits' (rapids) of Canada. Later on, Nellie had to join in and sometimes took paddle in rough water. But, all young warriors, be warned: gosh it's awful to have a woman in a boat, specially if it's a canoe: they're so stupid.

When you are just cracking on a rock, they do the wrong thing; then laugh.

What grown-up can ever do quite the right thing all the time, for a child of that age? The tiny child is producer, actor *and* critic, whilst becoming Emperor despot of the physical and emotional circle round it's body. Only later comes the complicating discovery that other people have their private empire too.

COMMENT

These impressions from early childhood show how the senses impinge on memory when the first elementary contacts with the world are being made—elementary noises and smells. Something of the bewilderment caused by a parent suddenly disappearing because of war is here also and the deep record-cutting on the mind of particular remarks by adults. Notice the intense desire for individuality, even to making a cut hand last longer, so as to wear a bandage to be different from an elder brother. Finally, one may only feel a *person* when at last you are dressed differently from an elder brother, that is dressed with supposed distinction.

I suggest exercises sometimes, to music, for students and older people, to enable them to discover textures or colours about a room and to rediscover a few moments of pleasure in a very simple way, either for themselves or with the purpose of understanding children better. One of the lessons of this first description is that one should take the young child's dramatic play seriously and see that it can have a perfectly natural cathartic effect. The child's discovery of its own individuality is bound up with this too—how one expresses at all, then what one expresses and finally discovering that other people express too. Discovering the private empire of other people is part of learning to live with others successfully. Parents help individual children to integrate with friends or family and teachers help children to deal with the larger unit of a class. It is not always realised how bewildering it can be for a very young child to meet so many children at once in a new school. It sometimes tends to have the effect of difficulty in making a relationship with anyone. Spontaneous play can help here if, in their Child Drama, children are allowed to have their own space, their own circle, their own empire; and if teacher is telling a story each person can then take each part or character as the story goes along. Formal casting of parts is nearly always done too early. It is doubtful whether it should come much before six-and-a-half years of age at the 'dawn of seriousness'.

2. The Public

A child's first performance, about 1918

In Fleet High Street there was a smallish cinema. We went sometimes; though, except when 'speshul things', i.e. supposedly suitable for children, were on, it was rather dull. My mother never
came that I remember. We went with a maid, but whenever there
was a murder or anything 'unwise', we had to hide our faces. One
visit, my eyes had to be almost permanently hidden. It was so
dull that I resolved never to go again. But I did, for in between
times a sudden idea came to me. Next visit, I hid my face all right
but opened my fingers and saw the lot. It was a cowboy film and
set me off galloping miles over heather and silver sand on every
walk, particularly with my Aunt Liz, shooting every pine tree in
sight and my elder brother in the back when he was not looking.
How we hated each other, particularly as he had a peddle car and
I mustn't use it. But my beloved grandmother Franks gave me a
tricycle and this helped a lot. It was my friend for years till my
knees hit the handlebars and it finally broke under my weight.

But there was one occasion, when we didn't hate. My brother
had been 'shooting' at me and running sideways. After the final
shot, he tore into a maid bringing hot coffee and hot milk out of
the dining room. Why she was, I don't know to this day, because,
normally you take hot coffee into dining rooms and cold coffee
out. However there was a sort of explosion. The pots shot up in the
air, the tray sideways, the maid backwards and a sheet of scalding
white milk descended on one side of my brother's face, the side
nearest me. He screamed and I stood transfixed with horror, my
hair prickling, hating to look but having to, and in that moment I
loved him. The terrible agony was a shared suffering of the deepest
kind, my first real experience of sympathy. Then I was sick.

One of the unfortunate things was that milk was terribly scarce.
I had grown so thin, a little earlier, that my mother had taken me
on show to the milkman and it was this undernourishment that
was a part cause of my T.B. neck that plagued me at boarding
school and affects my speaking sometimes still, after all the chopping and X-ray they did to get it right.

My first public performance was at six years of age. It was a charity show to collect funds for wounded soldiers. My mother, hush-voiced, talked me into it in a tone rather like pre-marriage advice. I never know why grown-ups adopt this form of speaking to children. It makes you feel so guilty. I was to be pushed in a pram, talk, get out, sing a song, dance, talk again, sit in the pram, turn round suddenly and see a man in a big hat, white gloves, and burnt cork on his face. Then I was to scream and my mother was to push me off quickly. I loved her very much so it was easy to agree. There was only one rehearsal, on a wonderful sunny morning under a monkey-puzzle tree. My mother seemed satisfied, so let me off for a time. I wandered off past the apple trees. One tree had a heavenly perfume and I leant back to smell it again, then standing face-on to it, put my weight on one leg and bent over sideways. That took me past it. If you leant on the other leg you were with it again. Past it, with it, past, with. Finally my nose wore out and when the smell no longer worked, I ran off past lilies of the valley. It was then, it now seems, that a big proper lily first caught my attention. I remember it's staggering beauty for it didn't mean Death to me. I knelt down fascinated, staring at the high folded collar until my nose touched where white became blue-green on the stocking of the stork. I touched the yellow thing in the middle with my finger and it left stuff on me. After this I ran off. The stones in the path are very clear in my mind. I took up a butterfly net. Lots of 'Cabbige Wites' about. But I couldn't catch the darned things. A sort of bee came by and I somehow caught that. Fumble to get it out; then suddenly a sharp violent pain in my thumb. A yell of anguish and running to the house as my thumb became alarmingly bigger. It was going to burst, I think, like a paper bag. Not tell mother, she would talk in 'the voice' and make me feel guilty. Nellie. Nellie pulled something out and did things with blue bag. It got better.

In the afternoon, my mother actually came with me to the picture house. It was a terrific programme, a mixed affair of film, acts and singing. I was on the same bill with Charlie Chaplin and Fatty Ah-bukle. It was all very hot behind the scenes. The sun had melted the surface of the road, I saw, as I hung over the side of the pram when we crossed it near the cinema. In places, it was obviously pudgy like a horse's skin and we made railway lines with our wheels. 'Sit up, dear.' I felt guilty again.

A lot of women grinned close at me till I had to lean back to see them properly. They came forward though and I couldn't get my head farther back because the pram stopped it. They went out of focus but not before I had seen that they had red mouths and they put red on mine. They smelt of powder and of hot, but mostly of powder. Large men in blue suits and red ties with huge white bandages stood about smoking and whispering near the stage. My mother whispered off and away amongst other whisper-women. The whole dark place was wis–wis–wisp all the time, with another loud voice farther off and occasional coughs and laughter from 'out there' behind a curtain. One of the blue men leant over to me, now entirely alone. 'Going to scream aren't yer? Goin' ter give a nice loud scream. That right—eh?' I looked at him but didn't answer. My thumb hurt. He tried again. 'You're going ter *scream* aren't yer?' he hissed. 'See that man behind. That's 'im as yor goin' to scream at, aint it—eh?' I looked round; sure enough it was the man who'd put burnt cork on his face. He rolled his eyes at me. I rolled mine back. He rolled. I rolled. We both rolled. They couldn't frighten me that way, so the next touch came. 'This is where you're sposed to do it. *Now*. Look round quick see 'im and SCREAM. That's right, en it Jock?' 'Yep', said cork face, 'course it is.' 'Really?' I said looking from one to the other. I looked for my mother. Not there. 'Go on, you'll miss it.' 'Yes, you'll miss it.' 'Come on now, I'll give you a bit of chocolate if you look round sudden, see 'im an' *scream*.' That did it. I looked round suddenly, cork face had gone, but I screamed all the same.

Blue man smacked his hand down on another man's shoulder then held it out palm upwards. For some reason the other man put some money into it. Then there was a heavy silence—very long, like when I let off a revolver at school lunch some years later—then a roar of laughter. My mother reappeared. She was very distressed: 'What have you done? Not now, dear. You've ruined the show. We did it all together before. How *could* you be so naughty!' Luckily, it wasn't 'the voice', so I didn't feel too guilty. Anyway, there were reasons. Oh grown-ups, how bewildering

[17]

they were. The laughing stopped and soon we were 'on'. Hot lights and a large, smoking, silent throbbing sticky them-ness out there—a great amorphous octopus collective body of attenders-to. Words remembered. Mother—Eau-de-Cologne; pram pushing; silly songs, then building up to the ecstasy of the dance. Doing it longer because people began to clap. Pulled gently into pram by Mother—oh, dressed as a red cross Nurse. Then the quick turn. Cork Face—SCREAM. It was the loudest noise I could make and hurt all my neck. There was another pause, but shorter, then laughter, then another wave of louder laughter, as when audiences see a further joke and enjoy it more. They now knew who had screamed before. Much clapping and off. Pause. Back on again, I didn't know why. Out of pram. Short dance, bow and off. All of 'out there' was clapping now and cheering. On again. Couldn't see past the lights properly. I felt hot all over, desperately happy, filled with a strange power. Out there liked me. For one splendid moment I wasn't guilty, but redeemed in joy. The curtain fell but my joy remained. Thus, far too young came the dangerous drug into my life, the realisation of being able to move people, to make them laugh. My addiction was to last far too long, indeed until deep unhappiness made the cure and taught me to respect my power. But oh that first feeling. Oh that golden hour.

COMMENT

Here I have been further concerned with putting down the sort of things that stand out in a child's memory, not now only with *what* was said, but *how*. It is strange what small things can influence one in later life, the tone of a voice for instance. My mother induced the most frightful guilt feelings in me until I blushed over quite insignificant things that were not really sins at all. Parents, take note. Correction can be made in quite an ordinary voice and teachers, beware that you don't put on a special voice for infants.

Observers of children's behaviour may be interested in the part describing a swinging from one leg to the other. It can often be seen in street play, adventure play grounds and nursery schools—sometimes in corners of school playgrounds if momentarily quiet! It is sometimes found in unfrequented passages of schools too. Sometimes adults feel this sort of behaviour is silly, but it nearly always has a reason. A similar situation appears in my first book, *Child Drama*, where I describe a child pushing backwards and forwards on a tricycle chanting a sort of litany. The

A wild mustang. The author's younger
daughter Clare, at Whitmore House

Below left: 'Land ahoy!' Reaside Drama
Playground, Birmingham

Below right: the Queen in her carriage.
Adventure Playground, Lambeth

'They had pulled me in on adventure playgrounds'. Birmingham, 1954
Dance of the Christmas cracker. Used as Christmas card one year by author

Children's evening, Rea Street Drama Centre, Birmingham

actual words are given there too. In this description I was discovering and savouring the delight of the smell of apples and how to banish or bring it on at will. I had never had such experience before. This is the sort of reason which can cause such behaviour in young children. To know it, recognise it, appreciate it is to understand better. We can also be 'shown it' and share the experience and thereby come much closer to children's minds.

Finally comes the experience of being on a stage. Young teachers today do not know how lucky they are. The atmosphere is much milder now. But in about 1946–8, as described later, the controversy in education and theatre circles was hot. I met Charles Schiller H.M.I. about that time and he had been endeavouring to explain the harm which experience of a formal stage can do to very young children. Very few people could understand what he was talking about and I could not see why they could not. Documentary evidence is hard to come by, so possibly for teachers, parents and psychologists this particular description may be of interest. I hope it will not raise old controversies all over again. To offer children other experiences than that of being on a raised proscenium stage is not in the least to say that one is against all theatre—a thing I have often been accused of. Indeed in later reports it may slowly appear that it is not only the child and his supreme spontaneous actions which one attempts to guard, but because one's own standard of what the art of theatre ought to be is fierce and high, so one sees the primitive and unformed attempt as unacceptable. There are so many important in-between stages as part of life that ought to be experienced.

Another lesson of this particular report is the mother's swift reaction. The child is 'naughty' because it screamed at the wrong time—even after rehearsal. But parents, foster parents and those in charge of Cottage Homes anyway, as well as teachers, particularly those dealing with E.S.N. children, Home Office staff, social workers and all those dealing with delinquents, must often beware of swift 'judgment'.[1] We tend to leap to conclusions too quickly. There is nearly always a reason for human behaviour. Have we bothered to find out what it is before apportioning blame?

Also, there are several aspects of language itself. The tone, the actual music, of a misjudgment can be a main cause of hurt, for in early development a child associates itself and its reaction with sound just as much as with meaning. Hence, if a tired or lazy adult says 'No' and still allows a child to do something forbidden, it will learn that the musical sound 'No' has the allowability of 'Yes-ishness', i.e. No means Yes. Thus the intellectual *meaning* becomes clouded because the adult was not loyal to the sound. My own strong feeling is that deep inner disobedience can start this way and have apparently unexplained behaviour symptoms later. It often happens in a child whose father is away.

[1] To follow up this point at greater depth, read *Mr Lyward's Answer* by Michael Burn.

3. *Blood Sacrifice*

First love and unholy children's games, 1919–20

A boy from my brother's school was coming to tea. Charlie was reputed to be too rich and very spoilt. He was not liked and had been socially foisted upon us. I was told there was a wheeze on. Despite having signed an armistice for Europe, there was still a great need in me to vanquish and symbolically to overcome difficulties, so it was an enormous pleasure when my brother started a short but entirely new war and was prepared to let me in on it (my first real experience of cooperative play as against solo play). We had dug a trench in a sand pit and gone on digging into the clay under it. Our trench was of a depth that allowed his head to stick out a little to see the enemy, but it was quite over the top of mine, which made clay lump bombing a little inaccurate. General Joe (my brother) got very narked about this at times. 'Waste of amnishon, waste of amnishon,' he would shout, all purple. But it was wonderful to half climb up, then throw yourself flat on the clay and let it go all over your suit when the enemy fired.

But now for the wheeze.

'We need a dug-out,' said General Joe. 'We'll put boards here, nice and strong so I can walk on them, but specially for Charlie, we'll put some loose ones here.' So we firmed in some boards and 'forgot' to put much more than damp sand under the others, shorter ones that didn't bridge the trench wall. Then we covered the lot with sand and clay on top, partly so the enemy wouldn't see from the air but mostly, I fear, that Charlie wouldn't see either.

'Seems a bit mean,' I said.

'Sposed to be, you fool. But I tell you what—if he behaves, we won't do it.'

Charlie came. He was ghastly. He bossed me of course. For I was younger and he had been before, pulled my hair successfully, kicked me in the stomach and dropped hard apples on me whilst on the ground. Then he gagged and locked me in a sort of coal cellar for the whole of one afternoon. I couldn't take to him somehow. Though he did become a romantic figure later, because grown-ups said (in the voice) 'he had an unhappy home'.

But now he made his great mistake. He tried to boss General Joe.

So the time came when the dug-out was shown off; then it was suggested we stand bravely on top, as 'there was a truce on, in the war, since early afternoon' (really, because we had our best suits on). Charlie was a bit dubious. 'Oh come on,' said General Joe and strode on to the good roof. 'See? Now, you go.' Charlie moved carefully over on to the good part (visitors first and all that). 'Cha – cha – cha – cha – cha!' screamed my brother suddenly. In the burst of machine-gun fire, he lurched against Charlie. 'Down everyone.' There was no need to say it, and of course *we* didn't, but Charlie in turn had lurched onto the looser boards. The sand foundations gave way, and as the boards were not really wide enough in span to be held by the real clay walls, down went Charlie in his best suit to the bottom of the trench, with wood, sand, clay, old branches, nails and everything on top of him. He started to yell his head off. General Joe and I looked on, grave as granite—thrilled. At that moment a bob of dark hair struggled through a hole in the fence and a small girl appeared, asking what the noise was about. She saw and giggled, as young women sometimes do. She had heard and watched the battles before, she said, and wanted to join in. 'Girls is sloppy,' said General Joe. 'Anyway, we're busy.' However, she helped us get Charlie out of the trench and helped to shame his animal howls and tears. So we made a date for later and escorted 'poor Charlie, bad luck Charlie, jolly poor show', back to the house, only our footsteps and occasional rhythmic involuntary after-tear snorts, from him, to challenge the calm triumph.

Charlie left early. He was obviously unwell as he didn't eat much tea and everyone else was rather quiet.

So we kept our appointment with the girl next door and struggled through the gap in the hedge. 'Must see to that,' said General Joe thoughtfully, 'get it bigger.'

For me it was the first of numerous visits, for next door proved to be a quite fascinating other world. It was all trodden down and mostly mud, spades and old cans lay about, so you could dig anywhere. There was only one small bit of grass and a cat rolled on

[21]

that. A shaggy dog came by sometimes but only inspected things and went again. There were lots of bicycle wheels, for hoops or whizzing against fences or pinging the spokes, because dark-hair's father owned the 'bike' shop, she said. We had seen it from the High Street, but it lay back a bit and you did not notice it much when out walking.

But perhaps the greatest, most wonderful thing about next door was the pit. This was past the cat on its grass plinth, near the end of the garden. It was full of everything. Fish bones, bacon rind, old vegetable, orange skin, meat bones, half-chewed buckets, a lampstand, cardboard, tins of every size, sticks, an old jersey, one pyjama leg, three shoes, half a strap and, above all, egg shells —hundreds of them; shovels of old tea leaves, some still brown and some blue. And a whitish grey dust sprinkled all over everything like sugar on a cake. Tea-coloured water was half way up and some things floated. It gave off a strong and curious odour. I can smell it to this day. 'Gosh,' said General Joe. I am not sure that he approved. But I did. To me it was unbelievable and dark-head loved it too. She was friendly to me and shared her toffees. Joe did not come much more but I came again and again and began to dream of the pit, the digging and of her. In fact, one might say that this—apart from my best stuffed monkey—was my first love affair. I spent every moment of every day there and only partly to avoid the gardener in our own spruce place. Nellie began to laugh at me for going—a matter of mystification and extreme discomfort. But Joe did come once more, for the day of the Blood Sacrifice.

'You must come tomorrow,' said my maiden at sundown and calling-out-of-names-for-bed-time. She spoke hoarsely and in dramatic tones, partly because she was upside down over a bar, as she often was. This always made me vaguely uncomfortable. It was not easy to talk to people like that, unless you did it too. 'You *must* come, Dada's goin' to kill a chickun.'

With his usual effectiveness, General Joe had seen to the fence. No need to squeeze through now. Dark-head had even danced through onto our side sometimes, whilst General Joe, in stand-offish mood was up a pine tree constructing a sky raft, and when neither the gardener, Nellie nor the hated young temporary nurse were about. If they were, she danced back again and we both felt guilty. Sometimes I went too. So, this morning, General Joe and I, hands in pockets and rather blah, sauntered through the fence.

Up curtain at once on the other world—sun, a chattering gang of three or four children, some rather ragged, whom I had met before and liked a lot. Toffee from dark-head. Then came the 'Chickun'.

What took place now may seem distasteful to properly civilised minds, but I must try and tell about it in all honesty and as it really happened.

The proprietor of the bicycle shop walked down the path grinning, holding by its legs a cock. The cock did not like being carried this way and arched up occasionally, trying to peck his hand. The circle of children closed in. Over one edge of the pit a stake had been driven in slantwise. Bicycle man produced a bit of string and suddenly there was a turmoil of screaming and fluttering. He was trying to tie the legs of the bird, whilst still carrying it. One or two boys rushed to help. Finally the cock was tied by the legs and swung round a bit. The circle of children widened. It tried to peck the masterful holder once more. 'Ah, try to bite me again, would ya?' said bicycle man. 'Take that then for a beginning,' and he swung the cock hard so that it's head banged against the stake. We all gasped. He then attached the cord to the top of the slanting stake so that the bird hung out over the pit, like an ancient picture of humans in Hades. After this he took out a pen-knife carefully and deliberately, selected a blade and plunged it into the neck of the cock. My little girl screamed, the cock only fluttered, but then the man drew down the knife in a savage cut almost the length of the neck. The cock screamed. He turned the knife round several times. Once or twice the cock fluttered. 'See that,' said the man, 'that's when you touch 'is windpipe.' 'Let's try,' said one of the boys. One after the other the older ones put a finger in the cock's neck and touched the windpipe to make it flutter. They stood back. 'Think that's enough for a bit,' said bicycle man. 'Now leave it be or we won't 'ave no dinner,' and he strode off.

I looked round, there was blood everywhere on the hands of the older boys, all over the cock's head and on the egg shells.

[23]

Suddenly a great flicking started. It became suddenly exciting. We had forgotten what was happening. Now we were just flicking the red. It seemed more 'everywhere' than before. We even picked up egg shells full and threw them at each other. Then the chanting began: 'Cock's done, ya, ya, silly 'ole bird.' It was taken up, 'ya, ya, silly 'ole bird', and in a sort of group sensitivity we began to stamp in unison. General Joe snatched up a tin and soon almost all of us had something to bang. We chanted and beat and created our own Child Music. We roared out in our stamping dance, round and round in a circle (no doubt with hearts to the centre, as nearly all children do): 'silly 'ole bird, silly 'ole bird, ya ya, silly 'ole bird'. Then we broke off into a sort of yelling Indian dance with much more development in the percussion. It was tremendously exciting, full of deep comradeship and colossal group expression. And we actually had and were Redskins. Then it suddenly stopped. Silence and a slow half circle forming round the cock. Different now; a darkening sort of gloom and a feeling of menace and catastrophe. I shall never forget it and I think the others felt it too, for they sloped off one by one, wiping themselves down, hand on grass, or in mud, as they went. 'Come on,' said General Joe, 'I'm going.' But I couldn't move yet. Dark-head and I stood looking. Her hand stole into mine. 'Think it's dead?', I said.

'Dunno.'

'Try touching it.'

'Oo I dursent.'

We played for a bit, sometimes coming back to look. But we knew he wasn't dead because occasionally he blinked. Like another King, he seemed to take 'an unconscionable time a-dieing'.

Finally his eye went glassy and I found the courage to poke him gently with a stick, but not in his wound.

''E's dead then,' said my companion.

'Yes.'

'Should think 'e'd go to 'eaven.'

'Yes.'

She stretched up her little neck, then almost like a chicken herself. Her eyes opened wide and she called to Heaven: 'God, 'e's cummin'. Cock's dead. 'E's cummin' up.'

[24]

We turned and looked at each other, smiled in mental agreement, as children sometimes do, and both turned to Heaven. In chorus we sang: 'Cock's dead. Cock's dead. 'E's cummin', God. 'E's cummin' *Now*.' Then we looked at each other and laughed. It was a sign of innocence. We laughed because the poor bird was free. We were somehow purged, purged of the whole frightful affair and of our enforced complicity. I still looked at her, the smell of the pit in my nose, then suddenly ran off and left my love. I knew she was free.

I never saw her again.

The grown-ups had heard about 'next door' and told my mother. At any rate they teased me so unmercifully that a young man of 6½–7 years should want to play with a little girl next door and laughed so loud that I could not sleep at night for crying and blushed all over with guilt, but I didn't know why. Next time I went to the fence, it was boarded up.

Soon after that I went to boarding school, after a fearful struggle to dress myself, in new tweed suiting, lace-up shoes, braces, loose collar, tie and terrible things called studs. The agony of being sent away at that age, never having been allowed to do anything for myself (often to my anger) was not in any way calmed, after only one try on, one undress and one get up, for practice, by being told, in the voice: 'Really dear, you must look after *yourself.*'

COMMENT

There are many lessons in this story. How children are often not given enough opportunity to do things for themselves. How guilt is unnecessarily built up in the younger child and what a thin dividing line there is, at the start, between innocence and delinquency. We never know what may begin it all, whether it be something said or done by old or young, or an uncalculated experience. How did this one affect all of us there? It is a memory I shall never forget. Of such and other far worse stories I have been told by youngsters since, one is reminded constantly of ancient advice: 'Judge not, that ye be not judged'. This had been my first remembered experience of that dangerous and incalculable thing we call the herd instinct.

'Blood Sacrifice' gives an example of a young child in some emotional danger, hitherto unable to cooperate much with others, except the occasional adult, but now joining in with a group in over-excited play. The adults play a slightly different role from another child during spontaneous dramatic expression, being a living prop, antagonist, or a guide (if sensitive enough), companion for short moments when privileged, but otherwise, for the most part, just a dog's body to be ordered about. If they do not actually get fed up, they tend eventually to laugh, either because the child is so self centred or they think the activity ridiculous. Even Nellie (in No. 1) laughed when accused of incompetence over shooting the rapids on a kitchen table. But in 'Blood Sacrifice', we see a child starting to cooperate with an elder brother because there was a purpose in so doing—that of 'continuing the war'. It may be noted that this is the general pattern—a child alone, then play with a partner and then the group. In taking spontaneous work, it is well to bear this in mind as a pattern of man's behaviour, for it works with adults too, particularly in the realm of movement and dance. I have written at length in a book being prepared on Movement on the particular function of the guide who must arrange things occasionally so that cooperation, as needed, may take place.

Parents particularly, but also nursery school and junior school teachers ask me again and again about natural play and guided play. Psychologists and doctors often ask how to help spontaneous activity to be constructive. In *Child Drama* I talk about the difference between the wild flower of the street and play, which may take place as it were in the 'garden' of school and be nurtured into a civilised plant.

In this report it is made absolutely clear how delinquency, or near delinquency, can creep into unguided child play. It is always likely to happen, of course, but the description should provide a fairly vivid answer to those who say—' Why bother to use Child Drama in school, children do this sort of thing on their own anyway.' But there was the terrible newspaper story some years back of a 'prisoner' being left in a dustbin. Indeed children do things in their own way but spontaneous creation is one of the most dynamic things in man, and if that is the way we tick, one may just as well make use of the fact in order to gain 'cooperative learning'. Besides, if left alone, it can go wrong.

We might notice, in passing, a child's wonder at the 'fascinating other world.' next door—because it wasn't kempt—a fact that has been appreciated more in recent years, giving rise to such things as adventure play grounds. One had the chance, though, later on, to plead for huts on adventure playgrounds on a national scale, so that guided Child Drama and other things could take place in a smaller space, to allow imaginative exercise side by side with the physical, but also to help achieve loyalty to the site during winter months. There are huts on many adventure playgrounds today.

Early love for the opposite sex appears in this description and incidentally adult mockery can have a devastating effect on very early affections of the kind. This child was put off women for a long time afterwards. My brother's statement 'girls is sloppy' became my own, but not for the right reason. With him it was temporary masculine contempt, with me defence against my hurt.

Then follows the elated blood dance. The group activity, after my one companion activity (the normal pattern) happened to be gruesome. It has the sort of quality of William Golding's *The Lord of the Flies*. How near an adult can bring children to delinquency and how close the abyss. As it happened the event ended in naive but fervent prayer. But it might not have. It might have been just the first taste of blood.

At the very end, parents might note that a feeling of insecurity could easily be started by unthoughtful criticism of a child trying to don unfamiliar clothes, and alone, before being shipped off without ceremony to a school away from home. One of the fatal mistakes is to go on 'putting on a child's coat' for it too long, metaphorically or actually, but it is not wise to drop the aid suddenly and entirely in a totally new situation and on the eve of an emotional event anyway. Children need to be weaned into responsibility, though weaned they must be, for a sentimental or over-selfish love will make them dependent too long, and they may suddenly find themselves bereft and incompetent.

4. Kings and Chemists

Crashes and fire in the playroom, 1924 perhaps

Soon after the First World War we must have left Fleet, for I seem to remember further days in London, for a time. We even bought a house there after staying on and off with my grandmother Slade, but things did not go according to plan and my father had to get rid of it before moving in and we soon found ourselves in East Anglia, in a fairly spacious house in Ely.

In a back part of this, my brother and I had a special room where we played 'Kings', and later 'Studies'. 'Kings' was where we projected our minds into the inanimate bodies of leaden figures and made them come alive.[1] I think my brother's King was at one time a toy Station Master and mine was certainly an R.A.M.C. Colonel. He had a hat like an Admiral only his head had been shot off, so he had a match stick neck to keep it on again. Our Kings went for fearful excursions in toy cars and trains, often suffering terrible pain in dramatic crashes and sometimes flying to different countries in a small tin box, to recuperate, comfortably lying on an eiderdown of padding from a King George V Chocolate box. We had saved up and bought a gramophone and records. This saved us humming ourselves raw in the throat—though between us we could do a creditable rendering of the band at Hove, so the Kings could now review the troops

[1] An outline of the difference between personal and projected play is to be found in *Child Drama*.

to 'Marche Lorraine', 'Pomp and Circumstance' or 'Oh for the Wings of a Dove'.

My brother had devised a great many crashes that morning and I had got fed up with the dents in my new engine and supplying new necks for the Royal Army Majesterial Colonel. So we turned to 'studies' and, after heated debate, curtained off portions of the room. For those interested in the investigation and observation of children's behaviour, we then started to indulge in a sort of mixture of personal and projected play, for we became professors *ourselves*, but set up a chemical laboratory in a further partition of one of the 'studies', for creating explosives still for our Kings and scent for their wives. This needed music too, so crank crank and final squeak of the old Decca once more and 'Land of hope and Glory' to fizzing coloured waters in tins on the gas ring.

Unfortunately we tired of this and changed the mixture to Pears brilliantine and as much candle wax as possible. The smell was terrific. Much joy in royal households would accrue, we thought, and aimed at a lump of wax that the Ladies could rub on themselves, retaining a coloured smear of smell too. But in taking off my cardboard lenseless professorial glasses with too great a flourish during a certain peak of top level discussion, I inadvertently touched the handle of the experimental pot. In one moment the whole stove seemed ablaze and there was a solid sheet of fire from floor to ceiling.

My brother threw everything at it and shouted for my mother. She was in time to see a large pot of pink water and my new jersey emptied onto the exciting brightness, whereupon the blaze and ring went out and the main fire gasped, let out an enormous regurgitation and 'blew back'. This was even more alarming and my poor mother now fully alert snapped off both taps. She was not very pleased with us, particularly when this mild and charming lady found the gas mantle had also been broken; then, as when a policeman asks for your papers after apparent small misdemeanour and finds a mounting volume of things wrong, so with us. There was a crack in the glass shade, paint mysteriously off the door, a terrible green wax mark all up the wall, a black scowl on the ceiling, one broken chair leg, a torn sheet (holes for the arms of famous chemists) and final and worst thing perhaps, for her, I had chopped the head off a small wooden foal she had lately given me. In vain did I try to explain that it was beautifully chopped—it could stick together with chewing gum—look—when it was wanted as a foal, but it could be a wild beast's head over the fire place of the cardboard palace of my King on ALL OTHER OCCASIONS. But it was no good. Even my brother's last attempt at conciliation failed: 'But Mum, you have to *expect* occasional explosions in a chemical factory, partikly a munitions one!' However, she was near to tears and sent us outside. 'Silly ass,' said my brother, 'you would do a thing like that.'

We rushed out then to the yard and capacious stables where we kept our 'motors'. Joe jumped on his bike and I on my trike (aforementioned) and quickly adjusting our bits of three-ply wood to roar in the spokes properly, we whizzed off round and round the yard, round and round, then occasionally backing, occasionally breaking into the eight shape to be seen in the play of all absorbed and happy children in full flight, until the morning was over. Another swish and our father's car purred in under the stable arch. Immaculate as ever, he took off his pearl grey hat and clean gloves.

'Well, what have you two been up to this morning? Been good boys?'

'Ooh yes, Daddy. Of course!' came the indignant answer. How extraordinary grown-ups are.

COMMENT

It used to be argued that the only division in child play was that between realistic and imaginary. But this is clearly not so. At any moment an imaginative idea or an anachronistic one can come into play, even of a neo-realistic kind. Hence a straight action between ancient kings, generals or modern Big Business men can be interrupted by a spell, or these days a message from Mars, at any time.

We might note here, in passing, the constant repetition of 'lazy magic'[1] in the play of many children. This is where a quick happening can get you out of a difficult situation without explanation. It is worth saying 'Yes, but what did the spell do?' or ' What did the message *say* and what had to happen because of it?' This may

[1] For fuller recognition of this I am indebted to Miss P. H. Lutley, former Headmistress of Nansen J and I School, Birmingham.

enrich the plot without any further guidance. Guidance there often has to be, particularly in schools, for that is why children go there. Teachers of infant and junior children, as long as you draw things out of them and occasionally suggest *what* to do without showing them how to do it, be assured you will do them *no psychic harm whatever*.

But to return to our main point, although all play is fluid the only genuine division of child play is between personal and projected. When first writing of it in *Child Drama*, I drew attention to the existence of this division and tried to explain it. Since then there have been more years in which to see its very great importance both in education and therapy. Briefly, projected play is where the individual is generally quiet in his own body and projects out of his mind a dream or idea into, onto or around objects outside himself. Then the objects take on life. Personal play is where the individual gets up and does the thing himself. There are fascinating borderline actions, to play with as red herrings on Leaders' courses. For instance, what is riding a bicycle? It is half and half really. But do not let us get bogged down into this. In 'Kings and Chemists' there is a situation which fascinates me now, seeing it objectively and from afar. We two youngsters got up and *became* chemists ourselves (personal play) yet our purpose (this important word in guiding a good lesson), our purpose in the situation was still to produce something for the Kings, i.e. the toys, the objects with which we had recently played and to whom we gave life (projected play)—a life so strong in our imagination that it remained still, even after we had discarded them temporarily, albeit in commanding positions, to devote ourselves to actual living chemistry. In projected play, man builds unto himself a monument, then walks away, but the symbol or memorial of his doing remains there after him. In this case the toy kings stood there whilst we took action.

I am now convinced that each of us tends to be a personal play or projected play type, not unassociated with extravert and introvert. The personal or projected in us can be suppressed or at least the potential energy of it wasted, which leads one logically and ultimately to an ideal of an almost individual timetable for each child, though some grouping could be made. When it comes to school life the three Rs are of the projected realm, being symbols into which we breathe life—or fail to, as in the case of a backward child. A feeling of success can only then come through the other field, of personal play. We see an example of this later in 'Dance Drama on the Downs', p. 40.

Note the use of music also. Children often use or need music for their play. They do not always listen as adults do, but draw upon it as an emotional background to their creations.

At the end of 'Kings and Chemists', it is typical that momentarily these two children had entirely—or almost—forgotten their earlier fright, though it remained a sharp memory later. It was probably true that they thought they had been good boys when suddenly asked by father. A little time later they may have remembered otherwise, but they had been very absorbed in their motorbike play since then, so again we must not jump to conclusions and call them liars.

5. *Illegal and Unrecognised Drama in a Prep School*

Eastbourne, 1926

I had learned to be very happy at my school here and at the end of my time was prefect, an Empire Marksman and not only a school colour for shooting but for Rugby and Association football also.

This did not prevent me from smoking in the bushes, I am afraid, nor from belonging to a gang, nor from indulging in imaginative drama of a boisterous nature. I had passed my common entrance well and all seemed to be pretty right with life, except that there was never enough to eat.

It was this preoccupation with food that first gave us the idea of making dramas about eating. One gang—which shall be called 'Hunt's'—got the idea of staging enormous pretend feasts in the playbox room, where some people had managed to smuggle grub. But not for long. There was a huge iron cage over a boiler in this room and that too, no doubt, contributed its inspiration to the ritual. The gang to which I belonged shall be called A gang. We went in for bloodcurdling knives of Red Indian appearance, cutting up birds, cooking queer soups in the woods and taking boys from a nearby school prisoner. Hunt's gang was less civilised, they used to chase new boys, capture them, tie them up and prod them with specially prepared sticks. A notch was cut in a Hunt chap's stick for each small boy brought to tears and bleeding. We treated our prisoners comparatively well but with the contempt that members of another school deserve. I remember one wonderful wet afternoon, however, when two friends from A gang and myself had been playing at gentlemen burglars, who dressed in immaculate evening clothes and always escaped the police on roller-skates. We had been swerving and dodging and flying for a considerably time, drawing with the wheels of our skates those sublime basic shapes that I now know (and have since described) to be the permanent patterns of movement in Child Drama the world over. We decided to go to the box room, like Hunt's gang.

Somehow a discussion on food started, and one of my friends

was made King Umboola (from a frightful puppet show that was brought to the school and nearly hissed off the premises). Umboola spoke something thus:

'I am the King, I am Umboola. I am the great ghastly puppet . . .' (Umboola's speeches always started that way.) 'But I am hungry and I command a skating dance, then food—lots of it: sweet grub, biscuit grub, and human grub. Slade-oola, arrange the dance.'

I rose. 'All skating warriors, line up against the wall, and then form fours. Skate fast and don't hit a play box. Anyone hitting a play box shall be punched by Atkinson-oola.' This was a fearful threat. Genial 'Akkie' thought everything amusing. He used to just beat me every year in the hundred yards. A great one, Akkie. He had a punch like what our P.T. instructor would call 'yorl fancy a elephant's kicked yer'.

I don't remember how many people got punched, but I do remember arranging swirling flights of six and six skaters intertwining amongst boxes and each other. I remember a beautifully graceful cartoon love scene between Punch, Judy and Atkinson-oola waltzed and lilted on skates to the drumming of playbox lids, and I remember it was the first time I had consciously used large monuments of bricklike boxes as scenery in any production. The finale was a pile of boys high on three sets of boxes, sitting with hands round knees. At a sign from Umboola I let out a great cry and led horde one, swiftly followed by hordes two and three, down to the floor from the heights to weave and counterweave to a rhythm of banging, scraping sounds and weird cries. Such skating as has never been seen. Never such felt. Oh never, never to be forgotten skating.

But there was to be no allowance, no 'near-finish'. Our creation was cut, cut like a dream of film by some Super-Snipper Dictator.

'Enough,' cried King Umboola. I can see the beads of sweat on him to this day. He always got them on his eyelids when excited (what extraordinary things one remembers). 'Enough dancing, Slade-oola. Now for the feast. Atkinson-oola, form a guard and search all the playboxes.' There followed the most disgraceful intimidation, when playboxes of every sort and kind were forcibly broken open and food deposited before the king. I am ashamed to say that Umboola, Akkie and I ate most of it before a thunder-struck and sullen, sweating mob. But to this day it seems to me they thought it appropriate to the occasion. We were the chieftains, not ourselves. If they had just seen *us*, surely we would have been lynched. But the best was yet to come.

After the mob had been encouraged by being allowed to share the remnants of their own grub, Umboola shouted: 'Now for Human Grub'. The most extraordinary thing then happened. A member of Hunt's gang got up and said 'I, oh King Umboola, will arrange it.' Now Hunt's gang and A gang had never co-operated before. We had always been at daggers drawn—or rather throttles clutch. It was my first lesson in diplomacy on a grand scale. I have since seen many occasions when common need, greed, envy, hate, fear, ambition or sheer economics have welded nations, groups or persons into curious alliances. But that was a real snorter for most of us. However, it worked. Hunt's gang liked catching new boys, and catch 'em they did.

Practically the whole of the bottom two forms were shanghai-ed and thrust at one time or another into the iron cage to tremen-

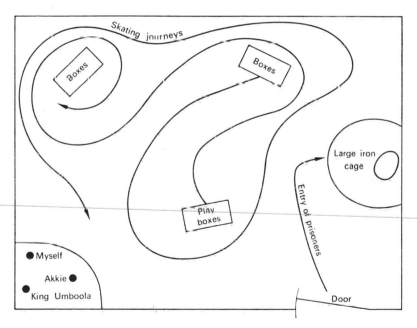

dous cheering and drumming. But just near the very peak of the climax when the prisoners' eyes were dilating with terror and King Umboola was about to demand that he should eat his first child, the school bell went.

The King's fierce countenance relaxed into a cheerful and friendly grin. 'All right you kids,' he said, 'better shove off now and get washed up.' In five minutes the Jungle Scene had dispersed, in twenty we were all singing hymns in chapel, our hair plastered flat, our faces shining, our voices strained in boisterous praise. Praise for the sheer love of living.

COMMENT

It is sometimes thought that prep schools are somewhat delicate places where the effete and diminutive pale male learns by one method or another how to be, or ape at being, what was once admired as a gentleman. He incidentally learns about fair play and how to pass exams. The last part is probably true, the first is less true. In my own experience, the inmates were extremely normal exuberant males but on appropriate occasions they did learn how to behave. They must have been for the most part exceedingly robust for they were practically starved for years. The description of happenings at this school is included on purpose, for this book is concerned with the unfolding of the personality of man, as shown in spontaneity and must show a cross section of society. It is important to realise that in selected places such as private schools—many of which are extremely good schools and this on the whole was one of them—there are still human beings. It would be a pity for any propaganda or unworthy feelings of envy to delude us over this. So let us consider that in this place boys worked very hard and very well but in their off time, which was not much, they had their unguided amusements. Too unguided they were really, and being over organised the rest of the time behaviour-revolt came somewhat in excess.

It is natural for gangs to exist. They begin in most infant schools and are rife between the ages of seven and nine in junior schools. Our gangs were going on a bit long at this prep school and the over-organisation of life tended to make free behaviour rather younger in pattern than it should have been, as nearly always happens. It is this inner 'youngness' which is a draw-back for the clever child being crammed in every type of school. They just don't have enough time to grow up. Thus it is that at colleges and even universities, students revert sometimes to extremely young behaviour. But they must have their outburst too. If it is not actually a nuisance, it can appear to the rest of the world as fun and perhaps, on the whole, it helps to keep us all young.

For those particularly interested, in this description there is a repetition of youngsters re-enacting in personal play an idea which came to them from a projected play experience (seeing the puppet show) but at a slightly higher level and perhaps more successfully than in report No. 4.

The skating which we did went on and on whenever there was a short break and mostly we preferred it in the semi-dark. Years later I was to find that many people prefer to do spontaneous dance in semi-darkness and that E.S.N. children often enjoy complete dark. One always seemed to go much faster at night and imagination roamed more freely.

People, particularly theatre folk, often ask how one makes a bridge between spontaneous child play and theatre, for most of them these days see spontaneous acting as valuable and probably use it themselves, it is only the old-fashioned who cannot see the point. In this report we see the beginnings of theatre and production arising out of improvisation. My arranging of the swirling dance and use of built up boxes was intentional and far more conscious than the earlier and mostly unconscious child play. So the answer is that, in part, theatre grows naturally out of Child Drama but it is probably all the better if it is not hurried. I feel perhaps that Gordon Craig and Grey of The Cambridge Festival Theatre might have been impressed by the use of those square boxes, those little rostra.

The allusion to 'near finish' will be familiar to those that know the philosophy of Child Drama. It pertains to the moment when a young child is becoming disengaged from deep absorption in play and may thus receive an adult command with less emotional conflict. With all children the near finish is worth watching for. With disturbed children it is essential.

We note here also the fantastic power of play. That the throng allowed their food to be eaten seems almost incredible. It could not have happened without the magic of the imagined situation. This is what happens in herd behaviour, sometimes for good, sometimes for evil. The situation is the primitive forerunner of political propaganda and outlook and national belt tightening before war.

In a moment, though, the experience is over and the boys are in chapel, able to switch from one thing to the other. It is a good example of the opposites in the nature of all men.

6. A Christmas Fantasy with the Family Next Door
Ely, 1927–8

For years I had been acting in plays in the holidays. I can hardly remember a time now when I wasn't. Regularly since the age of about eight, and sporadically before that. These were not by any means only children's productions or games. They were often script plays in which adults took part. One particular group was a family of neighbours and friends who finally bound themselves into the Fen Players. I hope to write of them at greater length one day in a book on theatre proper; but for the moment will content myself with describing one Christmas evening after we had acted a lurid play about murder, aeroplanes and lunatics written by my brother.

We never kept strictly to the proscenium shape in our productions, though the family next door put up with considerable inconvenience at having their drawing room turned into a theatre each year. The proscenium was raised like a Big Top and struck out little ice-sugar blobs from the plaster each season it was put up, until a permanent socket was formed. Meanwhile the family would inhabit the far end in half shadow and cower round the big fire. Often the plot of the shows would be changed because dogs or other animals in the 'audience' would join in and come onto the stage area. The actors would continue the show and either use the animal or lead it back across the footlights, if there were any, and continue action and speech amongst or even with those at the audience end of the room. But after shows of this kind we always had a big feast on the stage; then the serious work would begin. We would make up dramas by the hour, dramas about fun, hate, hope and life, death or glory—anything and everything in fact that had happened or one could imagine might happen to a man.

Here is an outline of one such imaginative drama that remains in my mind. My father had been called not long before as a witness at a trial of some undergraduates at Cambridge who had been had up for speeding and injuring a pedestrian. My brother and I had sat through the proceedings enthralled. It was my first 'court', and from this experience our drama of the Christmas I write evolved.

I was the judge and my elder brother was the police sergeant. The head of the ancient family whose house it was, and a director of a sugar beet factory were brought in as prisoners, tied hand and foot. They were given remarkable names which unfortunately now escape me. But they both pleaded not guilty. They were knocked about by the police quite a lot for not pleading guilty, but since they proved resolute I ordered the trial to begin.

The oath was taken on a Boy Scout's diary: 'I promise to tell the truth, the whole truth and nothing but the truth, swelp me .

[36]

and finished at that. But this diary contained a germ that it had got from the lunatic in the script play before, and each time someone took the oath they took the bug too and got the lie-disease. This, you see, was the reason for the strange tales told that night. It explains, for instance, why the policeman insisted on saying that he wasn't there at the time and was on the top of Ely Cathedral. It explains why the undergraduates of remarkable name swore black and blue that they were riding black and blue mules respectively and not a red roadster at all.

'Well,' said the judge, 'having arrived at the suggestion that these two young men (the father and the company director cowered) were not driving at all, can it be explained why they were riding at eighty miles an hour on black and blue mules respectively and knocking down innocent pedestrians on a perfectly respectable Cambridgeshire road near Newmarket?'

Policeman: 'It can't m'Lud.'

A prisoner: 'I was not going eighty miles an hour.'

Judge: 'You were.'

Prisoner: 'I wasn't.'

Judge: 'You were.'

Other prisoner: 'We wasn't.'

Judge: 'Kindly address your remarks to me in a quieter voice and speak proper . . . er, properly. You were just gently riding along admiring the rolling hills of Cambridgeshire, I suppose?' (This I lifted from the real trial.)

That is all my brother and I could remember of this part, but the next main part we were quite clear about recently, though there was a huge slab in the middle somewhere which is lost for ever. The following, however, is adequately vouched for.

My father came on as a witness but kept being interrupted by hiccoughs.

Judge: 'Will somebody keep that man quiet.' (You see how wonderful drama is? How marvellous to be able to say that to your father and get away with it! I remember a great load coming off my shoulders at the cathartic effect. My heart sang. I was going to make the best of it.)

Judge: 'Constable, stop that man heaving and hicking. If he does it again knock him unconscious or stick a pin in him.'

[37]

My father as witness (and so mildly for him): 'Beg pardon, m'Lud. I had fish for tea.' (This was his favourite joke and it stopped the trial for several minutes whilst various people overcame convulsions of joy. It was funny, I suppose, because no one in that room least of all my father, had *ever* had fish for tea and none of us then thought we were likely to, though most of us may have been grateful enough for it since.)

Judge: 'Come to the point, my man. Did you or did you not see the corpse?'

Witness: 'Yes, m'Lud, 'e was dead.'

Judge: 'Dead, how do you know he was dead? Was he cold to the touch?'

Witness: 'No, m'Lud, 'e was 'ot, 'ot as if 'e'd been runnin'.'

Judge: 'Constable, did you see the corpse?'

Sergeant (my brother): 'Yes, m'Lud, I sorn 'im. 'E was 'ot orl right, proper 'ot.'

Judge: 'Did you touch him?'

Sergeant: 'No, I could *see* 'e was 'ot.'

Judge: 'What do you stupid men mean? How could you see? Do you mean he was aiktually *steaming* in the cold Newmarket air?'

This remark literally brought the house down. Someone knocked the proscenium frame and part of it fell. The dogs started barking. My brother marched into the audience and started arresting people left, right and near the fireplace. A picture fell down. At this moment the two undergraduates escaped from the court by the second drawing room door. 'After them,' cried the Judge within me. The constable, witness, court and jury, dogs and one cat rushed down the stairs after them, together with half the audience—except my mother. We ran round St Mary's Green for a time and finally the guilty men were caught just opposite Oliver Cromwell's house. We 'hung' them from a lamppost and sang a carol. Then we collapsed into each others arms. I looked up at the clear stars and a moment of deep calm came to me. Would life ever be so wonderful again?

What did the shades of Roundhead Cavalrymen, who used to assemble on that green construe of our strange saga that night! Would they wince at our deep and simple joy or did some sardonic glimmer twitch their Fenny face? I wonder.

[38]

COMMENT

Happiness is a very elusive thing. Most of us may feel there is not enough of it. This piece records some transient moments, to show if possible some of the gaiety and joy. Those interested in the changing forms of theatre today may note the fact that even in the twenties our group flowed out quite often from the more formal stage which was there at all because, like many groups at the time, certain members of it were only acting at acting. They aped (hopelessly) the established theatre but when really being creative the small stage area could not possibly hold our exuberance. Our energy became a pageant and our audience was so wrapped in the experience that they became part of the flood waters too. When one thinks of it, the wild joy of the young, so different from mere quiet contentment or the normally quieter joy of older people, is nearly always associated with spontaneous outburst. It has something to do, no doubt, with the child's logical division of sound into time beat, rhythm and climax, for it enjoys music in an emotional way, to which the parent and clever teacher must add purposeful *de-climax* as a civilising factor. For me such outbursts of joy were special for, in my early years, every time I showed gladness, some maid or nurse or servant would say 'you'll be crying before you go to bed'. De-climax certainly, but not of a kind to bring peace.

From about 1946 to 1948, controversy was raging over any suggestion that young people might wish to flow on and off stage. Although this is now taken for granted in many parts of the country, there are still schools for which one has managed to obtain arena lighting who do not appreciate what it is for.

Psychologists and teachers ask about the value of drama as therapy. I think spontaneous play is a natural therapy (particularly and normally between seven and nine years of age); you don't have to try to be too clever about it, except with disturbed children and special cases. The director of a clinic once said to me 'If only all schools did your sort of drama, we should be out of a job'. 'Christmas Fantasy' gives a precise example of catharsis, details of which are so difficult to obtain. The child here feels the weight physically lifting and although taking full advantage of kicking back at his father of whom he was afraid and by whom desperately teased at times, he felt bound to him (father) in a sort of team during moments which he hoped would not pass.

Ultimately the flowing energy took us right out of the house and the strength of imagination held the drama and kept it going in a wider flight of space far beyond its original nest, like the travelling pageants of ancient Egypt. Years later, I was saddened in a certain arena production, when children invited to be birds were flowing up and down steps chasing an actor. But instead of using this absorption as a compliment he suddenly panicked and ordered them back to their seats. Unfortunately he did not know his Child Drama.

[39]

7. *Dance Drama on the Downs and Epic Drama on Horses*
A group of outlaws at public school, 1928-9

I became rather a misfit at my public school. Like many children who fall behind a bit in their studies, it was for me a pleasure to get out of school. Though backward in some subjects, it was no difficulty for me to write commentaries on Havelock Ellis, a four thousand word thesis on why Wolsey became estranged from Henry VIII, and another on the 'Foundation of the Church of England', and by seventeen years of age, I had completed the main theory and most of the detail of my method on Drama-Athletic-Movement, which fortune gave me an opportunity of testing and proving during a longish stay in Germany a little later in life, and which has frequently been my mainstay since, in the part treatment of cases of physical or psychological disorder.

One of the joys of those days was to go out with a few companions on the Sussex Downs and create improvised ballets. But on the way we played a game which goes like this:
1st Person: 'Quaker, Quaker, how art thou?'
2nd Person: 'Very well, I thank thee.'
1st Person: 'And how's the Quaker next to thee?'
2nd Person: 'I don't know, I'll go and see.'
Person No 2 then becomes Person No 1 and includes his other neighbour as Person No 2, asking the same question. This is asked over and over again as it passes backwards and forwards along a line of people, or round a circle. With us it was mostly along a line, for if you listen to the rhythm, you soon perceive that chanted loud, and with some stress, it is an excellent marching song. Thus would we tramp abreast out and away from our despair, this strange battle cry upon our lips, across the high green-clad chalk to some fairy dell away from adult tyranny.

Now, you might think that this verbiage is particularly trivial and inane. Not a bit of it. There are countless variations to invent, calling for extreme dexterity in the manner of putting the questions, and in the inflexion of the answer. Facial expression and gesture play a big part too. There can be a slight change of words also but with fearful forfeits for anyone who gets out of time. Example:

[40]

'How *is* that Quaker next to thee?' (in an overplayed 'ham' Shakespearean manner with much rhythmic lifting of eyebrows in time to the tramping feet.)

Answer: 'Don't aiktually *know*, old boy, but I *could* go and *see*' (in a very Old Boys' exaggerated voice, what we called 'smothered in blazers').

Then there is the joyful caricature of detested masters. Their voices entered the scene like fairy chimes oft repeated. 'Sounds and sweet airs', we called them; that (for once) 'delighted the ear and hurt not'. Sad to say there were many detested masters, so there were many 'Sweet airs'. But some of them, we felt, had hope. There was the 'Greek Bloke', who placed me and others amongst what he called the 'Old Men', on the back bench. We only got asked questions about once a year, but because they were either to do with deep human problems or highly intuitive in nature, rather than in any sense scholastic, we often got them right and every one felt relieved in consequence. I never learned any *more* Greek after leaving my excellent preparatory school, but oh the love of the sound of those words. Oh ecstasy. I named a stuffed monkey Luthesomenos at the age of eight. It is still one of my favourite words, though he perished in a fire during an exam. Even to learn the Greek alphabet is to share with the Ancients some of the poetry and culture of all time.

But to progress. The Quaker can be a cockney, or a Welshman or a Yorkshireman. We delighted in broad cockney, and one of us was a wizard at Welsh.

One day a conversation went something like this: 'What about doing a thing on the Quakers themselves?' 'How?' 'Well, let's think of a real Quaker.' 'Where will he live?' 'Brighton.' 'No—only Brighton College and Commercial Travellers there' (this was a stock phrase arising out of a friendly rivalry over an annual cricket match). 'Yorkshire.'

We agreed on that. As far as I remember there were about seven children in the story. There were five of *us* for sure, so we employed bushes for some of the fat progeny. 'Too fat to walk,' said a gay young man who has since become a successful parish priest I believe, but who in those days, we called the Outlaw. Roughly, then, the story became this:

[41]

'A very holy Quaker lived in York but hated pork. But he didn't mind eating anyone who didn't agree with his religious views. He particularly enjoyed eating the detested masters of his day. But when he ate *them* he began to want to teach. So he started a class on religious Algebra in order to instruct people in Latin. Amongst the students he discovered a girl who loved science. He discovered this, because in lessons on Light (which is all pins and dots) he stuck pins into her and the dots came out in the right way. They married and had seven children. These became the "Old Men" in their class, but grew up to be members of Parliament. It is upon such men as these that Democracy is founded, we decided. But one day the Wife died, and the Quaker was very sad. He became ill and streams of callers came to ask, "Quaker, Quaker, how art thou?" And he answered, "Terribly ill, I thank thee." "And how's the Quaker next to thee?" "She's dead, you fool, you can't ask that." But another time: "I 'aven't an inkling luv, but I'll gaw and see." Whereupon the citizens of York knowing that his wife was dead, clapped him into a Loonie Bin.' The tale ended with about forty minutes of strenuous improvised dance by the 'inmates' and their 'keepers', during which many detested masters were caught by the keepers and added to those who were best put firmly out of harm's way.

After such a session as this, we would be greatly refreshed, and more ready to face again the horrors of everyday school life and the dark cloud that descends every Sunday night on all those unfortunate enough not to get through their prep.

On other occasions, the themes were more sedate: I remember one very serious ballet about five fine men (us), who were brilliant at cricket, and who had been left out of all tests by sheer oversight, and therefore never got into the colts. (This had in fact happened to three of us.) But were they disgruntled? Never. They set to work like fine men should, and perfected their athletics by practice on the Downs. When they ran on the playing fields, they were obviously so fast that they all got into relay teams and won their colours. After becoming Varsity Blues, they were all decorated by King George, except one who became a missionary. (One of us did, but not that one.) This story included much ballet built upon the athletic movements of jumping, putting the shot,

[42]

throwing golden javelins dipped in poison, pole vaulting and hurdling bushes. Thus we perfected the style taught us by our school Olympic coach.

We also practised that day, and thereafter, the changing of the baton in relay racing, hour after hour. The perfect change is as exquisite a piece of art as the perfect flying of a hurdle, and to this day is for me one of the most exciting examples of technical drama. Determination, mastery, excitement, production, foot-work, dexterity, thought for others and 'good theatre' are all present in this wonderful moment of time.

Other things we danced were the stories and myths of ancient Greece. We placed great stress on sincere sadness, and always had forfeits for lack of agility or virility. Sometimes we spoke, but mostly we had no breath for it. The form of work was in itself a strenuous form of training, and at the same time a remarkable opportunity for acting out deeply, not only our own griefs, but the griefs and joys of the gods themselves in the great stories of the World. I look back upon that dancing as something, which instilled into me once and for all the deep knowledge of the stan-dards of effort and beauty, which have been my yardstick since, in the judging of professional and amateur work of every kind. Such dance as this was, many years later, to form the basic train-ing for the Pear Tree Players, and other professional companies that have asked my aid.

Towards the end of my time at public school a Riding Society was formed and in my turn I became a sort of informal Captain of it. The dance group had picked up another soul on its way, and within the framework of the Riding Society we became a special riding group too, which formed itself into the Six-cylinder Club. As obviously none of us were ever going to be chosen for prefects, we registered a club tie made up for us in Bond Street, as near the new Prefects' Tie as we dared. The 'Pre' tie was a thin dark blue stripe on a white ground. Terrific. We took the part House Colour of the Deputy Captain of our group, alternat-ing with a pale Cambridge blue one by my choice, because I lived near there and my father had been there. Alternative stripes, also on a white ground. Double Terrific.

Whilst out riding we also created epic. As the horses couldn't dance, we spoke and shouted a lot in these dramas. Most of them centred round violent bursts of galloping by 'Stew Green's Gang' after ghastly enemies, followed always by a slow sad walk home, our heads hanging low, our guns thrown away because our pal had died, with the huge orange sun sinking into Copenhagen China mist, as the Wild West slowly oozed back into the reality of the Downs, the grey stone of the school, a hot bath, Earl Grey tea and half a pound of Bourbon biscuits.

COMMENT

Again, this report is included partly because it provides a piece of cross section of society; and as an actual happening in a public school of all places, it may come as a surprise to many, but it is also factual evidence of the value of spontaneous outburst and creation which aids disturbed youth and gives courage to the outlaw. I want to stress that in many ways this was a good school. It tried to go a long way towards individual timetable and even at that period took boys from many different backgrounds. It was, as I understand the term, a good comprehensive school. Yet somehow it was too level, once fall behind and you were sunk. Most of the boys there were happy, I think. Most of them turned successfully into young men. My brother loved it. There was very little bullying, just cold disdain. Indeed after the warm, earthy, huge, robust family of my prep school, where you loved games and were encouraged and trusted by adults, the whole place seemed cold to me. An iceberg of cold grey. No affection, no trust, cold grey. It was cold grey teaching, cold grey flint and we wore cold grey tweed.

It may well have been that this reaction was part of an overwhelming humbling after considerable success and responsibility. To be at the bottom again after being at the top is part of life, but it is not always a good thing, particularly if the humbling is really humiliation. There was only one other new boy in my house and he spent most of the time with his brother. For many weeks I was entirely alone in a sea of grey tweed. It nearly sent me mad and on top of the pace of the cramming to get into this school, the sloppy and sentimental master, who happened to be my form master, disgusted me and allowed my brain to sink into apathy. Not that I had much and what there was of it craved for the rest, which probably it should not have had to quite such an extent. Another problem was that at such places you must conform. If you conform, you are happy. It is easier to be a convergent thinker and unfortunately I have never been that. Perhaps there are two main forms of intelligence, the first is what I call 'all frontal lobes', clever, can remember and pass exams but cannot necessarily think. The other is more intuitive and philosophic, does not necessarily remember things easily but *perceives*. This type of mind generally belongs to the slow developer and is often divergent in its thinking. Such schools as this did not usually aid young people of such kind. Those of us who were rather of this second pattern, not entirely by our own fault became outlaws. The experience was not a happy one but I would not have missed it. If it did not break you, it engendered or enlarged a sort of quiet moral courage. You must go *on* and you must believe in *yourself* whatever other people thought. It also taught me to understand the whole situation, attitude and feeling of the outlaw which has been invaluable in the treatment of delinquents later in life. But life then had some recompenses, for when the sun was out there was a beauty in the place, the ice lit up. And the Headmaster was one of the greatest raconteurs in the country and it was wonderful occasionally to meet his mind. It gave me a healthy respect for telling a story well. The experience of working under an Olympic runner was wonderful too but it was all too short.

'Dance Drama on the Downs . . .' Description No. 7 gives quite a lot of detail of disturbed and unhappy youngsters retreating in almost textbook manner to an earlier childish mental state in order to refind happiness and gain security. The type of moral courage mentioned above was typified in the standard we set ourselves and achieved in our drama-athletic-movement. This is also an outstanding example, I now see, of those who have temporarily failed in the projected sphere of lessons, making up for it like mad—and succeeding—in the realm of personal play. I am convinced that mental health, once shorn of all the long words and trappings of psychology boils down to a sort of psychic bank account. Too many failures and you are in the red. You must earn success somewhere. The moment your successes—even of an imaginary kind, for after all these affect the unconscious—add up to your failures[1] then outnumber them, you are solvent again. It is this sort of success to which spontaneous creative activity can contribute. It is invaluable for mental health. But it must go on regularly and provide countless imaginary successes and overcomings in struggle, to get rid of the overdraft. That is why Child Drama often contains an element of fighting. It is not delinquency, it is the symbol of overcoming. It is St George slaying the dragon.

It is interesting in its symbolism that pins were put into a girl and dots came out the right way—all to do with anima and animus, also rejection of what we probably wanted, i.e. the sight of any female at all in that monastic set up, for we were only allowed into a town once a year. Thus the loved or longed for thing is punished (like the hated one in witch folk-lore), but comes out all right in the end. No doubt it would also appear to some as a fertility image. However well this virile dance drama helped us to overcome our unhappiness, there was still the dark cloud on Sunday nights of not knowing your work for next day. This gloom is with me yet and no doubt will be till I die—every Sunday night.

The value of all this experience for me is beyond price, not only did it help me to identify again at will with the position of outlaws in actual prison, or in prison

---

[1] There is an important stage which would take too long to describe here in detail. But briefly, when a patient only just equalizes his successes with failures before actually outnumbering the failures in his psychic bank account, there may be a puzzling and prolonged hiatus in general condition. It is often to be found in mental homes and E.S.N. schools. The person is, as it were, brought down to par and needs to be built up again before being asked to face the world. I have written of this in *Dramatherapy as an Aid to Becoming a Person*.

of the mind in later years, but it gave me supreme confidence in spontaneity itself and techniques associated with it, which I was building up. For I must now admit that there was also a suicide club at this school and it was a very serious affair. Nevertheless, members who indulged in my drama-athletic movement began to pass their exams and finally wanted to live again. This really woke me up and gave me an interest in life as well. I did not know then that it would all become part of my life's work and touch people in so many lands.

At the end of this report comes the riding. This was not only fun and a way to happiness but no doubt deeply psychological. It was almost strip cartoonish in its primitive childish form of play. But the horse is also, of course, an archetype— a sort of demon affair, that which plagues. The gallop of the horses of the night (nightmare) bears the sleeper away in an onrush so terrific that there is no resisting. The dream-horse represents a dynamic instinct. Shakespeare refers to the 'Lubbar fiend', but this Lubbar, this Loob, plays the fool with us, for it leads us away to do foolish things. Thus it is unwise to give way to primitive instinct, it leads us to regret. Perhaps that is why nearly all disturbed young people treat a pony badly, not necessarily in a cruel manner, but without thought. They don't handle it and manner the animal, they gallop it like mad. I have noticed it again and again. They treat it like a motorbike, its modern counterpart. The ton up boys are merely riding their Lubbar fiends which lead them sometimes to do foolish things. At least one thing may be said of the gang I describe; after urging, each one, his Lubbar fiend to thunder him away from their citadel of distress in the maddest and fastest rush possible, they always returned—what is more with 'our guns thrown away because our pal had died', i.e. thinking of and honouring someone else, a *very* hopeful sign for future health—they always returned to face the music. Not one of them ever ran away from school, though they constantly asked to leave.

8. Nelson and the Battle of the Rhine

An unexpected event in the life of students abroad

About the year 1930–31 there were a number of remarkable minds grouped around, or linked with, Bonn University. It was my exceeding good fortune to come into contact with many of their owners—artists, doctors, educationalists, psychologists and musicians. From them I drew on a deep treasure store of knowledge and wisdom, which has since stood me in remarkable stead and must have been a source of considerable inspiration to any young person who took the trouble to work hard and immerse himself in that atmosphere. My companions were of many types, gay, despondent, thoughtful or athletic. We played music, we acted, we read widely, we rode horses and played violent rugger for the town or province, then discussed, often through the night. There was one group, that met on Wednesday mornings over a late Frühstück, consisting of such people as the son of a famous London society portrait painter, the son of an English diplomat, a German university professor, Austrian aristocrats, Russian Princes, and a number of perfectly ordinary and delightful young people. It was a gay group of younger folk unlike the other serious groups to which I belonged. This lot changed girl friends so often that one was in permanent danger of having to fight a duel with some cavalier because of getting a fair maiden's name wrong. The maidens had the main things about them identical —they were all incredibly beautiful, all blonde, all with fine teeth and silky brown skin, very good company, slightly podgy, ate far too many strawberries and were absolutely dumm. Sometimes we used to sing a song: 'Oh—a principified Prince is a very pretty Prince but a princeless Prince is POISON.' One of the reasons we loved them was that they always sang it loudest themselves.

One particular morning (I can't quite fix the date now) we had been discussing the resurgence of the Stahlhelm, the crop-headed little man in a cellar who drew a plan of how the Germans were going to come round the flank of the French fortifications in the next war (which they eventually did), and the day that two companions and myself, just after the wearing of badges had been rather hopelessly forbidden in Germany, had bought three different political symbols in a slum shop and been shot at from behind as we went out; then there was the tall young German in the club cap and wearing a very long neck, who passed us most mornings in term time on our respective ways to work. The portrait painter's son said rather loudly on one occasion, 'Look at that giraffe, we meet him every day', and the young man turned round with a charming smile and said in perfect English, 'Oh dear, all my friends call me that'. These and many other things, that no longer come to mind, we talked over, when one of the lads declared that he couldn't waste any more time on such a wonderful day. Who wanted to come for a tramp in the mountains, sleep out and return next day? Three of us said we would. The

[47]

weather held and later on four young men in assorted shorts and carrying weird bundles crossed the Rhine to set out for the Siebengebirge.

I had done some walking up hill before in Switzerland, but may there never again be a forced march in my life at such a pace! Surely the Roman legions would have approved. We obviously intended to pitch camp before *prima luce* and all its roseate hues. It had been decided not to go to the castlelike hotel on one of the hills: there was another hill with a clearing of trees and a much better view, we were told. We found it, and finally we were at the top. It was to furnish me with a mild triumph at having achieved the climb, but also with one of the deepest experiences of peace and beauty of my life. We shared the day's slow death as the heat turned to an olive warmth under the trees. The castle and hills shed their third dimension and became cardboard against a splash of cool hurt sky, but away to the west a frantic flame spread fast and knocked on layers of cloud edge like mighty floodlights controlled by million watt dimmers in the wings of Heaven's pantomime. But far below, not yet caught by fire, a pale blue Rhine corded its way, removed and unbelonging, between these foster-parent peaks. And above it, lightly floating was its soul—a silver snake of gentle cloud with tones of kindred blue, but so sensitively attuned to the needs of the river that it danced the identical moves and shapes, eye to eye, heart to heart, like lovers at a ball. So a man might think that there were two dreaming torrents and see a higher second river in other realms of time, and be convinced at last that the one true river was the soul of cloud and not the one below. My thought was broken then at a sudden dimming by the unseen stage manager, and as the sun sank away the moon came in bright at the other end of the wood, till a sort of lost chord of light mixed within our clearing that I can never find again. And, as if that were not enough, the first glowworms came crawling. But, again, some Alfred Hitchcock angel kept the tension going. With a clutch at the throat I received Titania's subject host of followers. A thousand fireflies fled across my sight, until the whole night and every leaf and tree and creeping flying thing was bright with cooling ecstasy.

I do not know how long we sat there. No one spoke. Nor could

[48]

anyone tell another of their happy suffering. But the midges finally woke us to reality. We slapped on anti-bite lotion, ate our sandwiches, drank our gleaming wine and fell asleep.

The birds always wake me when I'm sleeping rough, and the day always starts heavy with golden slumber and a ghastly feeling in the stomach for lack of being unconscious. It was this moment which one of my companions chose for the opening remarks of a discussion on Freud and God. One of the others somehow deftly turned it, via nursery rhymes, to the philosophy of Nietsche. When it came to my turn, all I could say was 'Nietsche Nuts!' To my surprise there was general agreement and we moved farther down the slope to a bigger clearing in order to sunbathe. After a lifetime of chattering torture it was half past seven, and before eight the sun was so hot we had to put pfennigs over our eyes, until in turn they burnt us too and we had to keep changing them for others.

I think the drama started from this really. Someone said, 'God, I wish I was Nelson, at least he only had one eye. Good idea on a day like this.' And I said something rather inconsequent like, 'All these Naval chaps have good ideas. I remember one coming to give us a lecture on Zeebrugge at my prep school. He sure fooled our present hosts. Why don't we get into the shade and have some good fooling of our own? Come on John, you be Nelson.'

Eventually they agreed grumbingly. Once out of the sun we began to wake up, the association of ideas came smoothly and although none of my present companions remembered doing this sort of drama since childhood they were soon quite deeply in it:
Self: 'John, that mound's your ship.'
John: 'Who has my t-telescope? You blighter, *you*'ve got it.'
He ran at one of the others and tickled him till he screamed, then said: 'He had it in his p-p-pocket.'
The diplomat's son shouted (mixing his history a bit): 'Himmel, Nelson, I'll get you for verdamfte dics, du Schwein-admiral.'
He then shanghai-ed me into his ship's company and I found myself fighting for the enemy. The fourth man joined John and became, in turn, a gun, a mutineer, a mast and an albatross. Nelson shot him with a 'one-eyed catapult'. 'The b-b-bogus bird',

[49]

he cried. Then the trouble started. We, the enemy, having stalked through green grass waters up to our chin and many waving mists of foliage, uttering ghastly fog horn noises the while and finally reciting Milton ('. . . as when the Arimaspian . . .' which can sound infernal enough for any horn, if you care to make it), came of a sudden into clear light. And there, clear before us in the German day, lay the British Fleet, all athwart with gun-cocks gleaming and a sly Ango-Saxon smirk amongst its crew. 'Shootenheimer! Es ist der perfidische Albion selbst.' screamed my boss leaping onto a fir branch to direct the fray.

We threw. Everything that came to hand ended up on the luckless Nelson. 'Blast,' shouted John, 'I n-nearly lost my other eye.' Then, after an interminable battle and many adventures for us all, he fell to one knee. 'Hardy,' he called, 'I fail, I fail.' 'Don't we all,' muttered my boss, who had never passed an exam in his life. 'Coming, my lord,' called Hardy, taking the longest and most difficult route over fallen logs, mounds, ditches and even upright trees where necessary. The tension was fright-ful. It created temporary chivalry even in us, the foe. We held our fire for the terrible last moments.

Nelson, by this time, was very uncomfortable. He was leaning over rather like the Tower of Pisa, only worse, and hanging on to a 'flying briddle on the taff-tusset' to support himself from falling quite, till Hardy's interminable journey to him were done. At last Hardy arrived, and the inevitable 'Kiss me Hardy' was spoken, but with the unusual addition, '. . . but go steady, old man'. Hardy went as if to kiss Nelson, then suddenly emptied the remains of a bottle of water over him. 'Ow, you swine,' shouted John, no longer Nelson any more. 'I've known some g-girls and aunts who kiss wet, but nothing anything like this.' He then chased Hardy hard, who, being a runner of some repute, got away easily, to return later with myself hurdling bushes in pair with him, to bomb the remains of both fleets from the air.

That is all the detail that my notes can give, though the play lasted some fifty minutes. I wrote things down to put in my weekly letter home. It somewhat surprises me now to think of the ease with which these different types of young man entered into the joy of that creation, and for so long too. Upon it I was later to

Improvisation to music. St Philip's EC School, Cape Town

Beginnings of individual spontaneous dance. Children's Evening, Rea Street Drama Centre, Birmingham

Below: knights fighting with axes. Senior boys letting off steam. It is useful to have weapons of air. 'Experience without sin', Rea Street Drama Centre, Birmingham

Learning to shake hands and welcome people. (Social Drama) Rea Street Centre, Birmingham

A situation beginning to develop. Top Group, Tuesday Evening, Rea Street Centre, Birmingham

base my first really big arena production, in the baths at Bad Godesberg, a feature programme pageant entitled 'Nelson to Kaiser Wilhelm', in which swimmers were battleships, Nelson died on the high dive and aeroplane raids on London and Berlin were enacted by athletes running and hurdling in a sand pit near by. Thus do ideas grow when the poet in us plays upon the embers of them.

But the four of us then, the famous artist's son, the possible future diplomat, the reputable runner and I, wound slowly down the mountain in search of late breakfast-lunch, which we eventually found across the Rhine in that hotel where another Englishman, some ten years after, was to have an historic discussion with the would-be Nazi Emperor of Europe.

COMMENT

This description really speaks for itself, you either like it or you don't, but there are a few points worth mentioning. One sees this through the eyes of a young man who although having had a good deal of experience as an actor is only slowly emerging out of the stages of Child Drama, but is now apparently able to organise even unwilling companions under uncomfortable circumstances until the spontaneous spark is lit. Wise elders had felt a 'bit of time abroad' would help and how right they were. It restored confidence enormously to meet a wider world and particularly the minds grouped round Bonn University as mentioned.

On the evening on the mountain one sees also a mind now very concerned with theatrical production on an enormous scale and although this scale was rejected in later years in favour of something much more simple, it was a period that had to be gone through.

I hope the reader will just relax and enjoy the sheer fun of the Nelson episode and perhaps be able to share *something* of the mountain with me. But those particularly studying spontaneity might marvel that these particular people actually did it. The Language Flow[1] was superb and one notes often the different sense of humour which creeps into the creations of youngsters who have had special advantages in education. Something sticks. The Perfidious Albion *himself*, in pidgeon German is absolutely wonderful, the 'selbst' makes it so strong. One becomes suddenly aware of some fearful collective hypocritical monster and aware too through the flash of wit and fun in spontaneity of a deeper hidden truth about how others may see us. My 'boss' and I were role playing the part of Germans but representing maybe something of continental thought altogether (überhaupt!) at that moment.

[1] First explained in *Child Drama*.

Language Flow is a wonderful thing, it is an arrived-at form of emotional as well as mental and physical fluency to express in words. It should be achieved by at least seven years of age, if enough improvised work has taken place. But generally it hasn't and then the break through later is much more difficult particularly for serious students. These were not terribly serious students but their flow was somewhat unexpected all the same.

One should add that spontaneity is such a remarkable thing that it is possible for people to hold conversations in foreign tongues yet catch a deep sympathy and understanding. It is the principle underlying my suggestions for 'blah-blah' talk with a baby, for communicating and for extending vocabulary, partly, it is true, by the emotional music, but finally with the more intellectual association of meaning by one added real word. I have known older children create most moving dramas in 'jabber-talk' too and have used it as a bridge for different nationalities working together, for disturbed children, for those unable to express (at university level), also in the training of salesmen for export trade. It can offer a tremendous release and I hope it will be used soon as a step for helping children who are learning English as a second language (I was speaking at a centre of such training this very day). One must break down the inner barrier of being unable to converse or fluency dries up. To speak in any way at all is the important thing. Jabber-talk can also help stammerers. Talking of this, it is worth noting that one of the young men in this report has a stammer and stammers also in the improvised play. It may be that the stammer was too well established or that he was not too deeply involved in the play, or even that he enjoyed it a bit, for 'b-b-bogus bird' is much better than the usual way of saying it. But in younger folk it is often noticeable as an extraordinary fact that during spontaneous creation a child may entirely cease to stammer until he becomes himself again. As a stage of development from jabber-talk we find here joy in invented words that often comes during Language Flow. 'Hanging onto a flying briddle on the taff-tussett.' What could be more nautical!

The experience of the mountain as well as the Nelson episode may have influenced my desire to produce huge pageants for a time after this, as well as the drama creations with children in the forest (partly influenced by Ben Greet[1] too) perhaps).

At least it is a splendid piece of dramatic irony that we should have enacted Nelson of all things in the high clear air above the Rhine and then gone to eat at the very hotel where Chamberlain met Hitler afterwards.

[1] A well-known travelling company that took Shakespeare to schools, performing plays in open spaces, on green terraces or amongst the shade of trees.

9. Hockey in Regent Street, the Fish's Eye and the Little Yellow God at Four in the Morning

Young City men, artists and students in London, 1932-3

Most young people like to dress up and most of them that I knew in the early 1903s did so in one way or another. Strangely enough they were interested in the Edwardian period even then, and also the late 1800s. The vogue was for bright ties, extremely clean gloves and expensive walking sticks. No sloppy loose overcoats, they had to be extremely well cut. But evening dress was the best of the lot. We had not come to the period of double-breasted satin-faced American dinner jackets. That came later. Full evening dress tails, and top hat were the thing, with a white scarf, plus monogram, from Austin Reed's. One night several of us had bust the savings of a month to go to cheap seats at some show and had gone on to a very simple party afterwards—the kind where you drink weak beer, eat kippers and dry bread and talk about politics, education, women, Russia and God, to a background of Bach and Leslie Hutchinson. Somehow it ended up with a game of cricket with rolled-up gloves and someone's too perfect ebony silver-knobbed stick. This employment became dull after one side had declared several times, and everyone seizing their own, or a stick, took upon themselves the democratic readjustment of the game until it evolved into a compromise of hockey.

It wasn't hockey proper, because tooth-mugs, bread crumbs, beloved gramophone records and lack of space do not present a good pitch, and thus it was the red door opened and the hockey began to ooze all over London. Out of the Museum district it started, and then split into numerous games. One veered east towards Red Lion Square, another called out 'Meet you at Lord's' and presumably fought north, one sped off to Trafalgar Square for a date with a lion, and my group slashed their way south-west to Soho. I still see the disposal of forces very clearly in my mind. Where *did* they all end up? One wonders whether they are 'bullying' away now, one in the North Pole, another in Scandinavia, the third in Mid-Europe, at the place where one cannot get any further. Ours at least remained within down-to-earth

[53]

limits, for it is still possible to plot our course. In a way hockey is a down-to-earth game, a very good training for maintaining a position likely to lead to permanently keeping the nose to the grindstone. But you can cover a lot of miles, and travel we did. Round and round St Anne's Square after a change of course from Shaftesbury Avenue, down around and past the many sleeping little eat-shops, cutting across Dean Street, saluting the Lex and gambolling into Golden Square. Up north again behind landed-gent 'Liberty's' shop and all athwart to Oxford Circus.

Now at the south-west corner of Oxford Circus there is or was (for life changes so quickly now) a slicket, much beloved by all who wish to break left towards Marble Arch and catch a bus at a hoped-for cheaper fare than if you actually got on at the Circus. And at the point where this slicket narrows to venture into Oxford Street is, or was, an eatables and fish shop; and two feet from the well-known-to-dogs-and-cats- (who hope to cadge a bite at a cheap rate) curbstone, lay the fish. It was high, yes, no one can deny that. Indeed it was blue. But it made a wonderful hockey ball. I can feel again something of the splendid sense of satisfaction as I think of the poetic curve it made in the air after the first successful hit. There are, no doubt, proper terms in the realms of ballistics for what happened, but in plain English the fish burst like a bomb in mid-flight, its body went up Mayfair way towards the expensive dress shops, its head cometed (comet, says small dictionary, is a wandering or planetary meteor) practically into Regent Street. It was a splendid shot. But the paper was the most romantic thing, it gently disengaged itself and glided away sideways in a moon of light and a zephyr of unfelt wind, like the veils in a Ginger Rogers film.

We pounded after the head. Oxford Circus became one goal. Piccadilly the other. It was all very exhausting. I remember thinking, in a short pause, that there was something unfurnished about London at the Piccadilly end, then realised it was so late that the hansom cab (relic of other gay days) that should be standing outside the Café Royal had either been hired or gone home. We should probably all have died of exhaustion, if one of those small but important strokes of Fate that change history had not occurred. The eye fell out of the fish's head.

[54]

A German friend of mine, who had been studying at a Poly-technic, started to recite the 'green eye of the little yellow god'. One of us thereupon became the yellow god and stood in terrify-ing posture outside Oddenino's with his own eyes tight shut. The fish's eye became his and it was stolen and made off with in a hurried way into Vigo Street, then back again into Regent Street towards Oxford Circus. The eye was wrapped in some-thing by this time, but not very securely, and if you caught sight of it, you were not actually turned to stone or salt, but some terrible catastrophe caught up with you. Thus most of us were blind, dumb, or lame long before reaching Hamley's and one unfortunate man was decapitated and had to continue the journey with his head tucked underneath his arm (a top hat was used for this and imaginary boiled sweets were popped into the non-existent mouth below it by way of comfort). Another person got changed into a faun, so we enacted a good slice of the ballet 'L'Après-midi' and hummed the music in ghostly chorus with white scarves falling each like a tabard in front of us from clenched teeth. We intended to weave back via Bond Street to see whether the Burlington Arcade was locked up. I was arranging a bet that it was, then we remembered old yellow god, and rushed straight back along Regent Street. We had been away quite a time. But there he was, still in the same place, loyal to the drama we loved. He was still a god, but his eyes were open, and he was furious! We returned the extra eye to pacify him but he still didn't like being left. He complained that people would have thought he had jaundice if he'd had to stay until breakfast time. But he didn't, we pointed out. Then with a roar like a dragon an old taxi came round Swan and Edgar's corner. We suddenly felt tired, hailed it and bundled in. During the round tour home we decided to crown the German as Polytechnic King. He was given the eye as his orb, a stick for his sceptre and my top hat for his crown. Near Holland Park he scrambled out suddenly and I never saw my hat again.

There is no need to draw a diagram of this drama. The stages of our journey can be seen in any map of the roads. The only thing that astonishes me now is the energy of youth. I always walk miles when in London, because it is so wonderful, but it makes me feel quite terrifyingly old to face the fact that most of that night we ran.

COMMENT

This is a period piece and again exemplifies a curious elation which comes from participating in such group activity. Activity is the operative word in this description. I am particularly fond of this one because in a way, it was the end of a period, historically and personally. After this, one senses a young man putting the good fortune of plenty of varied opportunity and experience to more constructive uses one hopes, indeed slowly, almost inexorably becoming involved with drama as a profession, using it not only as an art but for the good of other people. I must have been round about twenty or twenty-one by this time and the great depression of the early thirties was still upon us. It was still difficult to get work. The gay twenties had now really gone, gone forever, but the gaiety of youth was not quenched. There is no point in going into one's general way or condition of life here, as it comes into the 'histories' later on. So, considering the example itself, one should note that this night's fun was also enacted by people even older than myself, not only artists and students but young *business* men—normally bowler hats, umbrellas and all that. The power of spontaneous creation—or self-originated activity as my small dictionary calls it—will bind together remarkably different types of companions. But perhaps, in a more upstage way, this was not unlike the apprentices of all types combining together in fun at a much earlier period of history and evolving the first elements of hockey and football at all.

The fact that we dressed up then should not be assessed as merely snobbish. It was the fashion to dress at that period; for instance one dressed to go to the theatre in those days or to go out. In a way it was rather brave, for we had practically no money, but nothing would have induced us to go out improperly dressed. Of our kind, we were also Teddy Boys, but of a very modest sort, we did not go as far as the later T.B.s in any way and certainly did not have long hair. But we did admire Anthony Asquith, not just because he wore a cloak, but because he directed first-class films too. Our standards were high and our taste broad. For instance, note the interest at parties in Bach *and* Leslie Hutchinson. I have drawn attention since, though, to the similarity in the running Chicago Bass to the left hand of the French Suites. There is an aristocracy in many forms of music. It should be good of its kind and we knew it. 'Hutch', of course was supreme. He is part of the history of the period. Not only were his harmonies rich and his syncopation wonderful but each one of his records was a poem—always the opening, then chorus then nearly always a marvellous piano solo in the middle then final chorus, terrific climax and you'd had it. In his prime he had form, emotion, tremendous spontaneity as well as technique. He could always make something even of the most mawkish songs. This is the sign of a first rate artist, surely, like an actor or producer making something even of a bad play—which they often have to. The

[56]

thing that fascinated me and still does, for I have some of the Hutch treasures still, is that during his piano solos he obviously heard the words of the song continuing in his mind, but at a higher, more poetic and grander level, for his playing at such moments almost always gave us a reiteration of the chorus. You can hear him say-sing the words again, though only the piano is calling, yet he astonishes at the same time by his inventive sounds and remarkable use of rhythm (breaking away from mere time beat and back) in full command of the jazz idiom. He always appeared in immaculate evening dress too, by the way.

On somewhat the same sort of theme, I heard a piece by the Beach Boys recently and I could not think what it reminded me of. Suddenly it came to me. The intervals were the same as Gregorian chant—but this was in harmony and the quality of spontaneous gaiety was infectious, *wonderful*. The same sort of gaiety combined with grace was to be found in the beauty and dancing of Ginger Rogers (also mentioned in this episode), partnered and set off by the precise and accurate genius of Fred Astaire. He always gave us the thrill and illusion of spontaneity though one guesses at his hours of practice by the complete but easy-looking mastery of his technique. Talk about athletic-drama-movement!

Where this account says that if you caught sight of the eye of the little yellow god 'some terrible catastrophe caught up with you', youth leaders and secondary teachers might care to note that this is really a development of 'lazy Magic' of the more junior type of play, mentioned earlier, but now it has reason and more form and individual and separately imagined effect on each person. Thus it is no longer lazy, for each person had to think hard—or 'flash' hard and invent; or if the idea just came like a flash out of the blue, then each individual must have been very involved in the creation. Notice the absorption that must have gone on for the yellow god to have even remnants of recognisable godlike quality when we had been away so long. And even though he was now furious, he was still there!

The 'result' of looking at the eye is also a more grown up form of jumping on metal lids in the pavement as mentioned in 'Overture and Beginners' (No. 1) and of avoiding pavement cracks. The whole episode is an emancipation of pavement play, it has much more form and much, much more journey now, but although I hope the reader will again just enjoy this episode for the fun of it, you may judge that it still pertains to the 'wild play of the street'. This maybe is the last time we meet it in these descriptions quite in this form. All this is why the account, apart from anything else, is really a piece of history, as the end of a period (for after this the dangerous fox barks of Hitler began to echo across Europe more loudly) and for the young man I was, a more constructive period was to follow my coming of age. But anyway it is good even to have the names of the streets, for London is changing so quickly that tomorrow even the buildings might be gone.

III. Spontaneity for Others

A MORE ADULT STAGE WHERE ACTIVITY OF VARIOUS
KINDS IS USED FOR OTHERS RATHER THAN AS PERSONAL
INDULGENCE

From here on the descriptions change somewhat. 'Creation is being used to more serious purpose. Past experience is beginning to be used' (see comment in part 1). Hitherto, one might say that the experiences had been very largely for my own need, discovery or pleasure, though there were examples of organising people up. On the whole though, on these occasions I had been partaking as one of a group, if only after getting that group going. Now, it seems, I was beginning to use past experience in a more constructive way and using spontaneous opportunity for others. One could almost say 'for others' rather than 'with others', though this would not be quite true, for taking spontaneous work is very much 'with' also, as in producing a play, when you sort of suffer with each character. One ought to do this when taking spontaneous work too (it is very much ημν and παθος and all that) even when standing back and allowing people to do things for themselves. There is then no 'alien in the room'.

It might be felt that in 'Bernard Shaw and the Moon on the Yellow Beacon' (no 11), activity is of the earlier quality. Certainly it is boisterous and cathartic and of a group, but even here it is based more on script. It is a mixture of childlike creation and the adult art of theatre. It is no longer so unconscious, in places it is more intended, there is even some conscious pride in performance perhaps, and being more conscious about form of words, past experience is now used in a slightly different way. To that extent even this episode is more adult and, even on Hereford Beacon, I think I was more aware of the needs of other people.

ES–C*   [59]

Some of the first theatre training for others, through improvisation, particularly with young professionals, was one of the most exciting parts of my life, marred somewhat by lack of food sometimes and pain, which makes some general detail a bit blurred, though other detail on site became more acute. However, the low state occasionally gave me an inferiority and I would be shy to enter a shop for food. I would not have the courage to get on a bus, even if I had the pennies, and so walked miles. But so remarkable is the magic spark of spontaneity that, once having started work, play, creativity with others, then everything else was forgotten.

10. Acting-in-the-round; a Sudden Meeting

Spontaneous exercises with a group of professional actors in a studio in central London somewhere near the Arts Theatre Club, 1933–4

Self: 'You have no idea yet of group sensitivity, and none of you can walk like ordinary human beings. Dinah, you walk like a perpetual ballerina. John, every inflexion is per training school. No one ever speaks like that in life. It is quite unbelievable. It has to be larger than life, but it must have believability. I know every piece of music you are going to say several bars before you speak it. None of it belongs to you. And, in general, none of you think of the others. You are all thinking of your own chance, of your own performance. Come on now, we'll try *this*.

'I want you to try and believe you are ordinary people, and please speak like them. Just walk the full length of the room when the music is on. Don't pose. Don't show off to me, I hate it. Just be someone. This time I am going to put on Ravel again. A boy (you John) passes down the road, he is sad because he has lost his girl friend, sad with that deep agony that a sudden loneliness in London can bring. Coming from the other end of the street is Dinah. Now, as this new "Girl" passes you, John, as "Boy", feel something of the essence of a new personality entering your life,—you know how it is when you suddenly see someone wonderful in real life. You can't talk to them, because convention forbids it. You might get a clip on the smacker. But here, in this room, in our Dream World, you can. *Make* the most of it, make it lovely. Not for me, for you, for your own creative experience.

'Now: both Boy and Girl go on passing each other, but slowly a fire flickers up in each heart and they turn back to look. This is the difficult part. I shall take off the music at the end of a phrase. You have been walking to it, so your footsteps will keep the rhythm going. But then at exactly the right moment in time (I want you to catch it in sympathy) both actors must turn as one, and meet each other's eye. I want to feel an electric spark struck at this moment. Then a pause. Then everyone else in the

[61]

room is to start whispering—still in the same time beat as the Ravel—"a new life, a new life, a new life . . .". Bring it slowly up to full speech and a climax, and somewhere in that pause both Boy and Girl run to each other. Right, now we'll try it. Note the sensitivity practice for the first two actors, and, "chorus of whispers", you are to start together without aid. You must time it. If you really feel the need of the situation, and of the first two actors, and of each other, you *will* start together. Anyhow you will in the end, because none of us leaves here till you do. Don't forget. There's no audience, no proscenium arch, no stage. You are just two people in a street, and the chorus is the chorus of their thought and emotions.'

Self (after their first try): 'Not bad. Try again. *(After the fifth try):* At last, a spark. But you are still not getting the footsteps on silence. *Enjoy* it, use the rhythm Ravel offers. Absorb it with all of yourself, and then you will use the steps as an integral part of the production. After that, the second when you both turn is easy—why? Because it is demanded by the truth of the situation you create.'

Actor: 'You mean there is in fact only one moment it *can* be. This is frightfully exciting. Come on, Dinah, try again.'

Self (after the seventh try): 'Good. That was a moment. It's correct, but it's not electric yet. You've got to consider your next step too. Until you get this first part right and alive, the chorus can't find its moment. Try again. *(After the eleventh try):* Good. It was lovely, wasn't it.'

Actress: 'It felt quite different. The whole thing felt in rhythm, and each part sort of fitted into the other.'

Self: 'Yes. This is the sort of theatre we are creating. Each part of the play *all through* must have this rhythmic feel in it. Through our improvised dance we've mastered various things, but you must now master these small extra details. You've got to be better than you thought you could be. Burst through into the Dream Land. Enjoy it. Don't be ashamed of it and hold back.

'Now the next bit: Boy and Girl stand looking at each other, then disappointment begins like a worm in the heart, and slowly the whispering begins. "No. No. No new life, no new life, no new life . . ." Bring it to a climax. At the climax, fall away from each other, Boy and Girl. Leave your right foot on the same spot, but let the left fall well away, leg bent, and with weight hard on it. Use your hands in a gesture feeling "warding off", and freeze in that position. Now, chorus, creep up from wherever you are in the room to form a circle round Boy and Girl on the words "No new life" then—the hard part—exactly as Boy and Girl fall away to lay their weight hard on the left leg, you do the same. Try to get it *exactly at the same moment*, with the footfalls together. There must be complete silence, and feel the pleasure at the way you fill the space, near you and your neighbour, with your hands. Now—no wet, dead, trainee, bogus type of mime moves! Make it really true for you. Create something, which, though imaginative, really is worthy, exact and true. You will then have created something that exists. Only when it exists in its own right is it worth sharing or, indeed, only then is there anything to be shared at all. Perhaps that is the secret of good theatre.'

NOTE: *One would not repeat the improvisation so often with most groups. Certainly not with children but these were keen young professionals and could take it.*

COMMENT

Creation here is being used to more serious purpose. Past experience is beginning to be used. This shows how spontaneous beginnings can lead on to the polished improvisation and thence to a piece of theatre, also how it can be used as preparation and training for theatre. The skill of handling and guiding apart from choice of imaginary situation, lies rather in deciding how much to polish. Generally, one must watch that the spark of life does not die and repetition once or twice may be enough. But as mentioned in the report these people were not just here for fun, though they generally found it exciting. The handling is somewhat tougher than one would use with non-professionals.

I have often found that ultimately some such remark as 'Right, now make it your own' is useful during production. It somehow tends to release actors from merely trying to copy what the producer wants or what they think he wants, releases them from the bonds of being organised and sets them free again; it also helps children to see purpose in a lesson, to know how far they may go and to feel they are allowed to be fully 'in it' and not just to do it 'cos teacher sez so'. This is the moment when we may expect spontaneity to return again to the creation even after repetition. It does not return if the actor fails to gain freedom enough to create *something* at least in his own way. The acting remains dead and you can sense it at once.

These young actors were still suffering from being drilled in an old-fashioned way at drama school and had caught all the speech habits rife in second rate repertory at that period, hence 'I know every piece of music you are going to say several bars before you speak it . . .'

The message of good theatre is best put over by a team, though individual stars may dazzle us. However, when young it best behoves an actor to work in a team first. He may dazzle someone later, but it's better to wait till you do. People have different tastes over this though and have their right to them. However, there is something fascinating about a team, for only with a real team do you get a balanced show and the chance to use a genuine rhythm throughout, instead of a lot of separate styles. We could do with more really evolved rhythm in English theatre than we get, for it is rhythm in a production which is the real secret of how to hold an audience, where every click of a latch, pause and footstep is part of a symphony of logic. But the art is that it must appear even then to have spontaneity and, better still, be fully re-created at every performance so that it really has. Improvised dance can help greatly in building up this sensitivity to rhythm. Group sensitivity and group intuition are discussed and defined in *Child Drama*.

Regarding 'walking like a perpetual ballerina', it is very easy to fall into habits and to employ cliches in movement just as in tone of voice or words and you need an observer to guide you out of it. There are differences between formal mime, theatre school mime (of that period anyway), realistic mime, Laban's efforts, dance based on formal techniques, acting without words and spontaneous dance. Such differences these actors were learning. I was trying to help them find the appropriate movement and action to a given situation instead of mixing them all together. In the exercise on eye work, they were learning about timing and intuition as well as rhythm, but the falling back on one leg all together pertains rather to stylised movement and group sensitivity with a sprinkling of extremely simple choreography.

I don't quite know how all this started, probably with groups from the Polytechnic, as mentioned later but I soon found myself doing this sort of work in numbers of little studio theatres, which seemed to be littered around the Arts Theatre Club in London at that time, before starting my own studio. They were mostly young professional actors 'looking for something other than what they had found at theatre school', as they put it. I went to one for a short time and gained a first class certificate for acting, but it was not always easy to see what it was all for. It is interesting, in view of the fuss in later years, that we always worked in arena forms or in the round, even at the date of this description (and earlier) and no one questioned it at all. The creations demanded their own shapes and got them.

[64]

11. Bernard Shaw and the Moon on the Yellow Beacon or A Midsummernight Supreme

A group of young actors at Malvern, 1934

In the hot summer of 1934 it was my lot to play various small but interesting parts at the Malvern Festival, and to ooze myself into bits of extra stage management when and where possible. What a cast they had that year and what hard work it was.

But sometimes we had nights off, and whenever they played *The Moon in the Yellow River* I used to creep into the wings to watch Curigwen Lewis unwrap the parcel. What a sweet moment she made of it. It has remained a lesson in absorbed sympathy for me ever since. After this I would wander into the dressing-rooms where a few of us delighted in improvising situations in Irish dialect. On one particular evening two or three friends came in with me to find a handsome young actor, who used to dash about the streets in a small sports car during the day, cleaning the pistol he used in the play. Errol Flynn was in good form that night. He laid down the pistol and started to chat. We were in no hurry as we were going on to the Festival Club afterwards. Malvern is a romantic place in the summer and I was in love with the daughter of a local butcher at the time and wished the moments to pass quickly until we could meet in a party after the show. A spell in the dressing-room would help things along. This was the night Errol made his great prophecy that he was going to America and would become a film star. After this he gave us a long and superb piece of improvisation in Irish dialect on the perils of alcohol for the young. Then it was time for him to be 'on' and we sauntered off to wait for the club to open.

Eventually the party was over, and the farewells said. But I and two others were in no mood for bed. The night was dark purple and warm, and the myriad lights a-glow on the Worcestershire plain offered the sort of removed but solid security that many young actors need. We started to climb, up past the hotel where Miss Elsie Fogerty stayed, leaving St Anne's Pottery behind, where Miss Bell (now Mrs Lanchester of puppetry fame) had created her incomparable pieces. (I still have a set of coffee

[65]

cups with some dust off the Malvern Theatre's stage in them.) Up and up till we felt we were on the top of the world. We glanced haughtily down on the foreign Hereford slopes and moved as Staffordshire striped ponies over Heaven's promontory, the stars about our hair. The music of our footsteps brought words to our lips, and we found ourselves muttering part of the play and expanding further Flynn's discourse on perilous pints. This would be punctuated occasionally with 'Up the rebels!' (from *Moon in the Yellow River*) or 'and that a good knock' (*Interlude of Youth*) or some mock-Latin lingo ending up with 'burn thy books' (as pertaining to Faustus). Eventually 'rebels' and 'books' were followed by loud cries of the kind appropriate to each and we broke into a run, with arms out and knees bent. We were now the winged horses of ancient legend, avoiding the planets and out-flying time. There is nothing like the fleet joyous running of youth. I have tried to describe it, since, as it appears in happy junior schools and in the playground of the street. But that night we ran ourselves into a New World.

It was then that the Drama started. I remember saying: 'There's a gob-stopper' and promptly swallowed a star. We then saw other stars in the Yellow River, but instead of silver they were gold. Then the other two danced the Old Men of Gotham to the words of the Macbeth witches. When that was done I recited the beautiful speech from the *Interlude of Youth* beginning:

> Lo, masters, here you may see beforne,
> That the weed overgroeth the corn;
> Now may ye see all in this tide,
> How vice is taken, and virtue set aside.
> Yonder ye may see youth is not stable,
> But evermore changeable.

The others rested. There followed a very long and passionate outburst by Fine Spirits against those damnèd arts of necromancy, and three sturdy voices led an imagined host in choral condemnation that shook the patient Beacon: 'Faustus, BURN THY BOOKS!' But the Men of Gotham finally returned, chuckling with evil and sought for Faustus in the Yellow River. But all they saw was the Moon. Faustus had fled. But as they watched into the depths of the water a man appeared unto them. And, lo, it was the Man in the Moon. And they looked again and, behold, it was Bernard Shaw.

That is almost all I remember of this Olympian Night. I do not know how we finished, nor how we came back to earth. What journey did we take from Beacon to banality? We noted no donkeys nor other evil spirits. There were fewer lights, no doubt, and we probably hoped our landladies had not locked their doors. But one thing I do remember, indeed I shall never forget. We had just turned a corner in the midst of Malvern when an owl's-lid cloud lifted from Heaven's evening eye. A sturdy upright figure strode past us in the silvery light, his hair a frothing halo, his beard suffused in splendour. No mistaking the cut of that face. It was the Man in the Moon *himself*—or was it Bernard Shaw?

COMMENT

So great is the desire for creation in many young actors that they like to go on acting all the time—or would if they could. But an actor is at a disadvantage compared with a musician, sculptor, painter or writer, as theatre needs an audience. But there are other ways of blowing off steam, particularly in the type of imaginative creation described. We can use the poet in us too and enjoy to the depth those precious wonderful moments of sheer *living* and the joy of our individuality. On these occasions you do not need a separate audience for, as in Child Drama, you and your companions are audience and actors all in one and the shared appreciation and joy in spontaneity as it flashes to the surface is enough.

We had had some gruelling hot weeks rehearsing at the Old Vic and the dressing rooms were very crowded at Malvern and despite the fact that the fantastic cast gathered that year were, for the most part, kind and delightful people, Sir Barry Jackson being perhaps the kindest of them all, it was a relief to get right out of the theatre and away. It was rather like getting out of school and racing to the playground.

We note in this account a new item coming into the improvisation, that is the inclusion of allusions to and even chunks of the actual script plays being performed at the theatre, but oh what a different type of production! It is perfectly possible to include pieces of script in improvisations, indeed they often gain a certain freshness. A mixture of the two, in fact, is the best way for teachers of, say, thirteen-year-old children to make the bridge between unconscious creative drama of a junior kind and theatre as an adult understands it. For theatre is an adult art. It is a point about which one is asked time and again.

Those who are familiar with the philosophy of Child Drama will recognise in 'we broke into a run, with arms out and knees bent . . . the winged horses of ancient legend . . .' an adult example of what I have tried formerly to describe as Running Play. It is so interesting that, given the same conditions, the same spur and once alive to opportunity, adults will create very much as children do and often behave (creatively speaking) in a similar way.

It is a curious fact about human nature that we tend to get into a rut, in all sorts of ways. In delinquency youngsters can get into a rut of rôle playing, and spontaneous acting is one of the few things which can help them out of it. They see themselves as a pirate, a gangster, an outlaw, a great leader of revolt; their teachers are unfair, their parents are terrible. All these things may be quite untrue but once let an outlaw get into a rut of being one, whether he is or not, and he will endeavour to remain one as long as he can, over-defending with a permanent chip on his shoulder unless he is fortunate enough to find someone or some *thing* to help him out. (Nothing like a disturbed child for creating completely inaccurate images. Adults too for that matter.)

In my own case, as described earlier, the 'thing' that gave me and others courage and ability to refind happiness was spontaneous creation. At base, of course, because creativity is an outflow of energy, interest must be outside yourself, at least partly, and explode into action. Nothing like being interested in things *outside* yourself for mental health, it stops you being 'sorry for you' inside.

The type of rut we were in as young actors was the eternal repetition of passages of the plays at the theatre and eternal mimicry of the way other actors played their parts, until we and everyone else got fed up with it. We rehearsed so much of the time that we absolutely lived in the parts. It was probably very good for us, therefore, to fling ourselves out and against the heavens on those sturdy hills. It will be guessed what deep pleasure and satisfaction this experience of spontaneity gave us on that huge avenue arena.[1]

Isn't it extraordinary how, in the rhythm of life, coincidence can play such a part? Come across an unusual word or name and you will probably meet it several times close together in the newspaper, on the radio or television soon afterwards. We even have the expression 'talk of the devil'. It was just perfect, and a great piece of the drama of life, that we actually met Bernard Shaw after making him our Man in the Moon.

---

[1] For those dealing with emotional problems, it may be noted that the situation was not unlike the special pulpit arranged for 'the *super*-ego', as Dr Moreno of New York described it to me.

[68]

12. The 'Ideas Game' and a Good Bit of Blood

With students and young professionals, some of whom later joined the Parable Players, Broadhurst Gardens, London, 1935–6

The year had been a varied one. I had finished playing in *Henry IV* at what was then His Majesty's Theatre, London, had taken juvenile lead during the summer in a repertory in the north of England, had taken the main part in a 'new' version of the ballet 'L'Après-midi d'un Faune' in my own studio in London, and had started training a group of students and young professionals in modern and what would now be called Arena Theatre. I had also written innumerable stories for children, and eaten the world's record number of sausages and mash. But, before going off to join a new repertory being formed in North London, there was a job to do. This was the training of people who were interested in the sort of work being done at my studio. Some of them later joined the Parable Players, an already established professional company I had started, with the intention of keeping alive an interest in the old morality plays, but which also dealt with Children's Theatre. Later this group split up into numerous companies. The first company toured London and the Home Counties during the 1930s and subsequent companies toured the Midlands and West Country.[1]

Most of the training was based upon improvisation and great stress was laid on the music of the feet in ordinary acting— rather in a filmic manner. But apart from the flow of words, there was a lot of dance too, and I was learning to mix the proportions, for different types of production, of entirely personal and freely expressed dance with the more rigid discipline of the Drama Athletic Movement already mentioned, which had its origin in the use of body weight and the saving of energy. This brought the type of control and finish I wanted to see in acting, and also the grace. But the improvised dance brought sensitivity and spontaneity. My knowledge probably did not extend at that time to the ways in which one may help a person to

[1] See Coggin's history of *Drama and Education*.

[69]

discover a purely individual style of dance nor how to aid them through the process of selfish emotional dreaming to the discovery of the sanity of *form* and its mastery. But it had certainly been my conviction for a number of years that there was a manner of dance, both important and exciting, which was discoverable, explainable and repeatable, yet based on no set idea either of ballet or modern dance or any other accepted tradition. That I was right is now borne out by numerous educational experiments here and abroad, by my own professional companies that have been trained in the method, by the regular work at Birmingham Drama Centre (Rea Street) since about 1948 and by the gradual introduction of similar methods into professional theatre schools, not to mention the annual National Summer Courses organised by the Educational Drama Association. Any more detailed description of the training of the Parable Players ought really to belong to a book on theatre, but perhaps the following just belongs to this book.

At the studio that day we had been doing a good deal of work on freeing oneself from the habit of projection (as used in proscenium theatre) and developing the inner concentration and repose necessary for three-dimensional acting. The students had been asked to carry on improvisations not only in my main teaching room, but in order to learn the discipline of keeping things going, to walk through another room and back via a landing to the main room, acting all the time. I don't know when it was I first started using the Ideas Game. It is a great aid, either to a jaded mind, a mind terrified by blank helplessness when suddenly confronted with a group, or a mind somewhat permanently devoid of imagination. But it also happens to be a splendid way of building a bond with your group and of building their own confidence in their own work. The resultant story becomes in part their own creation, and thus has the dynamic of joint ownership, or at least a feeling of a finger in the pie. It can be used seriously or unseriously. Today we wanted a bit of blood to finish up with, so this is what we did.

Ideas were asked for. The answers were: *Knife Bread Death.*

My Story: The *Knife* lay there shining with a cold evil. The man entered the window. He sniffed slightly. Would there be food? The Knife lay there shining with a cold evil. The man slowly turned, and the moon showed green on his coat. He moved cat-like to the sideboard, and the Knife lay there shining with a cold evil. Then he saw it, the *Bread*, a dull grey lump. He grabbed it quickly and cut, cut for his life. It was a sort of tearing chop. He thrust the bread into his mouth. It was then that the Knife fell, and lay there shining with a cold evil. The man looked down at it, sweat starting on his brow. It was the noise, of course, that brought the old lady in. The light went on and they looked at each other a moment, then the old lady came forward a pace or two. 'What are you doing?' she said. He jumped and caught her. Quickly his fingers closed on her throat, she swayed and fell, they both fell. His fingers loosened and the old lady started to scream. There was the Knife, and he plunged it in. The scream died as it started. He got up. He looked at her. A crust lay near her. It was red. He caught her eye. 'No,' then he screamed, 'I didn't mean to do it.' He rushed to the light. Snap, it was dark again, except for the greenish moon. And the Knife stuck there, its haft shining with a cold evil.

'There you are, that's your scene. Work up for contrasts, get good changes in thought, and change of tempo in your move-ments, and this time we are listening to the music of the scene as well. Notice the sound of your feet. I want it in the right rhythm and the screams timed to that rhythm. We are building up a process that I call symphonic production. "Man", turn slowly at the beginning, and imagine that a green light from a half dimmed flood falls on your back.'

We worked on this for half an hour and polished until we were satisfied. (*See diagram on page 72*)

Second Diagram of work with those training to join the **Parable Players**:—

In order to train young actors and all who came to my studio at that time in the art of absorption in the task and sincerity in the way of doing it, they had to pass out of the main acting area in one room and continue in the same rôle whilst passing through

[71]

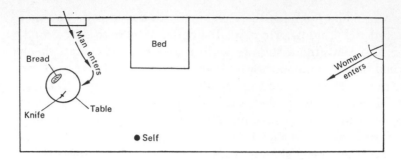

another room and one or more assessors would be there to see them do it. (*See diagram on page 73*)

COMMENT

The period of taking haphazard groups in little studios was ending if not over. According to this report, my own training studio was now established and both amateurs and professionals were coming there. From here on, my Ideas Game will be noticed more and more as a technique for starting creativity.

Figure 1 and the foregoing description show the Ideas Game being used as a training for Proscenium acting. Figure 2 shows how the method of a 'journey' was used for helping actors to concentrate—'walk through another room and back via a landing to the main room, acting all the time'. They all suffered from 'on stage', and 'off stage'. I tried to teach them to *be* acting before they went on stage and not to think it so clever to turn on an unbelievable smile and snap it off on their exit. In later years I have noticed actors in Theatre for Children groups walk off an arena area and whilst still in sight relax and come right out of the character. This, of course, destroys credibility for the child. It all becomes just vague fun instead of the emotional and aesthetic experience it ought to be—sometimes it is not even fun, just bewildering. Don't be led away by suspension of belief, disbelief, cynical unsuspension and all that. If people want any audiences for the future, they had better leave incredulity alone—and quick. The only way is to provide what the child can accept as truth.

My first Theatre for Children companies had presented plays rather in proscenium form, soon after I had come to London, probably because this was the convention expected by schools, but it was the observation of child play while wandering in the streets that made me see other possibilities and feel that I was probably wrong to present them in so traditional a way. It seems extraordinary that I didn't see it before, after all the work described. Perhaps the acting in space and off-stage had been largely unconscious (see the comment on No. 10. 'The creations demanded their own shapes and got them'). But after observing children very carefully, at considerable length and in a much more objective

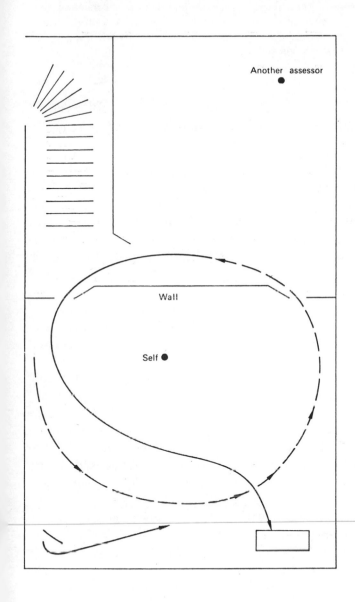

manner, I tried changes; and by now I was clearly training for a consciously different form of Theatre to present rather than only making creations for crowds of people to take part. But perhaps it is not so surprising, for children also quite often think of their own Child Drama as a different world to 'a play' which a teacher may put on. Sometimes they see no connection between the two. But then nor does the teacher sometimes.

13. The King of Pompatti, Podgebox and the Royal Balloon
A children's listening group, Birmingham, 1936 or 1937

When I returned to Birmingham in 1936 as the youngest 'Uncle' on any Children's Hour (a previous short term at the Rep had been my first visit), I had just watched my father die of cancer, had given up my training studio in London and was very short of money. By the time my washing and weekly bill for the bed-sitting room was paid, I had practically nothing left. Just enough for lunch sometimes, but never enough to go to a theatre, nor even a cinema. One walked everywhere. I remember some wonderful evening skies, which met me coming out of the old B.B.C. studios in Broad Street and stayed till just after Five Ways. The worst of poverty is not just the pain, hunger, dirt and loneliness—I'd had some of that too, earlier on—but it is so *boring*. Most of one's courage goes into inventing what to do. Sometimes I would get a bus, though, having saved up a few pennies. It would be a sort of dream to take a bus out past Harborne to Bartley Green. It was very reasonable country in those days and anything like a West wind brought a real freshness from Worcestershire. The reservoir always looked lovely and, going the other way, one met wonderful fields and woods.

It was on this part of Bartley that I sat down one Saturday to think over the lessons arising out of opportunities I had taken for experiments with children and their dramatic play. Not only with my Children's Theatre Companies in the last years, but just lately I had become sure of a number of things. It seemed that children (*a*) needed space for movement during play; (*b*) needed quite a different drama, mostly of their own making; (*c*) had an

[74]

imaginary world which was quite apart from ours and their form of presentation—if that was even the word for it—was in a completely different shape from adult theatre and from almost anything, in fact, that we expected them to like. I dreamed of a centre where one could develop this drama and interest adults in it and a sudden convincing hope flooded in me that, one day, lots of teachers would in fact be using it in schools for the enrichment and happiness of their pupils. When so many places had to be visited first and when world-shaking events had to happen, it would not have been possible for me to guess then that in a little over ten years' time I should be back in Birmingham and my centre established at Rea Street.[1] But the most remarkable thing of all—the sort of thing that happens to few people, perhaps, in their lifetime, and for which I am deeply grateful— is that on the spot where I sat ruminating that day, there now stands the hall of Woodgate School. And it was here on that floor space, after training with me and after leaving Steward Street, under Mr K. R. Scott, that Miss Jane Giddings (before her marriage) was to do her wonderful work with children. At the time of writing, her tradition has been carried on and they still develop Child Drama in that place, exactly as I had dreamed of it years before—only better.

The sort of experiment that had given rise to my thought was as follows. It was with one of the Children's listening groups which I had started,[2] to obtain real opinions of B.B.C. Children's Hour. I used to have sessions of imaginative drama with them after discussions. They had listened to a Request Week Programme in which a story of mine about a horse called 'Podgebox' had been included. So Podgebox was one of their ideas this evening.

IDEAS: *Podgebox   Cigar   Green motor   Apple*
Our story (built together by discussion and selection): Podgebox was in his field leaning over the gate as usual chewing a bit, and thinking about flies. Then he saw 'that man'. He was about to move off when the man offered him a wonderful *apple*. Podgebox

---

[1] Pronounced 'Ray'.
[2] I understand that these groups were some of the first of their kind, well before the general monitoring service, but believe that Mary Richards had a group or so about the same time.

took the apple and bit it and chewed and swallowed. 'Want to put you in the cart,' said the man, 'and drive you into Birmingham.' 'Not me,' said Podgebox, 'I don't feel like work.' 'It's not work,' said the man, 'it's fun.' 'Fun pooh,' said Podgebox, 'now if we were to go in a motor, that might be different.' So the man borrowed a *green motor* from his pal Joe, and he and Podgebox drove off in the front seat. When they got to Birmingham, people began to stare, and soon they formed such a crowd that the car could hardly move. Suddenly someone cried: 'To the Town Hall.' So off they went, and out came a reporter, and he said: 'To the B.B.C.' So off they went, and out came an announcer and he said: 'Come inside'. And the King of Pompatti was visiting too, and he took Podgebox into the Children's Hour Studio and introduced him to the Public through the microphone. And Podgebox spoke of many things that day, of flies and food, and green fields, and puddings, of leaning-gates and low fences, and the price of oats. When he had finished, in burst the Head of all Radio in Europe. 'Wonderful, magnificent,' he cried, 'such poetry, such charm.' And he gave Podgebox a Head European *Cigar*, which Podgebox promptly ate. But the King of Pompatti, not to be out-done, brought in his guitar players— all five hundred—and they played, whilst Podgebox danced in the studio, and all the announcers played the coconuts in time to the music. Then the King of Pompatti bought Podgebox for a thousand gold patties, and they flew off in the Royal Balloon, encrusted with toffees and diamonds. But the farmer was quite bewildered. 'Never mind,' said the Lord Mayor, 'you're a rich man now.' 'So I am,' said the farmer, and he drove home happily in the green car, and wrote to Podgebox every week for a whole year.

As there were only about ten of us, it meant that we had to change character suddenly and often. My parts were an announcer, a fly, a microphone, and Joe. At one time we were all flies dancing, and at one time we were all Podgeboxes. (Flies danced to 'Flight of the Bumble Bee', all Podgeboxes to a fast bit of Bizet's Children's Suite.)

Podgebox himself danced in the studio to a record of dreamy harp music. Announcers' coconuts were spoons tapped on saucers. The diagram shows roughly the shape of the main events.

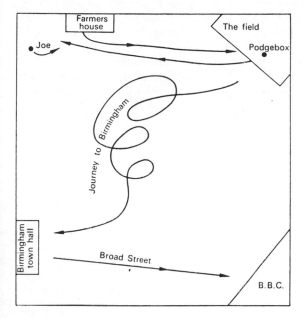

Then the whole room became the studio with me as the microphone in the middle. The Royal Balloon flew round the room three times then faded before our eyes. It is sad to think that I may never see it again.

Soon after this, I first met Stanley Evernden, who was to cooperate so closely with me some years later, when at the Birmingham Emergency Training College, before going to Loughborough. On this occasion he invited me to comment on a Grammar School production.

COMMENT

These listening groups were for the most part very different from, for instance, the children in report No. 5, but their play showed similar shapes. The flies dancing were very like those skating in the earlier description.

'Had to change character suddenly and often' is common in Child Drama, this I knew, but here it was associated with listening power. Restless and backward children are to be found in any group, but many more than expected could not follow one character very easily through a radio play and, of course, if voices were too alike in timbre or spoke too fast they became bewildered. Something to do with the fact that they change character often themselves but other people mustn't? Note again the earlier suggestion of not casting too early when taking children in creative play.

The noises introduced were partly because of what I had learned about children in the streets of London. Here a noise is used to represent another noise and accepted as perfectly natural—'Announcer's coconuts were spoons'. 'Me as the microphone in the middle' is an example of what was said earlier (No. 3) about adults needing to be a 'living property' quite often during children's creation of this kind, particularly in out of school play.

14. The Legend of the Lady of Shalott, Mr Growser of Toytown, Sir Jan and Lorna Doone (with apologies)
At a Women's Institute in 1937

The new year had brought a series of invitations to run weekend Schools on Drama all over the Midlands, also to give verse recitals and to lecture at Women's Institutes. It was not proving too easy, as my main job then consisted of being temporary Head of Children's Hour at Bristol B.B.C. studio, announcing there in evening programmes part of the time and continuing my work in the Birmingham studios on the odd necessary occasion. The only way it could be done was by taking a cottage in the Cotswolds,[1] half way between the two farthest points, and driving like Jehu about the country hoping to be at least in one and a half places at once, if not two—a somewhat schizophrenic form of existence. But I loved the work in country areas and did not want to give it up. A great many W.I.s were visited about this time and from my acquaintance with them then and during the years since, they have provided me with ample cause for profound admiration. One would not be far wrong in describing them as the unadmitted, but probably real, backbone of England.

One of the things that struck me as most interesting was that whereas many Institutes had their own little drama group,

[1] Chipping Campden, where a crippled boy used to put flowers in moss on my old English square piano, if he had liked my programmes. If not, I did not get them.

members of which would not be timid to go on a stage and do their bit, nothing would induce most of the others to go on a stage at all. But *all* of them seemed to be prepared to do drama on the floor of the hall—as long as it started near their own chair and not too far from the rattle of tea cups. They did some lovely work then—not quite theatre, but drama in a very wide sense, a kind of vivid folk art in three dimensions. I always remember a circular creation that my wife achieved (after I had cajoled her into this work), of Adam and Eve and a perfectly marvellous serpent, with a W.I. in North Staffordshire. But early in 1937 I had not met her yet and this is what happened tonight. One or two members mentioned that they had heard my production of *Lorna Doone* from Bristol B.B.C. Station, and one had commented kindly on my arrangement of *The Lady of Shalott* for three voices from the Birmingham studios. Quite a number of us admitted addiction to *Toytown* too, which it had also been my pride and joy to produce. So on the whole, though quite by chance, we seemed to have something in common. On this shared experience our drama developed.

The hut was fairly big and a reasonable space made things look promising.

My story: You know what troubles Lorna had. Well, one night when she fell asleep, a dream came to her about her Jan. She dreamt she was the Lady of Shalott, and was continually hoping to see Jan dressed in fine armour and riding a magnificent horse. The window was too high for her to look straight out, so she tried to see him in a mirror on the wall. Meantime she would spin, and what she spun was the hopes of mothers in dark attics in big cities, the cry of a heart when a sailor comes home, the perfume of an autumn evening and the smile of a child when it offers you a flower. Suddenly she heard hooves—the hooves of many horses, hooves of all the horses of all the lovers in the world, filing slowly past her tower. She looked at the mirror to see her Jan, but crack went the surface into a shivering star, like a smooth pool shattered by an arrow wide of its mark. When the guard brought her food that night, the lady lay pale upon the floor, an arrow through her heart. But though they put her body upon a gilded raft to float down the river of time, her soul floated free from the narrow window, born by two white swans. They took her to a hermit's cave and the hermit was Jan. 'Here we can live for ever,' said Jan, 'in perfect peace, for I too have left my body behind, upon a charger. I had become vain and proud and angry of mind. No longer was Sir Jan riding there; I had become Mr Growser, on a donkey. And after much suffering for my sins I have found peace here in my new home.'

Then the Lady understood why she had not seen her Jan in the mirror, for even the looking-glass could not bear to see the change and had broken its heart. But at that moment Mr Growser himself rode up. 'Ah, there you are, Sir,' he cried. 'I have been looking for my better self all over Arkville. Where have you been all this time? I'm surprised you're not ashamed to look me in the face.' But Jan answered quietly: 'Poor Mr Growser, don't be angry for once. Don't judge everyone so, don't grasp for what you can't have. Above all, never envy anyone. That I have learnt since I came here. Never envy *anyone*. There is always something unknown in their life, which you probably could not face, if called upon to do so.' And Mr Growser went sadly away.

But just then the two swans returned and started to peck lightly at each other's feathers. The Hermit and the Lady were surprised to see emerge a somewhat sticky looking dachshund and a panting little lamb. 'Oh, Denis, I'm afraid we've missed Mr Growser. Sorry we ca-a-a-ant stay Mr Hermit Sir, and Mrs Shalott, Ma-a-am.' 'No, after him go hurriedly is what we must, Larry my friend, didn't it?' Crying and barking the two ran off to find and comfort Mr Growser. And the crying of sheep and the barking of a dog is what Lorna heard when she awoke. She sat up in bed and peeped out of the window. The sun was in an armour of gold and riding upon a billowing cloud as charger. Below her, in the roadway, was a man. She looked down and met the smiling eyes of Jan Ridd.

To get people going, everyone was asked to stand up and use their feet on the boards to make the noise of the horses' hooves. We practised this for a bit, then added quiet stepping, as if from a distance, getting louder and disappearing again. Then we added a 'crack' noise for the shattered looking-glass. Somebody suggested swishing a bit of garden cane down on a ping-pong table. We finally used this noise together with the words 'crack', 'sausage' and 'mash', one of which was spoken loudly by everyone in the room. Altogether this mixture sounded rather what we wanted. Then I judged it time to dare further adventures and asked them to put their chairs against the wall. They came out bravely enough on to the floor space and I asked Madam Chairman to help me cast them.

Lorna 'went to sleep' on the little Institute stage. We made that her room. About ten members built a wonderful tower in another part of the hall from chairs and bits of stick put round a table, which acted as a raised floor and upon which the Lady of Shalott sat for her spinning. Others brought in and upturned a bicycle for this and she used the front wheel (the back one was too oily). We filled in little quick flashes of dreamlike acting without words for what she spun. There was one heartrending mother in an attic, and we could have spent a week discussing what they all suffered. Townspeople need never fear that country people misunderstand them, though it may happen the other way round. 'Sailor returning home' was rather fat—but he might have been, for all we know—yet tremendously sincere. And the 'child' who offered a flower was a bit tall, and wanted to use a toasting fork for this at first. Several others felt it was too big and I got her to settle for a teaspoon. There was a bit too much sniffing at the 'perfume of an autumn evening'. They didn't guy it, but they *were* a trifle robust. But the scene built up well to the 'many horses passing'. They remembered what we had done to start with, yet we went over it once again. Having pieced all the bits together in sequence we played through without check, up to Mr Growser meeting Jan the Hermit (his better self). They wanted to fit in the Lady winding downstream, of course, on her golden raft. We put her on a stretcher (what wonderful things you can find in village halls!) and turned out the lights, using a few torches and one bicycle lamp. It was stunning. The quiet tramp of many feet was accompanied on the piano by the 'Dead March', and a quite wonderful few moments ensued. I added the following short piece of narration after the bit about the Hermit and the exit of Larry and Denis, to introduce this part: 'But the world did not know that the spirit of Sir Jan and the Lady of Shalott lived on, they only saw the body gliding by.' Then, when those supporting the raft and lady had passed right down the winding river past the tower, they broke quickly into small groups, then spread out ready to be the barking dog and the sheep. Jan, who had been the front stretcher-bearer was thus able to pass down the full length of the hall back to the stage, where another person, as Lorna, lay waiting for the dawn and the smile which most of us are in need of but are too ashamed to admit it.

In all this strange tale, it is the quiet dignity and slow stately rhythm which remains most deeply in my memory. There was a long silence after we had played right through. Then Madam Chairman broke the spell in about the most sensible way: 'Well, ladies, I think after that praps we'd all better 'ave a cup o' tea.'

COMMENT

Up to this point we have traced creative action from childhood to young adulthood, but coming through the phases of childhood and youth, we see the unconscious drama—the doing of life—changing gradually into conscious theatre. As this becomes more serious, it turns into professional experience, but with a particular interest in children it was bound to lead to pioneering Theatre for Children. After this came production for B.B.C. on Children's Hour and the appendage of work with listening clubs. Sometime this would be bound to touch the parent and therefore some adult group other than the professional actor. This seems a perfectly logical development, for my interest was ever widening and was becoming more and more concerned with people. In this report we have just such a group for the first time and I include it because it also marks a special phase of writing. So many people, drama advisers, youth leaders, Home Office staff and social workers have asked me to follow up *Child Drama* and write on creative work with older groups and special groups.

We shall meet a good many different groups from now on (though we shall meet children again for a special reason) and perhaps the reader will share my delight in the fact that whoever they were, wherever they were and whatever their age, they all did somewhat similar things and a fluid sort of shape was common to their creation as well.

In 'The Legend of the Lady of Shalott' I put in quite a lot of actual dialogue for the story. At this distance over the years, it is difficult to remember why. It may have been just an actor wanting to act, it may have been done intentionally to

Man from Mars puts atomic sparks on the government. (Imaginative Drama),
Rea Street Centre, Birmingham

First Educational Drama Association Teachers Conference. Comedy story built by the author out of the Ideas Game. Invented and acted in seven minutes. Group on right are magic needles. Kneeling figure with finger up is the spindle. Hand over the top is tone arm with a spell in it to 'make a milk churn top into a gramophone record'. Man in centre winds, and those with arms on shoulders will revolve. Audience sings to make the music (audience participation)

First Educational Drama Association Teachers Conference. 'And the big wind was so great that a bough broke off from the highest tree and fell with a crash on to the wizard's head, breaking his magic blue spectacles.' Audience made a storm noise. From a story built by the author out of the Ideas Game

entertain and help the evening along (a) because it seemed sticky, (b) because one was finding the way. I would say now that it was probably wrong. They *may* have needed actual words to say but generally it is a mistake to give them, however tempting. It is better to say such things as 'he came to the house and asked for some water'. This is a step removed and they must invent: 'please could you give me a drink', and perhaps explain why he wants one. This is how to guide other people into creation rather than doing too much for them yourself or being tempted to show off.

But later I put in a piece of narration that was purposeful, 'But the world did not know . . .' this was just to link things up and had a totally different effect. It is just the sort of remark that is sometimes needed to keep creation going. They 'spread out ready to be the barking dog and the sheep'. This is a swift change of character too, what in theatrical parlance is called 'doubling', but in this creation it seemed rather more like the swift change of personality during play which you expect from children. How different this experience of spontaneity must have seemed from their usual village drama group production. They probably did not know how good the theatre effect was.

15. Electric Currant Buns and the Copper Tap Chaps

Getting happy and confident again. Backward and disturbed children, six to seven years old, Worcestershire, late in 1937

It was a sort of joke with some of us at that time that, on the hard job of radio, you either lost your hair or your eyes or your teeth. I started to go blind. With all the reading of scripts and driving, apart from studio work, it was not surprising; and apparently it was also partly still to do with previous under-nourishment. It was a terrible blow. It began to be painful and unpleasant to drive, as well as dangerous; and my performance on the air was beginning to suffer badly. I had always prided myself on reading ability, since prep school days, and hated the thought of becoming secondrate. However, they told me if I didn't stop and rest I might go quite blind. That settled it. In despair, I resigned; and by way of rest, started an Arts Centre in Worcestershire, having been invited into the county to lecture by the British Drama League. Fortunately there were others to do the writing for me,[1] which rested me enough to do occasional

[1] A local schoolmaster was a tower of strength.

serial readings of *Black Beauty* and to adapt *The Secret Garden*, and occasionally to broadcast from Bristol, still. In Worcestershire I started a sort of drama service, taking amateur companies round villages, swapping teams, running weekend schools into several neighbouring counties, starting non-competitive festivals and youth work, and percolating as far as Wales. It was all rather new and people were a bit shocked at it all then. They didn't really like one taking it seriously or energetically. Poetry readings, music and drama, you know, not absolutely English somehow. There were some village experiments in Cambridgeshire and exciting things in the West Country but no money at all for an Arts Centre in Worcestershire.

However, a strange thing happened there. People heard of my efforts and slowly came together, shopkeepers, printers, tyre-sellers, hospital staff and daughters of clergymen. And if they didn't come themselves, they began to send their children. One or two of these were backward or disturbed. After a time a considerable number went through my hands and I began to find myself in classrooms too. It was the exciting results of these experiments that finally took me nearer London again. For nearly all the children who came to me, their state seemed to be totally unnecessary and I determined to try to bring the results of my work to the notice of the medical profession; I also took an inner oath that I would one day somehow get similar but simpler work than my therapy into *general* education as a form of prevention. I went to a church in Ludlow and prayed about it.

Here is an account of one trickle before the flood of unhappy young; some of the first to come:

Self (to children): 'Have a sweet.' I offer them round. John remains over in a corner alone, staring at wallpaper. I go over to him. 'Nice pattern.' This is said in a low voice, and my approach to the child is from behind so as not to distract his attention sharply, but rather to attempt to join him and speak as with his mind.
John: 'It's got a 'orse's 'ead.'
Self: 'Yes, it has.'
John: 'It's a bad 'orse—like my teacher.'

[84]

Self: 'Some teachers are good.'
John: 'Mine isn't. She 'its me.'
Self: 'Does she?' The boy looks round at me then, saliva coming a bit at his mouth. Perhaps he is interested that I take all for granted, no surprise, no anger. Now is my chance. 'Have a sweet.' (Long pause.)
Self (as if I had not spoken): 'Have a sweet.' (Long pause.)
Self (in exactly the same tone): 'Have a sweet.'
John (coming to): 'Yuss'.
Self: 'They're over by the fire.' I had left them there on purpose. John follows me, and is thus induced to join the group without any commands being given, which might remind him of other experiences I don't want him to think of whilst he is here.
Self: 'Let's squeeze in near the fire. How is Janet? Do you want to read to us today?'
Janet: 'No.' I am secretly rather relieved. Perhaps everyone is. Janet can't read, which is partly the reason for her nervous condition. She *looks* at an open book sometimes when she comes to us, and either takes five minutes per half word or makes up a story, pretending to read. By letting her do this without reprimand, she is beginning to get confidence to *try* to read again. Her mother cuffs her, for not being able to read, which makes my task twice as hard.
Self: 'Let's have some ideas then, John. Have you got one for us?'
John: 'No.'
Self: 'Anne?'
Anne: 'No.'
Self: 'What, no ideas. Well I never did. How did you come here tonight, Anne?'
Anne: 'Walked.'
Self: 'Did you notice anything on your way?'
Anne: 'No.'
Self: 'No houses, no people, no trees —no buns—no monkeys with hats on?' A few little giggles begin.
Anne: 'Fat dog.'
Self: 'Good. That's a *lovely* idea. Anne has given us a fat dog.' The little group is warming up now. 'Bill?'
Bill: 'Warm fire.'

Self: 'Yes. Now, just one more. Let's have one more—Janet, have you got one for us now?' Janet shakes her head. There is a permanent drip at the end of her nose. 'Oo, I don't believe it, I'm sure you have.' Then, taking a dangerous chance: 'Tell us something you've read about lately.'

Janet: 'Sugar bun.' It's not very imaginative, and hardly her idea, but I accept everything.

Self: 'Grand. Now we've got Fat Dog; Warm Fire; and Sugar Bun. Once upon a time there was a *sugar bun*. He was a beautiful bun, King of all the buns in Bunland, and he lived in a wonderful biscuity palace surrounded by copper taps. Where shall we have the palace? Oh, over there I think, under the table—and his crown was a lovely blob of sugary spice, and he was fat—*my* he was fat! (*Giggles*). One morning the guards, those copper tap chaps, turned on their swishing noise to wake up the King, and he rolled over on his golden dish bed, and opened his curranty eyes. Then those currants nearly popped out of his head: "I must buy a dog," he cried: "a nice fat dog, that's wot's the trouble with me. I've got no dog." "Very dangerous, your Majesty," said a copper tap chap, "nasty treacherous things dogs." (Janet's nose drip wobbles and I bend over to her and whisper hastily 'not really'. After receiving a pale grin, I continue.) But the King wouldn't believe it and jumped out of bed, jumped into some frilly paper trousers, like you have on cakes, and jumped through the door—What did he do?'

John: 'Jumped out of bed . . .'

Janet: 'Jumped into some . . . (bursting into giggles) . . .'

Bill: '. . . frilly paper trousers . . .'

Everybody: '. . . jumped through the door . . .'

Then we all said this all over again about the jumping, until it developed into a sort of chant repeated several times. When it had been a satisfying group experience, I tried to get on.

Self: '. . . and then he rushed down the road, but he couldn't remember the shop, so he walked round and round for a bit—in the middle of the floor there—just to get his mind settled. When he felt giddy he stopped and there straight in front of him was the pet shop. In he went and bought a big fat gentle yellow dog. Now when he got outside the gentle dog didn't look gentle

[86]

any more, suddenly, and with a slobber noise he swallowed the King all in a gulp. Was that King cross!? But the dog didn't know what he had swallowed. You see you've got to be jolly careful what you swallow whole in this life. And two things suddenly started to happen. The King sent out electric currant messages for help, inside the dog, and from all the streets there came a marching sound—big buns, little buns, pancakes, rolls, rolypoly puddings, swiss buns and doughnuts. Every brand of bun you can think of marched against the dog. And when the King heard the marching sound he got boiling hot with excitement, and as he got hotter and hotter the dog got hotter and hotter too, till all at once he burst into flames. "Hah," said the host of buns—that's all the buns outside, you know—"silly old dog. Silly old dog. My what a wonderful *warm fire* he makes!" and they melted their sugar at him a bit. "Call the guards," someone said. So the copper taps were called. They turned themselves on and put out the dog. Then one of them got very cold, and made an icicle ladder and stuck it in the dog's mouth. So out climbed the King. But his crown was just a sticky mess. "Don't think I do like dogs much," he said. The fat dog said. "Sorry your Majesty, I didn't really mean it, I didn't really know, and he crept back into the pet shop. But the King soon felt better, and borrowing some sugar from two Swiss buns he quickly made a new crown. "All is forgiven," he cried and they all marched back to the palace and sang songs of sticky thanksgiving for the rescue of their King.'

When we had settled who should be what, the children wanted me to be something too, so I agreed to be the golden dish and was promptly sat on hard by John. My feigned discomfort started things off well. We imagined the hundreds of buns marching, and made knocking and stamping noises for their feet coming. We all 'swished' hard for the 'copper tap chaps' and to make everything happy at the end of the session, we finished up with the dance of the Electric Currants (twenty minutes violent improvisation to the tune 'Top Hat, White Tie and Tails').

It is essential that there should be no confusion between electric currents and electric currants. The latter are vastly superior.

[87]

(This report has been pieced together from various jottings taken at the time.)

COMMENT

This is an example of putting what has been learned to the benefit of other people. We are back at children again but for a particular reason, to help another group of adults, those many teachers, specialists and psychologists who have asked me how I would adapt Child Drama to the needs of backward or disturbed children. This is a description as near as possible of what I did, but anyway it came then in chronological order. (The description has been used and discussed at a number of psychological conferences since.) Perhaps it might help parents too because, as well as their child, they can be desperately unhappy over a situation and often they are so hastily judged.

'Tell us something you've read lately'—this is accepting the lie process. I use this often in order to allow a person their defences, then strengthen them till they can tell the truth. Lies so often begin because of misery or fear rather than sin. One can give great courage sometimes to children by asking them to read a book that is not there. They can read *that* book but you couldn't. It wouldn't be the same if they handed it to you, they would tell you you were making it up! You do not let them get away with this for ever; one day, during treatment, you will help them to know the difference between dream and reality.

I felt it necessary to state where the palace was. With less disturbed children I should have asked *them* to tell me. The chant which was encouraged was a way of helping them to share and communicate, it was to bring collective happiness from which the unhappy isolate is normally debarred. It is sometimes well worth pausing even in the middle of a creation to serve out a little happiness. Always one must ask—what is the purpose of my lesson?—To show how cleverly I can make a story or a play or to help these children with their inner growth? An honest answer will generally be the right guide.

'. . . he walked round and round for a bit—in the middle of the floor—' It is a direction, it establishes the geography for backward children so as to give them confidence but as it is wrapped up in the story the purpose for their action is clear (as mentioned before) and it does not sound like a command that these particular children might not obey. Try to avoid a command, arrange a *fait accompli* whenever you can, in early stages with this type of child: '. . . as he got hotter and hotter, the dog got hotter and hotter too'—intentional building of climax, all this part, in the rhythm of a drum beat to excite them into action, for I knew by now that children divide sound into time beat, rhythm and climax. I learned this from the streets. For withdrawn children, climax is especially necessary, for the hyperactive declimax and peace.

Direct speech of a character is given occasionally but here it only heightened the story, I knew these little moles wouldn't even attempt my version of actual

[88]

words. In case anyone is worried that I was sat on—this was an out of school group! In any case there was a sort of logic in it for I was the dish and it all had the atmosphere of games at home. Only these children didn't get games at home.

My near blindness had given me a special compassion for others, but next day, still thinking of these children, I went to the top of Clee Hill and practised difficult athletic dance steps for most of the morning. It took away my depression, when not certain if I would really go blind, and enabled me to come back and face the music again as of old.

16. Two Dolphins, Caliban and a Whale
Tempest in a Remand Home, with adults and lads, 1938

In the last year and a half more and more children had met me who had some backwardness at school or some emotional disturbance because of conditions at home. It was my work with these as previously described that finally convinced me not only of the value of drama as therapy, when applied in a certain way, but also that much of this unhappiness was unnecessary. It seemed some time since I had sworn my sort of private oath that one day I should somehow introduce a modified form of the method into general education as a means of prevention. It is some consolation to me now that thousands of children in various parts of the world have, since that time, had their lives enriched, or at least bolstered up, because of the fine work of teachers who finally came to believe the same things as myself, and despite the opposition of those who should know better.

But the first task was to bring the results of my research to the notice of a wider public and in particular to the attention of the medical profession. Accordingly I moved from the Midlands to the Home Counties[1] and finally back to London. My first contacts there did not bring me at once in touch with children, and I missed the times I had had with them in classroom or at home. But a number of interesting cases came my way, some of them passed on by the medical specialists with whom I had begun to

[1] Amersham first, then Chalk Farm.

At Amersham my radio play 'St Patrick' was written; since used in different form by Brian Way and others, when representing me abroad or on their own courses, as an exercise in arena and theatre.

work. There was the Director of a vast and well-known firm, who suffered from an inferiority due to his shortness of stature. He went through a course based on parts of my old method of drama athletic movement, began to hold himself better, feel taller, improve his speech and finally triumphed over the simple difficulties of his situation. There was a person with a stutter who turned out to have had fears about passing a gate because of a dog, all of which was re-enacted till the fears were dispersed. There was the railway man with asthma whom nobody had time to help, sent to me by the late Miss Elsie Fogerty; there was one person who didn't like lying down and another who didn't like standing up. Amongst all this, from some quarter or another, I no longer remember how, came an invitation to visit a Remand Home. I have visited a good many since, as well as prisons, mental homes and other institutions; old people's homes, old men's clubs and even policemen will do drama too, it seems.

After a somewhat exhausting journey I arrived at the place. The Home appeared to be inhabited by rock-faced militia from Mars. They had a way of looking at you that would have done credit to the Director of an Asylum for savage homicidal angels-gone-wrong. It was necessary to use on myself all the drama-therapy offered to others lately, and a good deal more, in order to have the courage to walk down those cold and terrifying corridors under such soul-piercing scrutiny. No children in sight, just the Martians. Left, right, left right echoed our feet. I did not dare go out of step. It might have meant my never seeing the sun again. A sturdy door got knocked on. A mixture of dentist feeling, headmaster's study and rocket elevator assailed my stomach. 'Come in,' came the bellow of some three-headed bull. This was it. Surely, Lucifer himself sat before me. All the detail —a dark, cavernous, terrible face, a long wide desk and a red ink pot. My sins began to crowd in upon me, when suddenly the mask broke into one of the most sincere and charming smiles it has been my pleasure to encounter. One felt tempted to over laugh, like a funny film star after a tight squeeze. But this man could put people at their ease as well as quell. He soon made me feel my coming was a sort of noble gesture, on a par with the exploits of some Gentleman-of-the-Lamp, and the tea he had laid on would have done some credit to the top secondary modern social science course in the land. After tea, I at last met some boys, but it was a mixture of grown-ups too. It appeared that adults sometimes used the Hall for a meeting place, and occasionally some of the boys were allowed in at the same time. The grown-ups, including some of the staff of the Home ran an amateur dramatic society. They wanted a talk about Shakespeare so I gave them that, rather stressing contrast, energy of attack and the use of vowels and consonants; how this particular author offered you the music and instructions about pace by his use of staccato and drawn-out sounds in the words.

Then we set to work.

First we had a tempest. Everyone was asked to make as much noise as they could: the lads were asked to make splashing noises of rain and wind. Half of them blew terrific raspberries, but with the banging of desks by the men, and the wailing of the women a very passable storm was concocted. It obviously frightened one member of the staff anyway. I think he feared the lads would get out of hand. But they never did. One of the secrets of control in drama is to make sure that those taking part see the *purpose* of what is being done, however unusual it might first appear. We turned the stage into a ship and there were some gruelling moments whilst people fell about, and into each other, to the music of "Night on the bare Mountain". The grown-ups were mostly the crew and passengers, the boys (off stage in the body of the hall) became huge waves, two separate dolphins and five of them became a whale. Most of the words were improvised and a few of the remarks remain to history. 'Get that perishing bucket out of my way or I'll bathe you in it.'

'Tell your Mother not to have any more sons.'

'Hang on or the sharks will get you and you'll look like a herring's backbone tomorrow.'

'I can't. Both my hands are full of the Captain's supper and your flaming cup of cocoa.'

In the final version, some of Shakespeare's original words were kept in, but the script was enlarged somewhat. To the words 'Farewell, my wife and children—Farewell brother' were added 'Farewell Uncle—Farewell Aunt—Farewell cousins—

Farewell Mr Gonzalo—Farewell Mr Anthony—well—whatever-your-name-is. Farewell anyway.' Then the ship finally foundered and at the word 'We split, we split' several things happened. All the people on ship (on stage) fell off over the footlight trough, which was closed for the purpose; even so one of them managed to get caught unseriously in a bit of wire and called out, 'blast this rigging'. The captain fell amongst the rough and (very) ready waves, who waited like the devils in Faustus eager to catch him; a shower of spray had been reserved for this, in the form of torn up pieces of paper in the usual type of basket. The spray shot up beautifully and flickered down past a spot light, like snow at a wedding: the words 'we split' were too much for the lads, who burst into joyful mirth; the two dolphins collapsed in tears upon the floor, while the rest of us finally stood round smiling in that special resigned way that uncontrollable laughter in others tends to make one do.

Finally the glee subsided. When I had first come into the hall the atmosphere was uncertain and it had been my task to try to lighten things by the attitude of the first talk. But by now it was quite different. No one group, young or old, staff or boys were walled apart from each other. There was a warm happy feeling everywhere, with a dash of surprise, like salt in a good stew, which was just what I wanted. Having started the business of the evening on 'Contrast', I then brought it in, by moving over to that wonderful speech of Caliban

Be not afeard: the isle is full of noises,
Sounds and sweet airs, that give delight, and hurt not.

First of all we got one of the men to read it and we introduced the mood by a little music of Debussy. After the experience and impact of that, we began to consider the passage and discuss it and asked all the lads to try and find some quiet sound which they liked. They dangled a bit of metal against a central heating pipe, or discovered some quiet tapping to be done on wood. We then evolved a little tune of our own to hum and finally fitted the whole tinkle-tap-hum to the words 'Sounds and sweet airs, that give delight, and hurt not', fading from Debussy to words, into Debussy again, and a flourishing cross fade into tinkle-tap-hum. Then we broke off again to discuss 'The clouds methought would open and show riches'. What sort of riches? If you could really have your dream, what would you like the 'riches' to be?

Answers were: Money, toffees, food, beer, chocolates, chance to go home to Mother.

Self: 'Well we've had some good answers for that. Just for the moment, let's have our own quiet private dream.'

The record was put on again. One or two of the lads smirked a bit at this, but the rest had begun to get quite serious and sat there obviously thinking. I wanted to get them up and let everyone try moving about in their own dream. But the 'one or two' weren't going to stand this much longer. I failed, but it was worth trying and then admitting it. They were not really ready for such a thing.

Self (changing my ideas a bit): 'All right, now we have to fit in the dream section. Would anyone think it silly to include Mother? That was one of the ideas you gave me.'

I expected trouble from the rough ones, but I needn't have funked it, no one thought it silly. Then one of them said, 'Could we 'ave a lady?'

Self: 'What, you mean instead of a Mother?'

Boy: 'Yeah, just sort of a lady.'

This was interesting—rather like a certain figure from *The Water Babies*.

Self: 'All right, we'll make it a lady. This is our story, then. Caliban was sitting on a bank and he looked up—and what happened?'

A Boy: 'The clouds opened . . .'

Self (fading in Debussy music): 'Yes, and he saw above him, high in the Heavens some great chests tilted on their side and as he looked a shower of pound notes came down upon him—rather like the spray just now (some laughter and cheerful nudging here). Then as he looked again his mouth fell open with wonder . . . Then what happened?'

A Boy: 'A shower of toffees came down and they—sorta went into his mouf.'

Self: 'Yes. And what's more, there were no papers on them, so he was able to start chewing at once. And he bribed all the sprites and goblins on the island to get him more and more food, particularly chocolates, until he got a terrible pain and he was rolling on the ground in agony. Just as he thought he couldn't bear it any more, a very calm lady appeared among the trees and walked slowly towards him. He looked at her and suddenly felt un-angry any more. She gave him some pink medicine from a large bottle, but said she could not wait now, but would come to him in his dreams, whenever he was unhappy, and lead him to a wonderful home. So he cried "to dream again".' (Not too much poetic language in this story, just straight reporting.)

We then played through the whole of this, starting with the music again, and with the man reading Shakespeare's words. We included our special 'sounds and sweet airs'. A large boy became Caliban. (There was some splendid private joke about this choice, which we didn't go into.) The rest of them and some adults became goblins and weird creatures, hopping around to the music of 'Aint misbehavin'', bringing wonderful heavy dishes of food and gigantic jugs of beer. The entry of the lady was breath-taking. A great quiet peace descended upon us and the fat boy fixed her with a steady stare, which became more and more absorbed as she walked slowly down the full length of the hall to give him his medicine. Her exit just fitted in with the last phrase of the music too ('Walk to Paradise Garden'). There was complete silence for a minute or so, then a quick burst of clapping. It was to this sound that Caliban, like other strong men before him, unexpectedly broke. He wept bitter tears, and his whole body heaved, as he 'cried to dream again'.

By now the whole group was well in hand and I was able to have some exciting but controlled battle scenes, with *Henry IV* and *Henry V* all over the hall. I have seldom seen such well-behaved and hard-working troops. Just before going, I summarised the lessons I hoped we'd learned and stressed the purpose of what we had done. On moving towards the door, three tough lads came up and said quietly, 'Thank you for coming, sir'.

The corridors seemed much shorter than they had before. Lucifer had lost his lugubrious light too. A very ordinary sensible man saw me off the premises, whom I just recognised as the Dark One behind the big desk. 'I came into the hall for a short time,'

[94]

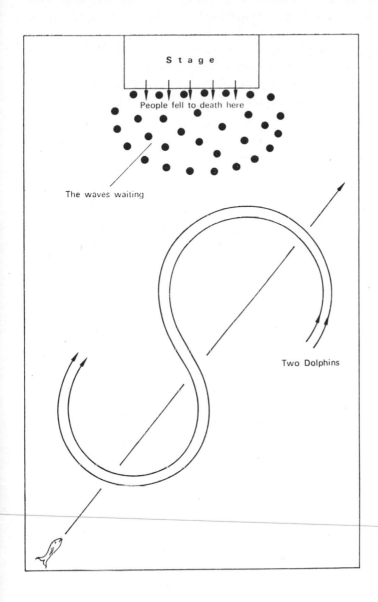

Stage

People fell to death here

The waves waiting

Two Dolphins

he said. 'We've never seen anything like this before here. I should never have believed it possible. It is the first time some of those lads have really cooperated and they were never out of control.'

Control, I thought on the train home, is a curious thing. It can either be personal or imposed and much depends on what behaviour is considered by society to be appropriate to the given situation. If it is not considered appropriate, we think there is no control.

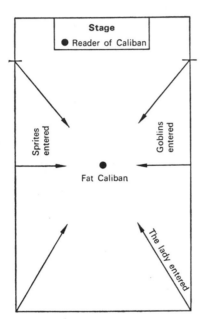

COMMENT

This is included because the situation seemed somewhat unpromising at first and one must have the courage to go on whatever you feel like inside, sometimes even if you are shaking with fright. Something evolves quite often, to help you. Although these were older lads, noises are used very much as in a junior or infant school but at a rather different mental level, though not much.

The 'flourishing cross fade into tinkle-tap-tum' is obviously derivative of radio experience.

[96]

The task of the narrator guide is shown again in 'Yes, and he saw great chests...' The remark links things together and keeps the lesson moving. Notice that soon after that, with these youngsters, a question is asked 'Then what happened?' And they answer. With the disturbed and younger children in report No. 15 suggestions are given, rather than asking questions. More direction is needed with the younger and different kind of child. A question can sometimes be a sudden test whether the children are with you and sometimes the answer or lack of it gives pathetic indication of 'where they are in life', i.e. in their emotional and mental development. Young teachers and social workers, take comfort. Do not always think that you have failed, though any of us can at any time, it may be only a test of 'where they are' in this sense. There is another example of this where I wanted to try and get everyone 'moving about in their own dream' but I failed, although some sat thinking about it. 'They were not ready for such a thing', but it was worth trying, it did not make me downhearted but helped me to know more precisely where I was with them and what they were likely or unlikely to do.

It will have been seen that jazz and classical music are equally used. One uses what seems appropriate to the situation, using a wide range of sound for them to draw upon for inspiration.

Here again we have a mixture of improvised speech and actual script in the creation, as on the Beacon near Malvern; the geography of the immediate environment is used too, but on a much smaller scale. Now the mixture of script and spontaneous speech is not mixed just for one's own fun, though enjoyable it became, but as in reports 14 and 15 the work is for other people, to share happiness and stumble into little pools of art and expression which may be arrived at by luck but not entirely without intention.

With this sort of imaginative approach, it is quite possible to bring the most unlikely groups to Shakespeare or other classics, but it is probably better to do it in short bursts.

Although this all happened at a Remand Home, it would be equally suitable for an approach in secondary schools.

17. The Genius and the Mouse

Visit to a Home for the Blind, 1939

I had had a little experience with disabled children, helping them to find hope and contact with each other by such things as exciting adventures, when police (who had to be static in their 'office chairs') phoned each other up all over the world in order to catch criminals; dancing with one's hands; pulling terrible faces at each other, guessing who such people were and then making

[97]

stories up about them; movement to music in wheelchairs of a limited kind and not nearly so good as I have thought out since. Blind children had also come into my life and there had been a number of episodes in a pretend garden—choosing flowers to grow, pruning trees, mowing lawns, digging and hoeing, sometimes to music, sometimes with words or words and music when a story developed. There had been the day when no one was serious, because blind people are often gay, and one little boy who had been sniffing pretend beetroot, cabbages and daisies, suddenly said—'*That's* not a flower, that's Annie!' There was also the Sunday evening when we visited the 'wonderfullest' garden in all the world and everyone moved about as in a dream to Debussy's 'First cuckoo in spring'. Some of the children said there was such a lovely smell in one corner that Jesus was there, and finally a little girl came up to me when it was all over and said 'That was a wonderful garden. Can we go again? I've never *seen* such flowers.' Blind people so often make that sort of remark: 'It looks lovely'; 'So nice to see you, do come again'; 'It's very nice country there'. They seem to build vivid mind pictures and develop tremendous sensitivity about the nearness of people or objects, so that it is quite possible for many of them to dance. Since the time written of here, I have seen blind and partially sighted children do the most remarkable circus in dance drama in an arena production at the Birmingham Juvenile Dramatic Festival. The first dance entry was like a gale of wind, and I shall remember the energy and surety of it all my life. One of the acts was of a tightrope. The 'rope' was laid on the floor, and the dancers went across it carefully with slight wobbles, umbrella and all. Remembering that all children love sound (separate noises of all sorts and kinds) was useful too. Blind children are sometimes a bit apt to get rowdy, but only because they are full of beans and need to blow off steam like everyone else. The function of delicate sounds and intentional 'declimax' helps here.[1] It was partly the particular type of theatre training I had developed in the early 1930s, but mostly from blind children, that I had learnt, later, how to use noises for teaching backward squads in the Army to do fine drill. The description of this

[1] For description see *Child Drama*.

is in *Dramatherapy as an Aid to Becoming a Person*. But today I had been asked to visit a Blind Institution for grown-ups. The place looked gaunt, despite the fine lawns and bushes. It had a sort of alcoholic nasal red about it everywhere, or should one say dirty purple. But inside, all was warm and smelt of beeswax and everywhere you went you either slipped or saw your own face. A crunched-up looking matron with a delightful smile welcomed me. I was taken into a sort of high tea first, because, she explained, she liked visitors to get to know the people there. It certainly helped me, because I was extremely nervous and there was the chance of picking up some background about the place. What struck me at once was the capable way in which everyone was eating. Gusto and a splendid aim. The only person making a mess was me. How did they all do it—chop, slice, spread; elbows lift and bang in the right place every time?

At tea they taught me about adapting to home life; what they felt like when with other people, their gratitude for aid but not liking to be patronised, and the importance of not having too much sympathy. Some of them were very frank, and one in particular described the self-centred person she used to be. After that meal I was no longer nervous but inspired—by their courage, patience and hope and by their sound common sense.

Now was the time for our drama. They spread out round the hall, but rather in little groups and there was a lot of chatter. I touched a gong and on silence we began.

Self: 'First of all I want everyone to find or touch something near them. Move your fingers over it and tap or scratch it quietly.'

This was a loosening up process. At first everything was very gay and they were a bit apt to get hold of a neighbour's ear or nose and one man started to scratch his companion's head. But this did not go on for long, and by saying that all the sounds were so far a bit too muffled, I got them to search a bit more carefully for more appropriate objects. It suddenly became more serious then and I put a record on a gramophone, quiet but with a pronounced time beat, and everyone tapped in time with it. One person gently jangled some keys. Next we progressed to a polonaise by Chopin (popularly known as 'have a banana', I believe), rather more difficult and with a less steady beat. Then having secured some serious interest and effort, I asked them to make their sounds without any music and then to tell me what they reminded them of. These were the answers: typewriter tapping; church bells; a mouse; a bicycle. Out of these I built the story.

My story: Over here is a house where an unknown genius lives (laughter and some applause, which faded out as I walked over to the place I meant and as they needed to listen for my where-abouts). He lives all alone and has very little to eat. He has no friends. His only companion is the *typewriter tapping*. But one day he felt he must go out and hear real human conversation, so he went into the market place over here (I moved again, then said to the people near me: '*You* remember that this is the market place, won't you?') He heard conversation all right, but it was nearly all about things he couldn't buy, particularly clothes and food. He stood looking at the food for a long time but in the end he had to go away. Finally he came to a pet stall and on it was *a mouse*. The mouse caught at his heart. It nibbled so and had a white blob over one eye. When the stallkeeper saw him star-ing, he asked if he wanted to buy the mouse, but the genius replied that he couldn't afford it. But he went on staring and in the end the stallkeeper became embarrassed and said he would give him the mouse if only he'd go away! So he accepted the mouse with surprise and walked off with it.

When he had gone back to the food stalls a man stopped him. 'What a nice mouse,' he said, 'would you sell it to me for my little boy?' The genius was sorely tempted by the smell of the food, but when he looked at the mouse, he couldn't allow himself to give him away. He went home instead and naming the mouse —what shall we call him? (someone answered 'Charles')—all right, Charles—he sat down to type. So, for the first evening for years he had a companion. He slept well, for him, that night but dreamt of mountains of food. Next day he was awakened by a tapping on the door. He got up and went downstairs. A small boy was in the street, with *a bicycle*. 'Won't you sell that mouse?' said the boy. 'No, I can't do that,' said the genius. 'My father told me about it. He says it's a nice one.' 'It is.' 'Well, could I come up and see it?' The genius agreed to that and he and the boy went upstairs. When they looked at the mouse, they saw that an extraordinary thing had happened—there were several baby mice in the same cage as Charles. 'Well, you don't want *all* those, surely,' said the boy. 'I haven't any money but I'll swop you my bicycle for all the babies.' The genius was worried about this at first but finally gave in. The father at first was furious, but finally, seeing the funny side of it, he bought the bicycle back for his second son, so the genius at last had some money. He spent it nearly all on food and was therefore so full of energy that he finished his first great work quite soon. The publisher, whose firm was over here, was delighted with it and offered him a large advance on royalties. This was the first of a number of great successes and the genius became famous, as all geniuses should.

Now in time the boy with the mice grew up and became mayor of the town, but there was an awful fuss about who should succeed him, and, sad to say, some bad miscounts on the vote. So everyone agreed they would ask the well-known genius to be mayor. The boy, who had grown up, led them to the author's house and they all carried him away in triumph. There was general rejoicing in the public square and a pealing of *church bells*. The genius looked round him with somewhat ancient and watery eyes. 'Is this really the place where I looked at the food on the stalls,' he thought, 'and couldn't buy it? All came well because I was true to my friend the mouse and wouldn't sell it. Everything began then.'

And though the genius has been dead for many a year now, his work lives after him. But there's one more thing (I moved one last time), here in the museum is a special glass case. And in it, eating, sits a large mouse with a white blob over its eye. Underneath is an inscription which reads: 'This mouse died at the ripe old age of twenty-one years. Its name is Charlesia.'

There was rather a lot of joyful noise and it took us a bit of time to get sorted out. The pet stall was a great success and somehow an elephant and an octopus came into it, but we decided that they couldn't stand *on* the stall, they would have to sit by it. They finally had to be moved, because both of them kept nibbling at passers-by or entwining them. But after that the genius managed to get near enough to 'see' the mouse. Church bells were largely tea cups clattered by spoons plus singing. One final remark stands out in my mind. One of the Aldermen said: '. . . and now Mr Mayor, you'll be feeling tired perhaps.' 'Tired,' replied the genius, 'I'm never tired. That is the secret of my success. I'll only be tired when I'm in me box.' Well, it never does to tempt providence, for in our story he died soon afterwards.

COMMENT

It always seems un-humble to take work or try to advise on highly specialised groups and I sometimes start by saying I am fully aware that the people I am talking to are the experts and one can only hope to contribute a little and share ideas. Usually, of course, you are only there because you have been asked, but then you have to avoid possible disappointment at not being able to give loads of detailed advice. However, I always feel that descriptions may be helpful, if analysed and thought about, because the specialist will see into it, see further and probably adapt and develop.

So, if anyone particularly interested in teaching the blind should read this, perhaps they will take it in that spirit for the description simply says what happened. My own eyes were gradually getting better, at the period this account was written about, but I still had a particular sympathy for those worse off than myself. In the third line of this report, for 'office chairs', of course, read 'wheel chairs.'

The Ideas Game is arising out of noises, just as in an infant school, yet this is with adults. Blind people enjoy sound and will often make a noise unexpectedly and with gusto. In the part '—and naming the mouse—what shall we call him?' we have an example of the test questioning again, to keep the group on its toes to test whether they are with you and to help them feel the creation is a joint one, that we are all doing it and it is a community creation.

It is important to get the geography straight, with all groups, but with the blind even more so; that is why I moved round the room to get areas identified, as in 'You will remember that this is the market place, won't you?' so that, if necessary, they could call later to their companions. 'This is the market place—over here—we are the market' etc. If done with glee, so much the better, it lightens proceedings. To give confidence and happiness is partly what we do this work for. I want them to have experience of spontaneity too. Sometimes people come up and say things like 'Of course you couldn't do this sort of thing with the blind (or some other group), could you?' almost as if they didn't want you to, that it mustn't succeed. I always feel sorry for them, only rarely furious, because I think they must be rather unhappy somewhere in themselves. It does one good therefore, when a person comes up, as they did recently, and says 'I see all sorts of ways of adapting what you have said. Thank you so much for opening my eyes.'

In November 1965 I was touched to hear that my second book, *Introduction to Child Drama*, had been chosen to be recorded as a talking book by the Royal National Institute for the Blind.

18. Jakes Heslop, the Injuns and his Girl, a Pageant on Motorbikes

Somewhere in England with an army unit in 1941

It is not always easy to get a perfectly ordinary unit of soldiers to do perfectly unordinary things. True, I had had some part in strange films about bombs, which blew up in a most inconvenient manner, had produced variety shows, in one of which two hundred men in the audience got up and danced and returned to their seats like lambs and at the right moment, had marched across a parade ground with one stripe on my arm and a film camera under the other and a bag of chips that would not conceal itself, whilst a khaki host stood glaring. It was then that I really knew what Milton meant by 'horrid in arms'. Before that I had just enjoyed the words. But never before had I dreamed up the notion of battling boredom by dancing on motorbikes. It happened like this.

One of the many strange orders that had been given me was: 'Teach these men to ride.' Ten days we had, before this particular bunch passed through. But for some reason their boat didn't go and they were kept hanging about, too far from any place worth painting red and too close to the village to avoid getting into trouble. By this time they had learned the rudiments of their mechanical steeds, had done whatever damage their bespattered spanners were going to contrive and had just about been allowed down a muddy shute at about forty-five degrees, which was the crowning triumph of their comparatively simple tests. After that 'they could ride'. Now there was a hiatus. Everyone felt put out. The pace of the last few days began to seem unnecessary and men were going about slowly unstringing themselves like ancient grand pianos that pass untuned—I saw one once in Switzerland that looked like a barrow full of spaghetti—a very dangerous state to be in. My commanding officer ordered evening parades. So one night my platoon was 'on' and I with it.

'What the hell are you going to make 'em do, sir?' said my sergeant.

'Something they've never done before, I expect,' was my answer, or words to that effect.

Then my mind began to clear, and when they were standing easy the discussion went something like this:

Self: 'Who are the literary guys here?' (Slightly startled laughter.) 'Come on, I really want to know.'

One name was thrown up. The rest seemed to go for very light reading and comics.

'Who likes going to the flicks?' (General enthusiasm.) 'What sort of pictures do you prefer?'

After the general sniggers and smallish list of sweet sirens had died down, we unearthed a fairly accurate majority yen for Westerns. Westerns they liked; Westerns they were 'at'; and being convinced that most successful drama activity starts only when you have arrived at the point where most people in the group really *are* in life and not where you wish they were, Westerns they were going to have.

Self: 'Right, now we're not going to have a formal parade. You've worked hard in the last few days and I know what you feel like, hanging around this place when the job seems done. So we're going to do something which I hope you'll quite enjoy, but at the same time you will be tested fairly strenuously. So take it seriously or someone may get hurt. We are going to do a story, like in a pageant, and I want some high-class driving as well, and some of it at speed. What's the name of the hero of our Western story?' (Laughter and some applause.)

We finally settled for Jakes Heslop. And the hero-ine (they would pronounce it as rhyming with 'wine') was Legs Amour. After some men had been sent to bring some motor cycles, I started one fair-sized group rather like one would in an infant school—not by casting immediately, but by letting everyone play each part.

Self: 'Jakes Heslop leaps onto his steed.' (Each man leapt onto his motor cycle.) 'He wants to get onto that hill-top there, to see if any Injuns are about. He digs in his spurs and off flies Brown Bess.' (All cycles except one started up and wobbled away at different speeds to the top of a mound. Several knocked into each other slightly on purpose.)

'Flaming ruddy —— !' said my Sergeant, 'you'll have a —— massacre in a minute, Sir.'

'Maybe,' I answered, 'but not the way you mean.' Then to the men (through a megaphone): 'Right, come back, you lot.' They returned, slightly sheepishly.

Self: 'Off the bikes! Next lot, you have a try, and don't bash into each other or the Indians may see you. Worse still, *I* might see you. You know our rule here. You'll be scalped pretty quick if I see any of that again.'

This went down quite well; the second lot saw we were serious beneath the fun and made a passable get-away to the top of the mound.

Self: 'Jakes Heslop looks round. He can't see anything at first, but suddenly he catches sight of a thin cord of smoke rising to the sky. He watches carefully and sees a skulking figure coming towards him—That's you lot.' (I indicated some of the others who were not yet in the story. Most of them took to it quite well, a couple sniggered a bit and held onto each other for brotherly martial support, but a few threw themselves to the ground and alternately wormed or stalked their way closer to the conglomeration of noise and smoke that passed for Brown Bess.)

'You two'll get a —— poison dart in your backsides, if you don't stop sniggering and get fell in,' interjected the sergeant helpfully, and just to show he was conversant.

Self: 'Jakes takes a quick shot at the Indian.' (Several different noises were made here, one or two the same as children make.) 'The Indian falls, but Jakes, realising he's short of ammunition thinks it's time to scarper. So he revs up Brown Bess, aims for the thin piece of rock there—that plank will do, over the ditch —and makes for base as fast as possible.'

All those being Jakes started off well, sorted themselves out very creditably and flew in single file, with only one skid, over the plank, down the farther mound and back to me. As the dust and smoke of these modern khaki Besses rose from the semicircle in front of me, I felt the old thrill of the theatre and had to restrain myself from cocking my hat on one side and flashing my badge like a sheriff, confronted by his posse. I noticed two Injuns still dying in agony under the withering watchfulness of Sgt B.

On these sort of lines we worked for about forty minutes, changing the groups, changing character, making the tests more difficult until remarkable absorption set in. The men really tested themselves too, and seemed to attain a certain extra dash and courage by flinging themselves into the simple story. By this time I judged that they had, what, in an infant school, I would nowadays call, 'reached their dawn of seriousness', and were ready for casting. I sat them all down, chose my cast and discussed the story and situation with them. They suggested some very remarkable tests. Out of what they suggested I built my final story:

'Some old campaigners, who have been set upon by Injuns already, enter slowly from the left there. They no longer have horses. Almost at once they are spotted by another band of Injuns (on bikes) who swoop down from the mountains (mounds) and start to circle round the old campaigners, shooting as they go. Luckily, Heslop is riding through the ranges at the right moment, whistling as he goes. He sees what is happening and starts a stampede of wild horses—That's you men, all of you who are not in it yet. I want you to charge as if you'd met Jerry in the village—between mounds one and two. Sorry we haven't enough bikes to go round. You scatter the Injuns, who leap off their steeds and hide behind rocks. As soon as the stampede has passed through, Heslop leads an attack by the campaigners on the dismounted Injuns. They overcome them—now, no bashing up of anybody; just shoot 'em with an imaginary gun, or stick 'em through with a spear that isn't there—and seize their horses. Then, with much jubilation, they make for the nearest small town and its saloon.'

We invented quite a floor show in the saloon and the story was

[106]

somewhat held up whilst one soldier sang, in a rich Irish tenor, one of our favourite songs. 'But the real reason why Jakes Heslop had come to town, you remember, was to see Legs Amour', I interjected hastily before another encore threatened. We were able to leave the saloon then. The singer was chosen for the Amour woman, and I shall never forget the way his bike was managed. He sort of put it on like a pair of high-heeled shoes and veritably minced out of the saloon on it in a most voluptuous manner, by judiciously turning his steering wheel from one side to the other in a gentle sway. It was terrific. Jakes and Amour 'embraced' by driving slowly towards each other and stopping dead in the right place, side by side, so that an outstretched arm from each passed across the battledress breast of the other. A mixture between a traffic cop signal and a spaceman's salute. It was stylised, balletic, fascinating. 'Finally they agree to marry and the sheriff holds a party and all the township dance.'

Here I stopped things a minute.

Self: 'I'm not sure of this bit, I just want to try something out. What I really want is for you all to drive over the top of that line of air raid shelters, up down, up down, up down, then come back here to the centre.'

I borrowed a bike and tried it myself. It was just as I hoped. One *could* get up onto the roof mound at one end of the line, drive along the top, drop down the far side, and by cutting the throttle back hard and applying a gentle break for a yard or so, then letting it free, could float up again almost to fall on the momentum of the machine to the top of the next mound in a rhythmic gliding dance, like children running over roads and pavements in the heart of big cities, or rather, like their dream of what they are doing when they do it.

So *that*, after a fashion, is what we all finally did. We, who had bikes, went rhythmically over the roofs of the shelters, and then we danced on the flat ground by swaying our machines in a sort of waltz, driving across and between each other, whilst some men without bikes did a sort of jiving knees up in the middle. All the others sang the Blue Danube to a ghastly raucous wailing 'dah' and beat on their messtins for drums. The sound, the concentration, the sweating men, the excitement and dexterity all seemed to ascend to Heaven in an incense of powdered blue exhaust, which billowed its way up to the stars and Him who watched, climbing a pale Jacob's ladder of light from the evening sun.

'Christ, sir,' broke in my Sergeant, 'I should never have believed it. Did you see little Candy Tuft [a pale carrot-headed Scot] take that bridge? 'E's never dared do it like that before. Did you see it?' I did and had. 'Oh well, sir, I always did say "Try anything once". Whatever we do in this crummy joint and 'owever much we —— up King's Regulations, we always 'ave the shine on your belt.'

I never quite see the logic of this remark when I have thought of it since, particularly as I was in battle dress. But it seemed entirely appropriate at the time. Perhaps it was a sort of symbol, a kind of poetry by mistake, for it held for both of us a deeper meaning than the words themselves convey.

COMMENT

'You'll be scalped pretty quick if I see any of that again.' The handling is much tougher than most of the previous reports, except the description of taking young professional actors earlier on ('because none of us leaves here till you *do*' in report No. 10). It had to be tougher of course. The Army conditions and situation are different. It was a risky experiment to be doing at all and I knew the only way to succeed was ultimately to get them to be serious and to show them as soon as possible exactly how far they could go. But I had faith in these men.

'All of you who are not in yet . . .' Keeping everyone busy, if possible, is a help in keeping discipline. It may be noticed too that after initially being firm, I was taking things at a cracking pace. 'I interjected hastily before another encore threatened . . .' We had had a longish pause in the drama and bound ourselves together because of the song but it was now time to get on. The timing of this work is so important, the quick remark to guide, lead, ward off an incident may be crucial, also the pace at which you are taking things. On the whole, a swift pace is best for discipline but the best moments of creation are often slow. As with a mettlesome horse, only let the reins off slowly and test. Tighten up again, if you can't manage, slow down again and aim at a slow collected canter, sometimes even a stop and standstill.

'Christ, sir—did you see little Candy Tuft—E's never dared do it like that before.' This is something that happens in P.E. too. Very often a child will do something more daring than usual in the gym if there is a drama, a situation, a story attached to the action. Absorption in the task takes away the fear. The same sort of thing happened to Candy Tuft. In this spontaneous creation he suddenly became a motorbike hero.

Something similar happened when I was taking patients in a hospital later; with leg and arm injuries they were likely to suffer pain during convalescence and were often being urged by the staff to exercise the limb. During the spontaneous work I started with them it was noticeable that once really absorbed in the drama, the situation, they would forget the pain, running a step or two, catching a cannon ball (tennis ball) and throwing a javelin (walking stick), such is the way we are made.

This motorbike episode is typical of a group most people would hardly believe could or would do this work. Yet they did, though I can hardly believe it myself sometimes, except that it is so vivid a memory.

19. An Agricultural Fairy Story
In a Women's Land Army hostel, Herefordshire, 1942

The time had come to leave my Slad Valley, with its Slade House and Slade Brook and everything else that seemed appropriate, from that far cottage on the hill to the golden stone I loved and Mrs Lee next door. It was from that upper window of next door that we first heard the strains of the violin, which introduced us to Laurie Lee, the poet. We had met his mother on the first day there and learned of her kindness and later on her intense inquiring mind and her passion for old china. In the hall of my house today stands an oak chest that was bought at a sale she told us of, and a 'piece' in our drawing room is from her own cottage. When it poured with rain on the warm living bank where that family had its life, the water would rush down into the Lee's house, causing the pandemonium that Laurie describes in his book *Cider with Rosie*. We could hear Mrs Lee 'going at it' and calling upon the heavens to aid her. When it was wet enough for water to pour through her living room, it poured, via a fresh air vent, into a cupboard where my best books were kept. My copy of Dr Viola's wonderful *Child Art* got damaged that way. It was in this house, after reading his book, that I had known my beliefs were right. There was a parallel to this concept of Cizёk's. I swore to write my own book, one day, called *Child Drama*.

With that and many other things to do, for just sitting at home was no good for anyone just invalided out of the Army, I started applying for jobs. One more visit to my cousin May (Julian Slade's mother) at Painswick, one more walk past the War Memorial, scene of the tragic account mentioned by Pat Smythe in her book *Jump for Joy*, one more visit to the swans by the lake at Steanbridge and I was away stumbling over the turnip fields in the early morning dark to catch a train for interview in Cornwall. Back again the same day to arrive at a small inn in a country town at four in the morning and to arrive fresh for another interview five hours later at 9 a.m. for a social service appointment. To my amazement (still) I got the job. The inn must have given me a very good breakfast.

Some chances for a bit of pioneer drama in Herefordshire had come my way from about 1936–37 onwards, running day schools in various places, and a course under the auspices of the Y.M.C.A. with its energetic secretary Mr G. Gordon (now County Drama Adviser for Northamptonshire). My job now was to collect hips, run propaganda weeks for aid to foreign countries, see about the price of nettles and visit youth clubs; dozens of other small tasks for the City Council too. Incidentally it involved trying to lay the foundations of a County Music and Drama Committee, and occasionally I was allowed to lecture for the Extra-mural Department of Birmingham University, if there was time. There were links with various factories as well, and eventually my production of *The Interlude of Youth*, in conjunction with the Arts Council (C.E.M.A., as it was still called then) at All Saints' Church. That was the evening that we all flooded out in costume, after the performance, and continued a lively improvisation between Charity, Youth, Riot and Pride all down Hereford High Street, then away down to the old bridge and nearly over the river. Lechery trod on her dress. She was verbally displeased. An oil painting of this production hangs in my house now. Pride has a huge tummy for some reason, and I, as Charity, appear too innocent to be true. One cannot associate oneself properly with that figure. I just remember the marvellous joy of speaking those lines and moving to Michael Mulliner's organ music—the most sensitive musician it was ever my pleasure to cooperate with in any of my productions. But tonight was something different. I had been asked to visit a Women's Land Army hostel.

This type of group was new to me and I had thought hard about it all day. When I entered the hostel a large number of clean and well-groomed ladies of varying shape sat about round stoves looking alarmingly comfortable. Having decided that they would be tired after their day's work, it seemed kind to start discussion with them first, not to order them bodily about but to try and stir their minds.

So we talked about conditions at the hostel, food, early rising. I inquired about hot water, privacy, transport and the people they worked for. Most of them were happy. Only one had met a farmer who was fresh, but plenty had met animals who were.

Thus somehow it all began.

'Who is the person in this room most like the bull in Anna's story?' I asked.

'Lucy,' someone shouted. One or two people began to sit up a bit.

'Who is like the sow that had a small litter?'

'Peggy,' shouted one or two. A slim slightly smashing blonde punched a neighbour hard. (I now see she *was* a trifle like a beautiful young large white, but I didn't see the connection then.)

'Who looks like a farmer—not the fresh one?' We chose another girl for that. Finally we were left with: Lucy the bull, Peggy the pig, Rose the farmer, the wicked stream and the green pullover. This was our story:

Mr Rose the farmer lives over there in a large pink bulging house to match his gently blooming nose. His acres spread over here and there round the corner of the L shape of the room. He has been worried of late because of the rudeness of Lucy the bull. This very morning of the day we are living he came out of his farmhouse, sniffed rhythmically through his rose nose and crossed the bridge of the stream. Just as he was half way over, a plank gave way and his foot went half way through. Mr Rose swore slightly. (*Self:* 'Not too fruity now, just a nice gentle couple of oaths about the *wicked stream*.') Mr Rose limped on his way until he came to Lucy's field. He tried saying a few nice things to the bull, but in answer he only got a roar of rage and narrowly missed having his block knocked off. (*Self:* 'I expect Mr Rose began to think Lucy wasn't the right name for that animal any more!' The real Lucy began to look approving. I didn't want to risk her feeling upset at being chosen for the bull.)

We agreed that farmers had a lot to do, so he continued on his rounds. When he came to the pig shed he was amazed to hear a certain type of snuffling. No, it couldn't be true! He pushed open the door and there she was. His beautiful gilt, *Peggy the pig*, had had a litter in the night. But what a rotten lot—only six and she had sat on one. When he had fussed round her a bit ... (here we broke off and discussed what he would do; I learned a tremendous amount about both farming and motherhood that I didn't know before) . . . he went back to the house feeling hungry. The morning had just gone in a flash and no one to cook his lunch. Well he wasn't going to have a wife (*Self:* 'Nor 'e wouldn't get landed with one o' they Land Army girls neither!') So he ate a rotten lunch and got a rotten tummy.

After that he went out to visit the far fields (round here) and as he was half way over the bridge a plank gave way and, we all chanted joyfully, 'his foot went half way through'. Mr Rose swore again. Then a strange thing happened. He saw a slim green thread of wool, gossamer in the afternoon sun, caught at the far end of the bridge on a slight nail. He unhooked it, followed the length of the wool, rolling it as he went, but didn't at once find the end of it. He limped on over hedges, over fields, till he came to the edge of the wood. It was then that he heard a clicking. He crept closer and there under a large green tree a green-eyed girl was knitting a dark *green pullover*.

We got a bit stuck here and they asked me to go on alone.
Self: 'Bright as the sun glows Mr Rose's rose nose . . . why?'
A land girl: 'He was annoyed.'
Self: 'Yes, I think he was in a rage at first because, remember, we agreed he didn't like women on his farm.'

But as time was getting on we finally decided this: As Mr Rose looked into the green eyes of the girl something seemed to happen. His rage slowly abated and he seemed caught by a sort of magic. He asked why she was knitting on his property like that and she explained that she had been told he was short of labour, had been deposited on his land by a lorry, had looked for him at the house, not found him and crossed the bridge, but just as she was half way over . . . (everyone very loud) . . . 'a plank gave way and her foot went half way through'. (Clapping and roars of joy.) As she had limped across the rest of the bridge her pullover must have caught on a nail, for as she made her way over the fields she started getting colder and colder and on reaching the wood she looked down and saw that she was wearing practically only a collar, so she started to knit it all up again quickly with a couple of twigs. Mr Rose shyly handed her the big ball of wool. As she thanked him with her glowing green eyes he felt he could tell her all his troubles—about the bull, the gilt, the litter, the lunch, the bad bridge and the wicked stream.

They then asked me to finish the story:

Self: ' "You know what's the trouble, don't you?" asked the girl. She went on to explain that the stream was bewitched. Oh yes. Anything could happen in remote parts of Herefordshire. It was quite well known. So that's what upset the bull, and broke the bridge and spoilt the litter *and* the lunch. But the girl cast her magic on the water by giving it a look, and cleaned the wickedness right out of it. Then she turned and looked at Mr Rose and cast her magic all on him. That is how he came to marry her, he just couldn't help it. And if you go to the old large pink bulging house nowadays it is never solitary any more. There's always a little bunch of Roses round the door.'

The joy of improvising is that these silly remarks often come out so pat that you even surprise yourself, and perhaps it is the element of surprise that has its swift effect in this form of drama, as far as comedy is concerned. Anyway we were helpless with laughter for quite a long time and it was very difficult to stop. Finally, however, we acted the piece in reasonable solemnity, marred only by an occasional snort near the beginning from Lucy as she went off again into heaving giggles and temporarily infected one or two neighbours with the disease. But the middle and end were sober enough. They got quite deeply into it. Everyone was something, if only an animal, gate or tree. Several chairs made the bridge, we used two pennies to make the clicking noise of the needles, and everyone still chanted when there was trouble on the bridge. My warnings about the oath were of no avail. We had some earthy self-expression here. The gilt was very affectionate to the farmer and kind to her young. We beat a tray for the 'bonk' when she sat on one of her litter in the night. A rolled up rug was part of the wicked stream under the bridge and after acting the story we all had an improvised dance to 'cow music' on the gramophone. Silly? Perhaps. But it wasn't our job to be particularly serious that night. My brief was: 'We don't know what to do with them. They are all stuck out there in a hostel and don't seem to have any interests or any fun. Finally we thought of you. Make them happy, do anything you like, but go and *interest* them.' I was trying to.

After our play, and arising out of the scene between the farmer and his girl, one of the others asked: 'How do you make love on the stage? Isn't it sort of special?' I said that I couldn't vouch for the way anyone else did it but would show them the way that I trained everyone in my own professional companies. It was important to do it well because you were the guardian of something important and beautiful at such times. We went into it quite deeply as far as it applies to proscenium theatre. I also showed them how to help a girl into and out of a chair from a sitting position (really a question of kindness and good manners) so that she had space to move and confidence in the sureness of her own and of the man's technique, finally ending with a reminder that you mustn't get imprisoned by technique, but master it until it is part of your natural ability, or use a few pieces of it as you feel able to. But that above all it was the sincerity and believability of the actual situation which counted; that improvisation kept these qualities alive in one's acting or instilled them; that the mixture of the highly imaginative and of the careful practical detail was what alone could produce the electric type of theatre experience, which satisfied me.

It must be efficient as well as exciting. We then passed on to a quite serious discussion about life and one's attitude to other people, and I talked of the relationship of kindness and sympathy to group work in acting.

[114]

'Will it burst?' Dance group at an early conference. Rea Street Centre, Birmingham

Passing moment when space is well filled. Object is first discovered. Dance Drama, early days at Rea Street Centre, Birmingham

Above left: Carrying Important Things. Training Course, Stockholm

Above right: recognising the injured, during an improvisation. Educational Drama Association Summer School, Saltley, Birmingham

Below: sword play during course in Stockholm (under Mr Brian Way when representing the author there)

It was getting late. I became aware of the blonde. She wasn't slightly smashing any more, she was—absolutely. It was then that I noticed she had green eyes. I left.

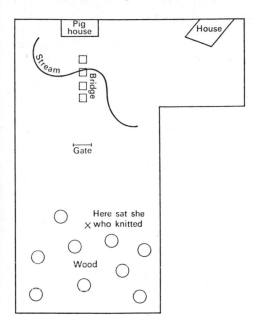

COMMENT

Again we notice improvisation very closely associated with a script play, actually arising out of it, after the production for C.E.M.A. at All Saints Church. A little later, the play was presented at Hereford Training College too. As to the second part of the description, of work with the Women's Land Army Group, the technique in this situation was a groping about for a basis for creation quite literally from 'where they were in life', actually where they were sitting, for the discussion revealed a little about their recent experience which one might use; as we had not met before, it was about the only thing to go on. 'Mr Rose the farmer lives over there . . . His acres spread over here and there . . .', establishing the geography again, a firm material basis upon which to build the imaginative story and hold the balloon of fantasy by a string to believability. 'We agreed that farmers had a lot to do' (reality) 'so he continued on his rounds' (the imagined story). This is another way of mxing reality and dream, but giving the dream some probability, however far-fetched. From these springboards one is more likely to weave a fantasy that is acceptable and somehow have believability.

ES—E

'We broke off and discussed . . .', a way of winning their interest by sharing their own knowledge. The creation then begins to seem to belong more to them. Timing is again very important—one minute too long and we all get bored and the original story is lost. It is like being a good chairman. Oh, how often do we suffer under incompetent chairmen: it is one thing I cannot stand. An example of chanting comes in again in 'his foot went half way though . . .' Note that these are perfectly normal healthy adults, yet they do the same thing as the E.S.N. children in No. 15 at the point 'jumped through the door, jumped into some frilly paper . . . There are more behaviour traits that we share with each other, large and small, than we know.

'We got a bit stuck here . . .'—this can happen in any group and the person taking things has to be ready to pop in a remark to help things along, particularly after a hard day's work. Don't go pounding away at adults with question after question. This is a technique much advocated by the adult education world and was used extensively with service groups in the war. It can easily be, and generally is, overdone. It is exceedingly boring at the receiving end. One lecturer I heard (suffered?) recently asked one hundred questions in about seventeen minutes. It is so uncomfortable that eventually the group gives up, becomes sullen and won't answer. This type of lecturer is still letting off cannon, though, blissfully unaware that they are narrowly escaping murder. Old-fashioned though it may be, it is sometimes comforting to hear a good straight talk by an informed mind. But then human nature is an old-fashioned thing, it is as old as Adam and Eve. Reasonable discussion is rather different, particularly if the leader is sensitive about taking on the burden occasionally and imparting at those moments an idea or even a little information.

'As time was getting on . . .', again a sort of chairmanship. Without dragging things and whilst we are still fresh, there must be time to play through or attempt the piece, if in your 'purpose' of the proceedings you consider it desirable. How often, particularly in schools, but in youth clubs too, a teacher or leader will mismanage the time, talk far too much themselves and fail to allow time to play out the story that has been built and is ready for the testing of spontaneity. It brings disappointment and less interest next time, if there is another time. With children, it is sometimes worth offering an opportunity next time, even if they don't want to take it. At least it shows you meant to play fair, particularly if several groups are working separately. If you *do* promise, you must remember.

It is fascinating how an unserious start can lead on to something more serious. The part about getting in and out of a chair, though part of theatre technique, can be used as social drama and has often come into personality training, taken by myself, or others who have trained with me, in day release work or in youth clubs.

The sincerity mentioned is part of good Child Drama, too, and is undoubtedly something which can slowly become a habit of the personality, with constructive results in the realm of honesty and fair attitudes in relationships with other people. It is these relationships which are the basis of civilised life.

IV. A New Era

A short preface to descriptions subsequent to becoming full time Drama Adviser

As one gets older, and when one has met hundreds of people each week and talked to thousands and thousands of children down the years, memories tend to get a bit blurred. I forget names very easily now, but have remembered faces for a long time. Now I tend to remember personalities instead. Sometimes one is unsure of small events, of when the detail fitted exactly. But I write notes constantly, because the history of the development of drama, attitudes, influences and personal relationships, fascinate me. I am very 'hot' on credit being given to the person, who really started this or that, and it pains me that these days this elementary matter of honour is taken so lightly. If a source of thought, influence, inspiration or action is not properly documented, or mentioned, it is impossible for students to follow an accurate form of study for their thesis or anything else. The history becomes warped, or there is a vacuum. For this reason, it is sad for me that a certain experience is a little unsure in my mind. I would like to think it was when travelling from Hereford to become Drama Adviser to the County of Stafford, sometime toward the year's end of 1942, for this was the beginning of a new phase, but I think it was perhaps only a visit to a doctor friend. It stands out in my mind, though, because there was an intense feeling of being all in a bundle. My wife and I and all our immediate belongings seemed to be on board, together with our first baby, in the back of a little red sports car. Apart from our furniture, still at Slad and guarded by Mrs Lee (which and whom we might never see again), we owned nothing else. Everything, down to the last pot and pan, was on board. It felt very safe somehow, like being a snail with the whole house on your back, albeit a fairly fast one. Perhaps the news of my appointment had come through and we were on that curious delightful crest of a wave, which you know can't last, still *at* a job but leaving and with the full relish of the new one, before knowing any of the snags. The whole situation was fantastic anyway, for my friend the doctor, with whom I had worked as a lay therapist before the war, was temporarily at my old public school; and more odd still, the school had been evacuated and was being taught Latin in the drawing room of my wife's old home.

There was one other occasion only, when the magic of one's burden had told upon me in quite such a climacteric manner, and this was in the same little red car when I had been asked to take the most important historical films from the British Film Institute to a secret destination, to get them out of London at the beginning of the war. I filled the boot with them and was in turn thrilled and agonised, as my exhaust pipe was broken and I feared for all of them. But we got there. On the way out, I was overwhelmed with the importance of the burden and think I would have pushed them all night in a barrow or rolled them separately, if anything had gone wrong and there was anything to save.

But the time I now speak of was special in another way. I had been developing spontaneous work and theatre applied to life, for years. At Hereford there had been extra mural teaching for Birmingham University, numbers of weekend schools on drama, and apart from the production for C.E.M.A. aforementioned, there had been work in factories and a vast revue. But so far, my advisory work had been mostly freelance, extra at times to whatever else was my main job. But after years of effort on the part of a few pioneers, full time paid advisory posts were beginning. Perhaps the final push came because of the Youth Service. Apart from occasional posts in private schools, paid drama positions in this country had, on the whole, started by being for adults, aided by Carnegie grant, mostly for rural areas. Then they included 'Youth'; and finally, because it was immediately obvious that it was hard to do work with Youth, without tackling problems earlier, it all began to ooze slowly into schools. This was the history of it. Now, at last, I was to be a full time paid Adviser. Someone would pay my lunch and reimburse me for my car! The permanent charity, the permanent loss, the permanent subsidising of every unusual undertaking would be over. It wasn't quite, but I thought so then. And on Stafford station, after first getting the job, I hugged myself and grinned all over my body, inside and out, like a dog. Apart from one noxious personality, my few years there were to be the happiest in my life and the only ones in which I ever felt deep inner security.

In my final house on the hill, I even forgot, for a time, the special depression that settles every Sunday evening on those who have been backward at school and unconsciously fear the Monday morning investigation of prep still unfinished, from many years before. I loved the work, I loved the people, I loved the place. I love them still.

Hitherto one could say that I had been a professional actor and producer, but because of being deeply concerned with reality and life had needed a broader canvas for the inclusion of education, therapy and prevention and was constantly trying to create a new profession. One had to win respect from medical men and practically bribe one's way into a class room. At last a very few of us had won through and I was a professional of that new profession. From now on, although there were going to be further occasions of having to subsidise schemes still (sometimes to a fantastic degree) and there would be many matters to fight through to establish position, respect and status for the subject,— from now on, things were to be different. It was the beginning of a new era. I bought some shoes to mark the event.

20. *The Gallant Captain and the Beautiful Matron*

Course for Youth Club Leaders and Senior Members, with a whole concourse of other young people from I know not where, at Rugeley, Staffs, about 1943 or 1944

The noise was incredible. I was frankly terrified. Take heart, all you who feel the same. 'Come on, do your stuff,' said a grinning Youth Organiser. My hour had come, but my mind was utterly blank. 'If in doubt, just start', I quoted myself at myself. So I started banging on a desk. The Youth Organiser valiantly helped. After about a minute the noise died down, and a second of surprised but uneasy quiet ensued. This was it, or else. I leapt into the middle of the room and started talking *loud*—or so they tell me—something to this effect:

Self: 'The war is on, and in the middle of the hall, here, is a hospital. There are twenty beds, and the place is guarded by a few soldiers and it's in the charge of a beautiful Matron.' (Roars, cheers, whistles and stamping.) 'Now, now, don't rush it—one day there is a bombardment' (the bombardment noises started, the Youth Leader used a whistle) '. . . fine, yes, just like that. And, after a bombardment what happens? Anyone know?' (No one spoke, there was a complete silence.)
Self (continuing): 'That's right, there's a complete silence.' (A few laughs, but they got interested about here, and I dropped my voice and began to build my bond with them.) 'And in this silence a gang of Nazis came. They seized the hospital, turned all the patients out of bed, tied them up in a bundle and pushed them over in that corner, over there. Ha, but they didn't know that gallant captain Archibald was on his way. In bursts Archibald and his few picked men, takes the Nazis completely by surprise, frees the patients, ties up the Nazis and pushes them in a bundle over there. Yes, that's right, just where those lads are standing—then dusting his hands very carefully on his trousers, freshing out the seams, flicking a lump of dust off his arm, straightening his belt, pulling his tie, putting one hair of his perfect head back into place—he uses Anzora, or is it Pears—he turns, turns

very slowly and meets the eye of the beautiful Matron. You know, it's an *amazing* life, isn't it? Do you know that officer and the beautiful matron had been walking out until the war came, and they *both came from Rugeley*.' (Cheers, whistles and stamping for some minutes.)

It took us some time to organise the vast crowds, the bombardment was a huge success. Everyone made noises, but were forbidden to throw anything. The beds were arranged quickly, an appropriate matron was put in charge, nurses were appointed, patients jumped into bed and were well tucked up. The Nazis took a lot of training, but were finally given to an N.C.O. of a Service Training Corps, to save time. He licked them into shape in part of the tea interval. After tea we all came together and played straight through. Part of the nursing became immensely detailed, because of what some of the girls had learnt about it, and some good contrasts arose in the characters of the English and German officers. The whole show finally finished up with a great party. Everyone in the hall ate imaginary biscuits, and drank pop that wasn't there. We sang some songs too. Then it was time to do something else.

This is the shape of it. There is not room to show the crowd which pressed round the hall. (*See diagram page 122*)

COMMENT

When there is noise, it is often better to use another noise than to try and shout. In the moment of surprised silence *you* speak. Timing again. After all, this is the way a referee controls a football match too.

My talking was fairly loud and fast at first. 'Attack' with the voice for attention and use speed for control. It is often worth picking up with something as it happens, thus to the noises of bombardment the remark 'fine, just like that'; also on the silence: 'Yes, that's right'; *use* or quickly comment. It can sometimes turn a barracking situation into a more normal one. You have to try and appear not to be put off. The silence here is used to drop down to the level of quieter speaking one is hoping to achieve.

There was a shambles of organising for a bit—'some time to organise the vast crowds'. Don't lose your nerve! The 'nursing' went on a bit too long, but I wanted them to have a good go without actually letting the others get out of hand. The old trick of putting someone else in charge (the N.C.O.) helped here. The point of the whole exercise was to show what could be done with that sort of crowd.

Fortunately it seemed to go off all right. It was important in my new job that it should.

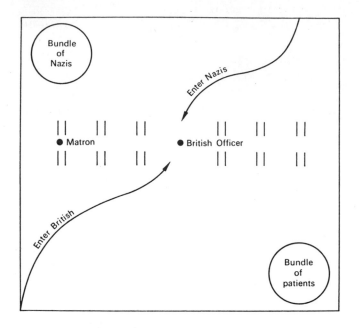

21. *Youth Ballet; or Murder on Page Four*
A Methodist Club, Staffordshire, 1944-5

Not all young people read the papers much these days; they mostly watch the 'telly' instead, perhaps, though father may take weekend papers distinguished by a near life-size symbol of hope and beauty on the front page. I would not go so far as an English master, who once nearly broke my spirit as well as my deep joy in words, and who insisted that we learned long political paragraphs by heart. But I would say that you can interest young people in life, behaviour, the needs of others and, arising out of that, national and universal problems, if you use a bit of imagination and go about it in a human way. I had done a bit of research on this and had been encouraging numbers of young people between the ages of fifteen and say, twenty-five, in clubs, training corps, service units, and factory groups to read more widely, more slowly and to reflect a little upon what they had read. Discussions would follow. I always, as now, took them from where I really believed they actually *were* in life—a very important axiom in all educational and social work, which it is easy to forget. It is much easier to start where we would *like* them to be.

Out of a large pile of notes describing how misfits, unhappy ones, part educated and just ordinary happy youths and maidens have been helped to read better, to read more widely—and to behave better, I have selected this example. Probably because it is gay and life needs more gaiety than it gets, or we give it. It was not necessarily historically accurate for its data or detail, but the story belonged to the period when certain international figures were already becoming a myth, and our British humour had stood us in good stead through some stiff and terrible years. This is what happened:

Self: 'Anyone read the paper today?' (Several had. Our encouragement had had some effect, it would seem.)
Self: 'What did you read?'
Answers: 'About an accident.' 'About Mussolini.' 'Horses.' 'Football.' 'There's a good murder on page four.'

Then we built a story out of some news items from my paper and some from theirs: Hitler, Mussolini, a smashing blonde, a professor who'd lost all his money on horses, a rich German banker, an ugly secretary, an accident, and as good a murder as on page four.

Hitler got fed up, and got a *rich German Banker* to fly him and his *ugly secretary*, Miss Sproshhcim, to see his old pal *Mussolini* in Rome, just for a nice weekend. When they arrived, Hitler noticed that Mussolini had got a *smashing blonde* for his secretary —much better than Miss Sproshheim. Being an evil man he sent for the girl's father, who happened to be *a professor who'd lost all his money on horses*. Hitler demanded that he should see her. The father refused, indicating that bad he might be, but he had not fallen as low as that. 'Ten thousand dammits,' said Hitler, 'I will woo her with loff,' which he did. And he arranged with the rich German banker to bump off the professor in a car *accident*. But Miss Sproshheim was jealous, and started to plot *as good a murder as on page four* for the blonde. She blew her up with a bomb in a powder puff, then stabbed the bits. But the German banker was in love with the blonde too, so he came in and shot the ugly secretary.

Hitler was sad without his girls, and Mussolini was very annoyed. So they parted, rather a bent axis, and the banker flew Hitler home. But Hitler decided that it was all the banker's fault, so he shot him over Berlin, and himself sailed quietly down to the Chancellery by parachute. Just a nice weekend.

As these young people I was training had not done their Child Drama at school, they were shy, and quite unable to move much, or improvise dialogue at first. Most of them were quite unable to read aloud too. So we all sat down and made masks, some of which I have to this day. Wearing these gave them confidence, and they were soon able to move about a bit. They were less shy about speaking too, though first efforts through the masks sounded as if most of them were eating cardboard, which indeed they may have been. After several sessions together at the club we achieved quite a polish on some of the movements, the rest remained improvised, but gained a quality of zest. The whole club joined in by banging doors and dropping things for the explosion, and one evening everyone 'stabbed the bits'. We shone old car lamps on the dancers as they moved, and, except that one line of speech, 'Ten thousand dammits, I will woo her with loff', remained in, we achieved what might be described as a ballet, only we didn't confine it to the stage, we danced all over a large Methodist Hall with tremendous vigour and enthusiasm, finding that free flying, which is of the birds and inspired by the personal dream in each young heart. This sort of dance can *only* be at its best when given space for the full 'journey' of its flight.

Girls and lads without masks helped to raise the banker, Hitler and Sproshheim off their feet when in the aeroplane.

Banker was unceremoniously dropped when Hitler shot him over Berlin.

Music was drum beats, foot stamping, hot jazz and Debussy.

Later on I used the masks again, and had other ones made for similar 'ballets' on youth courses.

During the construction of this piece of work we used to discuss a lot, and with great frankness. At one session we ranged over the field of morals, behaviour of young man to woman, the war, bad debts, loyalty and God.

COMMENT

Note that here there is a very pronounced purpose for the session—an interest in daily affairs, as part of the experience.

The type of dance, of course, was improvisation based on individual style. The word 'dance' was not used. English people, particularly boys, will often dance very well as long as you don't mention the word; if you do, as a rule they won't dance.

Masks are useful for all sorts of confidence building. I have used them for 'equalising of status' in factory groups, for patients who have had bad facial injuries, and I am now recommending them to help people from abroad who cannot yet speak English. Behind a mask, you often feel braver. The part of you which finds difficulty in facing the world is a small you. The You which grows behind a mask is a great big one. However, they are hot and you may find that after confidence is built, half masks are better. They still hide a lot of you, as a glance at a neighbour wearing one will reveal. Ultimately confidence may be fully gained and the mask is taken off—or the person in charge of the group may organise this, if carefully timed, as part of a therapy for strengthening the personality in an intentional test of doing without. Head angles are important and telling in a mask and, on the whole, should be a little larger than life, thus the apparent dead face will take on a life which is larger than life too. That is the fascination and strength of this strange device which we call the mask.

One line of dialogue was left in our piece because there are certain precise things which cannot be mimed or danced. That is why language was invented—to obtain more precision. There is nothing that happens more often in school and youth club than the inane hand on heart and pumping-away-of-air action. It is utterly unacceptable as representing any true emotion and can only lead to further cartooning of something we might try and make delicate; the delicacy of which we can teach young people to respect, if the Arts are used with taste, better than in almost any other way. The fact that this delicacy can sometimes come into the most unexpected stories is strange but also true. If you succeed—by chance or by intuition—you can lead on to the sort of discussion mentioned at the end of the report. Young people are often very grateful for this for, as they often say, nobody will talk to them about such things.

22. *Unserious leading to Serious*
Catholic Youth Club, Stafford, 1945–6

About this time, I was doing an enormous amount of youth work. Some of it was alarming, some of it amusing, some deeply moving and some just hard grind. It was interesting to visit every type of club and work with every denomination. There were some splendid Methodist clubs and a big Catholic club in Newcastle-under-Lyme, which particularly asked for my help.[1] Here I built up a sort of exhibition Youth Theatre before leaving the county and we produced a Morality Play, Obey's *Noah*, a Noel Coward comedy, and *Charlie's Aunt*. In *Noah*, we had younger members running round in a hall underneath, to get the noise of the animals, with an elaborate system of scouts to wave arms and give signals for the right moments to stop and start; and never shall I forget the tough gang that built a crane to lift away the hut from in front of the stage to clear sight lines for the moment when the family went up onto the deck of the Ark (the stage) and the sun came through. I am conscious that in these reports the figures of hero and heroine, boy–girl relationships, appear often. But this is because they *arise* often, if we are honest in our approach and either prepared to have fun where it is innocent or to go deeper and help young people over problems, should they wish it. An amusing skit has often led to serious and important discussion, ultimately leading to consideration of morals and values. It is part of the process I call 'beginning where people reveal they *are* in life' and developing from there.

Just such an evening did we have at another Catholic Club in Stafford, and one experienced a remarkable outcome.

Self: 'Now we have done funny stories and sad stories. Here is a

[1] Largely at the instigation of Father Denis Hickling, who had first met me at my Worcestershire Arts Centre.

[126]

serious one. A man is standing on high ground (let's make it the stage), and he looks out over the World (the rest of the room) and, just like Jesus, he is tempted. Satan comes up to him and whispers great promises, and you know how it is in life, sometimes we have great decisions to make. We waver on the brink. Sometimes we give in, but not always. We may choose, and reject, and go on our way, strong in the knowledge of right. So with this man. Satan slinks away. The man looks out over the world (the rest of the room), and sees diagonally across the room, in the far corner, his goal. Once his eye is fixed on God he makes his decision and does not waver. He comes slowly down the steps and walks on, head erect, walking the straight path till he reaches the far corner, his goal. But as he moves on his way the Evil Ones come to attack his fortitude. They approach with evil stamping sounds and talons out-stretched. But just as they are going to fall upon the man, Good Spirits arrive from the other side of the room bearing flaming swords. They raise their swords at the Evil Ones, who cower away. The good Spirits fall in behind the man and they are his guardians as he reaches his goal. What does he find? I want you all to think quite quietly and carefully for two or three minutes. If you were *really* that man, what would you hope to find? (Long pause.) 'Now then, face this, you *are* that man. Each one of us is, so what do we hope to find?' (There was another long pause of absorbed silence. It was not easy to judge the moment, but finally came the time to start.) 'Will you, X, be the man. Now, Evil Ones, here is a test for your group sensitivity. I want you all to start at once, and I want the footfalls to be as one. When the Good Spirits come, do not slink away by turning, stamp your way backwards in a group. Quite quiet, please, everybody. Absolute silence is necessary for this. It is a prayer, if you make it so. Make it true for you . . . quite quiet . . . now.'

It was very simple and all looks rather cold in print. But I can only say it was a wonderful experience. The resulting shapes are shown in the diagrams on page 128.

This outline has been used again since then, and points to watch for, or even to polish, are:

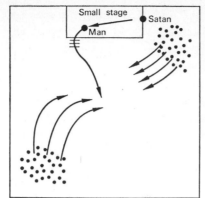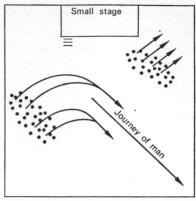

1. The grouping as The Evil Ones arrive.
2. The grouping as the Good Spirits arrive.
3. A great moment of good theatre obtained by hard mental work as the Spirits quell the Evil Ones almost with a look. Don't let the brandishing of swords be merely theatrical here.
4. Use of the music of the footfalls building to a climax as the Evil Ones arrive, and fading away to tiptoe sounds when they go.
5. See that a graceful accompaniment of Man takes place with, say, a file of Holy Spirits each side of him or in a 'V' like the wake of a great ship.
6. All stately walking must be exactly in step.
7. To aid, or possibly enrich, the creation, use the footsteps of the stately walking very purposefully as a complete contrast to the evil stamping. Or accompany the whole piece with appropriate sounds of the drum or clapping sounds by anyone not in the acting, or with rattles. Alternatively, use music, being careful to fade in well, so that the volume of sound is in harmony with the needs and beauty of the creation. If you use lights, they should be faded up, where possible, in harmony with music and movement too. Coloured lights often add interest; say, golden light on the Good Spirits and dirty green or red on the Evil Ones. Masks could be used too, though you may prefer the sincere expression of Man's own face and of the Good Spirits. If so, just use masks for the Evil Ones.
8. If you use music you might find something like the following

of value for such a piece: end of 'Walk to Paradise Garden'
—Delius; end of 'Air on G String'—Bach; end of 'Ave Verum'
—Mozart. Great care must be taken to fade in the music
at the beginning of a musical phrase.

9. One sudden spotlight to pierce darkness and fall on a large
   Crucifix might prove a good ending for some similar Creation.
   But that depends on what we hope to find when we reach
   our goal.

COMMENT

I sometimes get the feeling that now is the time one has to take a big chance. It
seemed right during the evening described above and at that exact moment. After
all, one might never meet these young people again and why throw away an
experience for them, when it could perhaps be achieved. Down the years I have
become less afraid of talking in depth. It sometimes proves the wrong thing but not
often, for so many people live on the surface; young folk notice this. Some of them
are in the midst of a desperate search and (as mentioned in the comment on
No. 21) they often tell me 'nobody will ever talk to us about these things'. They
mean God, love, death, duty and things like that.

Something of this wasting of time came home to me some years after this event
when someone had travelled half way across the world to see me for about half an
hour. Should I say what came like a flash into my mind? It almost seemed unjust
not to be honest. It was a calculated risk but I said it and they were very grateful.
Since than I have talked in lectures and at other times about things that are tender
if it seemed right to do so and people must take it or leave it. Some parts of this
book may seem like that but I have merely tried to be honest. There are technical
suggestions about the exercise 'man and his path through the world' at the end
of the actual description so there is no need for further comment here.

23. *Flood and Mermaids to the Rescue*

Spontaneous creation with miners sometime before the war
and again about 1946

'What you were doing was of interest to *us*,' said the social service
worker in the far North of England, 'but I don't think it would
go down with miners.'

This must have been before the war when I was rushing about

all over England and had pioneered some form of drama teaching in almost every county south of Manchester (excluding perhaps Staffordshire which was to come later), between 1930 and 1939, as well as doing stage work, running my own companies and other things described. There had also been the chance of a more permanent drama job in the West Riding and with Hull University, but earlier promises had made acceptance difficult, as they were to do, later, over the first county posts of Buckinghamshire and Kent.

However, another occasion found me back in the far North and with miners. They had wanted some help over a play they were doing in their club and I had been taking exercises in proscenium techniques. My ideas on this are very precise and detailed and possibly not acceptable to everyone, but they embody the method on which I always used to train my own professional actors from the early 1930s onwards and anyone that comes to me, or invites me, is always treated as an artist in the same way, however careful one may be about the doses offered.

We had been working on the precision of foot steps, before a quick turn and the holding of a sudden look diagonally across stage—one of those exciting moments of rhythmic silence when the *mind* can react to a remark and we all have the opportunity of watching or feeling the cogs work, until the next thing happens. I say 'we', because I think these Golden Moments can and should be a thrill for the actors taking part as *well* as their audience. A Golden Moment is a combined emotional and intellectual *assister à*, a total aesthetic creation and shared experience. It may happen by luck but can be to some extent, by art, contrived, as long as the actor can be sympathetic to the producer's dream and, rather than merely 'do as teacher sez', make the Moment his own.[1]
Self: 'Do you think there are other times in real life when this sort of training could be useful?'

There was a long pause. Then one man answered: 'Reckon down pit.'
Self: 'How?'

[1] This is also a healthy basis for teaching of Movement and Drama to young people. Time must be left for *them* to create. Teachers frequently talk too much, and instruct too much without pause. There can be no psychic conversation that way, only copying or bored obedience.

[130]

My notes say the answers were: avoiding bumping into people in near dark, saving you from bumping shins and not kicking a pit prop holding up a shaky roof.

Self: 'Would this be good?'

Answers: 'It would stop people getting annoyed with each other; make for safety; stop you getting hurt.' 'Save a bit of language too, reckon,' suggested someone. There was general laughter.

Self: 'All right then. Come off the stage now and let's think up some situations that might be real.'

Out of the process of group play making, an improvisation emerged. This was the outline of our story:

There was a very tough chap, who wouldn't go to the club, wouldn't take part in any of these wet things like drama (laughter). But he was very clumsy and was always knocking into people and hurting himself. He became a nuisance down the pit and generally disliked. One particular enemy arose, who threatened to 'do 'im', if he bumped into him again. One day he trod on the other man's foot and there was a scuffle. During the fight the other man—not the clumsy one—kicked down an important prop and part of the roof fell, trapping some companions. Finally everyone was saved by the strength and heroism of the clumsy man. The last line of the creation which they voted for was, from the angry man to the clumsy one: 'I'll never call you clumsy again', or words to that effect, which being interpreted came to the same thing.

Some of the Golden Moments in this were: an oldish man just standing and looking at the coal face before starting work; the careful absorbed filling of a truck; the footsteps down the pit, which we worked into a sort of group rhythm, broken by some slow, respectful or anxious looks at the suspect patch of roof as people passed; a very funny 'scrub my back' scene in a tub made of chairs. The higher level of the stage and the rest of the floor were used throughout. The tub was 'upstairs' (three steps) on the stage.

I have an idea that a pony came into this somehow, though this may have been with another group in Wales. But certainly the day finished with a remark *very* similar to one made to me by an old Welsh miner. 'I want to thank you, sir, for spending so much time with us and giving us so much of your 'eart. People don't want to spend much time with us, as a rule. But it's a mistake to think we don't all 'ave artistic feelin's just because we're miners.' I gazed into the old face (it is the Welsh one I think I see) with fascinating crisscross marks round the eyes and forehead—or is it both men by now? But in the case of the Welshman I know I kept thinking 'does he mean giving so much of my heart or art?' I was both shocked and touched and couldn't answer him. But, whichever way you took it, it was a great compliment.

A similar sort of thing happened in a weekend course for young miners in the Tamworth area of Staffordshire sometime between 1943 and 1947. Some of the young folk in the description of youth work at Rugeley may have been miners too, I am not sure. I had made several visits to Tamworth, having been introduced to organisers there by the Area Officer of the Council for encouragement of Music and the Arts, but this last occasion was rather formal. It was a sort of conference and weekend school, perhaps about the year 1946, partly arranged by the hard-working organisers of the Staffordshire Youth Service. It all opened in rather a formal and posh sort of way, but later we split up into groups of interest. Our group had been working on Joe Corrie's *Hewers of Coal* and trying to get some real characterisation into it, but, as usual with script plays in a large group, there was a danger of some people getting bored whilst not 'in it'. So we put down the books and started to create a very similar situation, with everyone joining in, and improvised that. It really arose out of *Hewers of Coal*, though, on this occasion. But a quite wonderful exciting part was when the roof fell in and chairs, forms and young men all fell on other young men from the stage to the lower level in front of it. I thought they might get hurt and stood nearby like a P.E. instructor, to catch or fend things off, but they seemed to get away with it. One young chap took a photo of a heavy beam (a long wooden bench) which the trapped men slowly lifted off themselves; unfortunately it did not come out or I would have tried to reproduce it here. One remark was rather

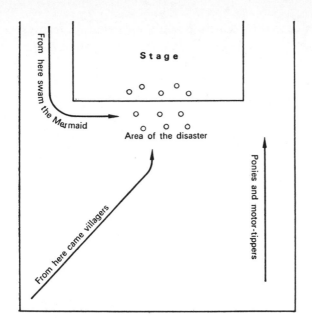

Stage

From here swam the Mermaid

Area of the disaster

From here came villagers

Ponies and motor-tippers

nice: 'Well we must be properly trapped or you can't feel it right.'
For this they were prepared to risk split skulls and broken legs,
if my proffered fending had been needed or failed in any way.
There were definitely ponies in this creation but they were discarded, with a smack, for motorised tippers.

The story finished differently though. Water poured through
from somewhere and there was danger of the men being drowned.
It got higher and higher but eventually they were rescued by a
mermaid, who took them to such delights, deeper under the earth
and beyond any coal face, that they never wanted to see daylight
again.

This last bit arose in rather an interesting way. I had been
warned to be careful, the lads might not want 'to do things about
their work'. But in fact they had chosen to do so. However, in
the way that sometimes happens with young people, there comes
a build up of confidence and a sudden breakthrough of what
they really feel and think, particularly after spontaneous work,
used in a wide and imaginative way, in secondary schools or
youth clubs. Somehow a discussion arose about what they would
rather be, if they weren't in the mining business at all. I was

[133]

further educated by learning about numerous different interesting jobs I didn't yet know in the industry, other than going down the mine itself. But some of them wanted to get right out of it and travel. One of them wanted to go into the Navy. There had been a long and serious discussion, which I finally thought had to be drawn to an end and joked a bit about the chance of seeing dolphins and mermaids. Perhaps that is how this particular alluring fishy damsel got into the creation. I seem to remember another such lady with young sailors at Portsmouth once, but no longer remember when that could have been. But I still have a tape recording of one in a submarine, devised with gusto by a group of physically disabled people in my London studio, during a holiday, many years later.

COMMENT

Expanding on the short description of Golden Moments, some of them in this creation arrived by luck, or rather they arose spontaneously because of the careful mental absorption of those taking part, who thought about the situation and imagined it so well, uncluttered by merely self-conscious or overplayed theatrical effect, that their quiet unexpectedness drove the message home. Thus the 'oldish man just standing and looking' at the coal face before starting work. Very relaxed, thoughtful, like a mariner contemplating that old devil the sea. Where should he begin? I should never have thought of this little touch quite as he did. He brought his own experience to it and shared it with us in a way which became sympathetically moving. The filling of the truck had something of the same quality. The footsteps down the pit were not quite the same. I liked some of the walking and also one man's anxious look at 'the suspect patch of roof' and worked them into an intended rhythm of walk—walk—walk—'look'—walk—walk, the occasional man each with his own type of glance. This is what I mean by 'it can be to some extent, by art, contrived' though it may at first have happened by luck and you can seize upon it.

The ponies 'discarded with a smack': not real ponies, of course, but so well imagined that when it was agreed to discard them, they had to be affectionately sent off as if real, not just dropped as a cold idea. This was splendid, as it contains the ability of an actor able to conjure up some real particle of affection for an object, animal or person so as to create a truth worth sharing. Perhaps the notion that 'we must be properly trapped or you can't feel it right' is more typical of the amateur stage actor. It smacks a little of getting yourself into a situation that you cannot easily get out of without some extra clumsy or time-wasting manipulation, and contains an element of risk. However, for these folk it was an example of their intellectual interest, and although it is easy to over-intellectualise and cause yourself unnecessary difficulties thereby, in this instance I was delighted by the unexpected remark and such a sign of our complete involvement together in the creation. It was clearly a cathartic moment to some extent. The feeling or fear of being trapped was something very real to them and they needed to include it.

24. *Umbrella Trees, and the Girl Without a Mother*

Teachers' Course for the northern half of the County of Stafford, Leek, 1947

IDEAS: *House   Mother   Umbrella   Sun*

My Story: 'Once upon a time a little girl lived in a big *house* in that corner, but she was a very sad little girl for she had no *mother*. Her mother had died. And every day the little girl would walk through the flowers in the middle of the room there and say 'Oh flowers, if only I had a mother'. And the flowers would nod and smile at her, and the bees would bring her honey. When it was wet the trees would bend over the little girl and be her *umbrella*, everyone loved her so.

But one day the little girl was wandering sadly through the flowers, and they were looking up and smiling warmly at her, when suddenly one of the tender trees could bear it no longer and fell with a rending crash to the ground, lying there covered in a dew of tears, her branches shaking about her. But through the gap in the forest the strong *sun* poured through and called out in a loud voice: 'I will bring you a mother. I will cough her up on the hill, out of the furnace of the heat of my heart.' And the little girl looked up, and there, surrounded in a glory of light, was a beautiful lady, walking slowly, walking towards her. Down she came from the hill, down amongst the flowers, and the wind smiled through the leaves of the trees as the little girl ran to the beautiful lady. 'Oh,' cried the little girl, 'at last, at last. You are my own lost Mother.'

'Yes,' said the beautiful lady, 'I have come from the heat of a great, great heart, and I'll never leave you again.'

So the lady and the little girl walked with arms round each other to the big house over there. And as they approached it,

[135]

the sun lifted up the fiery beams of his fingers and lit the windows like stars. And Mother and Child passed in at the great door which closed after them, but the windows shone for ever as a sign that love is not dead.

There was complete silence for a moment or two, then a spontaneous burst of clapping. One teacher asked if the story had really been made up on the spur of the moment. Several refused to believe that it had. These exact words were taken down at the time. There followed a discussion on creation, and then the story was acted.

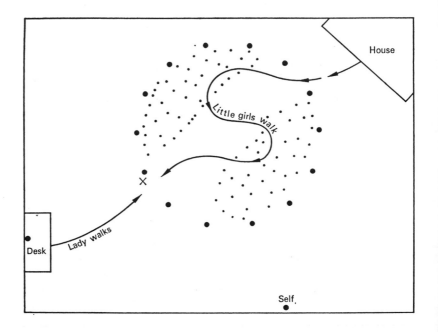

The small dots show the position of the flowers (people kneeling). The bigger dots were the trees, and X marks the tender tree who fell. The desk was the hill, the sun imagined above the desk.

COMMENT

This was the first of a series of courses planned in the county before my appointment to Birmingham. I was allowed to carry out some of them so as not to let down the arrangements made earlier.

Mostly teachers at junior schools attended this course and again I seem to have been carried away in a poetic flow and suggested the actual words to be said by the characters. As the work was with adults they were able to keep some of them and make them their own and add to them, whilst still keeping a sense of believability. I would not recommend it so much when actually taking children, they become more self-conscious in their attempt to memorise what you have said. It is generally better to say things like 'the little girl cried out with joy as she suddenly felt the lady was her mother'. Children will then supply their own actual words. However, in this case, at Leek, the purpose of the exercise was to give examples of and practise the art of story telling, particularly with use of the Ideas Game, so perhaps we may be forgiven for taking things somewhat at our own level even if the stories had an appropriately childlike flavour.

25. *The Blue Hat*

First gramophone record

Round about 1946, '47 and '48 there were a number of conferences on Education and Drama. At that time, opinion was very unformed and it was difficult to put across ideas that one had already been using for over eighteen years and almost took for granted. The Institute of Education at London University seemed to be my main ally and it is indicative of the situation then that a member of their staff asked me to come and discuss things with them whenever in London and to make a gramophone record of my suggestions and method, so that they could use it as a basis for discussion. Here is the script of that old wax. It is fairly elementary and full of generalisations. But it is very difficult to compress a long talk on therapy, catharsis, life opportunity, joy of living, personal expression, relationships in the classroom and emotional education into two short sides of a record and try to sound conversational at the same time. It was about the first of a series, the next ones more seriously prepared, on spontaneous work; and I am grateful to John Taylor of Messrs Hollick and Taylor for his interest, cooperation and patience in helping me to create some of the first recordings of their kind,[1] which have by now, been sent to or played in many parts of the world. I am also grateful to the Charles Henry Foyle Trust for aiding this venture in non profit making education. One is not particularly proud of this particular record but it served a purpose at the time and is now part of history.

With all its shortcomings then, the script of a gramophone record by the author recorded by Messrs Hollick and Taylor:

STARTING IMPROVISATION

Teachers and Club leaders often ask 'How do we get improvisation going?' There are a number of ways. You can read a story and then get the children to act it, they can mime to a story or poem while it is being read, better still they can make up something entirely of their own—give them an outline such as: 'A bad man is trying to get money from an old woman, he watches her in the 'bus. There are too many people in it to try anything on so he follows her off—then bonk! When he has bonked her what happened? They may then supply the answer—"Please Sir, the policeman comes"—"Yes", "Please Miss, the 'bus stops and the people jump off and surround the criminal"—"Yes", "Please Sir, they catch hold of the criminal and carry him off to the gaol." "Yes, what'll we do with the old lady?"—"Please Sir," "Please Miss . . ." and so on.' When they have done this sort of work for a bit they will not need an outline to start them off. Reading a bit from a newspaper is also a help. Bible stories are wonderful. It is important to try occasionally to see if they can express what they feel in movement to music or other sounds. Gongs, drums, hooters are all useful for this. It makes them conscious of sound. Gongs are vowel sounds, drums are consonants. If they learn to recognise and love sounds their English will improve. At first, do not be disappointed if the speech is bad, the whole thing is really a form of spitting out. They act out the many imaginary characters of their dream world and get rid of them. The children who do not act them out enough become self-conscious, and if after that they still do not act them

[1] Tapes have now been made of these, with further added comments.

[138]

out they *become* the characters in real life and you then have your problem child. The whole business is merely a sensible way of offering an environment for the child to express. If it *can* express it gains confidence, and with confidence *curiosity* and with *curiosity* the *desire for experience* and it is then stimulated to learn. Try acting a story then send the class off to write English. The *ideas* will improve—and aren't ideas in English as important as grammar and spelling? 'Katie comes in' is a useful game. She comes in slowly, angrily, sadly. Everyone can try.

Old Bill Blogs for boys! On a cold day the criminal is up one end of the room firing from his hip. The crowd rushes at him and some fall by the way blood gushing in all directions: *emotion, speed, vitality, violence,* and if and where possible *noise.* For quiet and calm—'Do you see that lovely pear tree? Pick a pear gently. Do you taste the juice? Concentrate, concentrate . . .' *concentration* the basis for study. Improvisation using the whole person is a basis for education. It develops imagination—where was the Pear Tree, how tall was it, was it in a garden, on a hill?

Now you may say—Yes that's all very well but my mind just doesn't work that way. I can't make up stories. All right—try the ideas game. This is one that I made up and have used with all ages from infants to Women's Institutes. Ask one or two people to give you an idea in one or a few words—'What is in your mind?' Sometimes they can't think of anything—well, 'Did you come here on a 'bus—did you notice anything, anyone *on* the 'bus?' (*Child*): 'Blue hat.' 'All right thank you—*blue hat.* Now someone else—you.' (*Child*): 'Please sir *food.*' (*Another Child*): 'Umbrella.'

'Yes, all right, thank you. Now we have three ideas: blue hat, food, umbrella. Will you help me remember them?' (Child-teacher relationship.) 'Once upon a time there was a funny old man and he lived in a funny old house over there *in that corner* and there were two things he wanted very much in the shops— *over there* but he was very poor and he could not afford them. But they were: (1) food (2) a blue hat and he did not know *which* to get. But he shuffled out of his little old house down the winding road (all over the middle of the floor space) and by the road were *trees* which bent towards him as he passed saying each in turn: "Good morning old man, good morning." But when he got to the shops it began to rain, and he *did* want a blue hat and he *did* want some food but suddenly he saw *what?*" (everyone): "An umbrella." "Yes he saw a wonderful umbrella." And he went in and bought it with his last penny. But he didn't know it was a magic one and as he came out of the shop he *couldn't* help wishing he had his blue hat too, and he was very hungry. But what do you think happened when he got home? (The house may be made of twenty or thirty human bricks if necessary.) He found that by wishing with the umbrella in his hand that his friends the trees had brought him two presents. "What were they?" (*answer all*): "*food—blue hat*." "YES, and he put the hat straight on although he was in the house. Not very polite but the trees said he might just for once. And they all leaned over him and filled him with so much food that he slowly—went to sleep—and all the trees passed quietly out of the house and rustled back into their places. There you are you made it all up didn't you—just from three ideas.'

They did not of course. You did, but they help and the ideas stimulate one's imagination.

Complete confidence should be given to the actors to say *exactly* what is in their mind. Regular use of this game promotes one of the most important things in education—friendly and trusting student-teacher relationship.

Note that in all this kind of work we are *not* concerned with a polished production. We are concerned with personal development and emotion and experience. Space is useful and the players act all round their body. Besides forming a valuable basis for education in this way, we incidentally offer opportunities for developing sincerity and absorption, the two most vital qualities in first class theatre.

COMMENT

In discussing the record afterwards, one university staff member said 'What do you mean by "Bible stories are wonderful" ?' They were right to pull me up. It is easy to make general, loose statements, when confined in time and space and I should have said 'wonderful as a basis for improvisation'. By the suggestion that if they (children) do not act out the characters of their dream world enough 'they become self-conscious' is meant, they do not release their inner vitality on the one hand, nor build up an efficient Language Flow on the other, suffering from consequent inability to communicate by lack of practice. They then become tongue-tied, afraid to move about freely, and their imagination is not fully enough stirred and used. 'They become the characters in real life' refers to the imagined image they may have read about or seen in film or on television as a character. Self-identification takes place and rôle-playing may begin. If there is not a place to go to or a time for acting this character out, under sympathetic guidance, the child may find its own time in or out of school and act it and act it and get into a rut in this rôle, thus to 'become the character in real life'. It is an unhappy state and in adolescence can be dangerous. The question is referred to again later in the book, in the history of the establishing of Rea Street Drama Centre (see p. 212) and in descriptions of helping delinquents.

'The players act all round their body', is the process by which children naturally act outwards from the centre of themselves all round their body. I have described the process as acting in the round, in the book *Child Drama*. It is different from theatre in the round, but is absolutely necessary to good theatre of that kind, yet alas is seldom used by adults who too often appear not to know about it.

26. *Deep Theatre, despite the Dancing Cows*

An adult theatre group, Birmingham, 1947

Another big chance had come into my life just now. Things were developing so fast nationally that I was finding it almost impossible to keep in touch and needed to go a little farther south. It was a big decision to make for the work was exciting, I had been offered new conditions in my present job and there was talk of assistants. The thought of leaving Swynnerton was a terrible wrench too. However, the decision was made. The City of Birmingham had offered me an outstanding appointment and I accepted. It is always fascinating and hard work discovering things in a new job and at once I was deeply 'in' it, lecturing and visiting schools and groups.

The group visited this night was in a small hall, not far from the Lozells Road, if I remember rightly. They had asked me what they could do in their small hall, which hadn't got a very good stage, and this led to a discussion on arena theatre and imaginative drama. Very high level talk on the attitude of an actor to his work. We then started practical work.

[141]

My story: There was once a very charming cow, who walked down
the street and saw a very snappy He-cow. She said 'tcha, tcha',
blinked her lashes a bit, and they got spliced, and lived happily
and had many children. They all lived in a field. In one corner
of the field was a trough, not of water but of magic tea. Now the
parents didn't like tea and—you know what parents are—because
of that they saw to it, or pretended, that their children didn't
like it either. So, for the children too, it was *'no tea'*.

Now one property of this magic tea was to make you dance,
and everybody was very surprised that the cows didn't make use
of it. But the cows knew a thing or two. They knew they didn't
need magic to make the world a wonderful, happy and beautiful
place. So they cried out: 'I know, we'll use our *imagination*. We
don't want to be the same silly people all our lives, we'll be birds
for a bit.' So they waved their horns like wings, and danced all
over the field till they were known in all that district as the
dancing *cattle*, and men would come from far and wide to see
them. But one day it was very hot. They got thirsty, and tired of
being birds, and they said: 'It's no good we'll have to drink the
magic tea'. So they did, and as they were drinking they wished
they were men so they could dance more easily. At once they
were transformed and found themselves drinking in a pub—in
that corner—(you might get tired of primitive cow dance, so
you see I am developing the potential theatrical theme). Then,
when they were nicely primed, they said: 'Let's go to the theatre.
They say there is some lovely *dancing in the theatre* tonight.' So
they all went to the theatre and watched the dancing. (We can
use your stage for this dance at the theatre.) But now a sad thing
happened, as it often does in life. The cow family had got what
they wanted—and somehow, in a strange, sad way, it wasn't
quite what they had hoped for, or thought it would be. The
dancing on the stage was cramped, the dancers muttered to
each other, they even glanced at the audience to see if they
thought they were good. They weren't in time to the music, you
guessed what they were going to do all the time, and they didn't
feel it with their mind. Oh, the dancing in that theatre—Oh the

dancing in that theatre—it was nothing like the dancing all joyful and enhancing, the gay entrancing prancing of the cattle in the field.

We discussed, for a bit, the difference between good dance and bad dance, which had been intentionally brought out in the story as part of the evening's instruction. We then acted the story. It began to get good in the pub, and some of the cow dance was very well tried. The pub part helped to get over any embarrassment, and then things got going. Those doing dance on the stage 'at the theatre' intentionally made lots of mistakes, making us fully conscious of what was bad. It was excruciating, and in fine contrast to the good acting in the pub, and the splendid moment of sincere sadness as the cows (now human) filed out of the theatre disappointed. This sort of finish always reminds me of Beatrix Potter's *Pigling Bland*, which moved me when I first heard it as a child, how he danced over the hills and far away. Where *did* he go to? It haunts me. Later I was drenched inside somehow, in the same manner, on first hearing that a certain ploughman 'homeward plods his weary way, and leaves the world to darkness and to me'. If you really understand and feel these words you will know how to fade your spotlight properly on a slow exit in an arena theatre production. And nothing less than this sort of 'best' will do for your criterion in vivid imaginative drama.

COMMENT

As this was a theatre group, one could have just given a straight lecture. No doubt there was some talking too, besides the discussion. But there is nothing like actually doing something yourself. 'They had asked me what they could do with their small hall.' If I had just said 'make it seem bigger by using more of the space available', they would have forgotten it almost at once probably, but they would understand and remember better by being involved in actual three-dimensional acting in the round, mentioned in comment on No. 25.

'Some of the cow dance was very well tried.' By this is meant, they made a good try at it and succeeded to a larger extent, particularly as hardly anyone present had tried improvised dance before and the story and their concentration on it helped them out of some possible embarrassment, as well as my offering them a deliberate 'natural' acting opportunity of just being 'in the pub'. This was not only kinder but gave them confidence. You could almost say that the made-human-by-magic cows coming slowly out of the theatre, disappointed, was a Golden Moment for they did it very well.

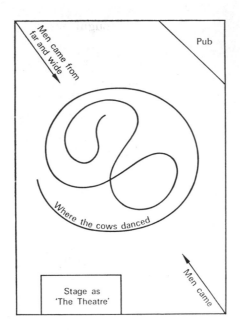

27. *Plumbottle Institute and the Corn that Clapped*

Course for candidates wishing to qualify as Tutors in Further Education, Birmingham, 1948

They asked for some training in Arena Theatre, and we had already discussed at length the actor's attitude to his work, and practised exercises for developing group sensitivity, group intuition, sincerity and absorption. They gave me:

IDEAS: *Wood   Spider's Web   Stream   Market place   Sun   Corn*

My story: A man lived in a house in a *wood*. This is the wood, and the house is over there. Now this man was no ordinary person. He had a great ambition to be a Tutor in Further Education,

[144]

and you know how special you have to be for that. So he kept a small magic wand in a pocket next to his heart, so that when he was teaching he could wish his message into the minds of his students. But even tutors have to eat, so the man set out through the wood to go to market in the nearest town, and as he went he would call out to the trees by name, and being good students they would always give the right answer. And he passed on through the trees till he came to a large clearing, and the clearing was full of *corn*, golden with hope, and tall with life. He pressed his way through part of the corn, but seeing that he was treading it down, he took the magic wand out of his pocket and made a *stream* appear. The he walked along the bank of the stream where the corn suddenly didn't grow now. But in a short time he needed to cross the stream, and seeing a *spider's web*, like a rainbow in the light, spun across the water, he used his wand again, and made it into a bridge. And all the corn on the far side clapped with delight to see him coming, but very softly though, by knocking heads together. By such means as this, and glorying in the day, the man came to the *market place*. And he bought there, cheese and buns, bread, butter, biscuits, milk and a bottle of Burton ale. Then he started for home and the corn cried out: 'Good morning, Man.' 'Morning to you', he replied, giving them teacher's best smile. 'You smile like the *sun*,' said the corn. 'That is to make you grow in wisdom,' said the man, and smiled again. And he passed on into the shadow of the wood, and back towards his home. 'There's something waiting for you,' called the trees. 'Good students for telling me,' cried the man, and ran to his house. He burst in at the door and on the white-scrubbed parlour table there lay a shining envelope edged with gold. He tore it open and read aloud: 'The Education Committee is pleased to inform you that your name has been added to the honourable list of Tutors for Further Education, and would be grateful if you would attend for interview at Head Office, at 5.0 a.m. to-morrow, just before lunch, with a view to becoming Tutor of Drama at Plumbottle Evening Institute.'

For just one moment there was a pre-thunderstorm silence— then a great roaring sound flooded the earth as all the corn and trees in every land burst out clapping, and a cheer went up that shook the clouds and the very heavens. Well, of course, he got the job. And now you know the secret—why Drama is so good in Birmingham. Such Tutors!

We laughed for a bit about our story, then when I felt they were relaxed enough, I started them off.

Self: Right. Now, part of an actor's job is to jump quickly into a situation, and although this story is a little unusual from the worldly point of view, now that you have worked together for some weeks, see how quickly you can make this situation believable. Concentrate hard and make it true—forget you are grown up. What does it matter? You still have hopes, many of you probably wish that things were easier, more pleasant, don't you? Some of you perhaps go out of the city at weekends to get clean air in the country. One of you, I know, writes poetry. Very well then, face the facts of what and who you really are. Let your dreams come true for a few short minutes, deep down in yourself, and apply that release to your creation.

They became very quiet and the acting went well. The 'man' gave us a wonderful first exit from his house, after shaving very carefully. His face lit up with the glory of the morning. After discussion they decided that they would like to have people kneeling, with hands raised and fingers extended for the corn. And we added a few 'flowers'. The trees carefully borrowed and held pots of flowers and leaves that happened to be in the hall. One man organised the wood to look like a place he visited at weekends. Thus does reality creep into creation. It became more true for him. A tall thin lady volunteered to be a kind spider, who not only spun the web on purpose for the 'man'; but *gave* it to him to turn into a bridge. The 'bridge' was a mixture of one fat man and two chairs. The 'corn' did not knock their actual heads together, but touched hands and fingers for the 'clapping of the corn' and clicked their tongues at the same time.

There was a splendid market place with a loud voiced auctioneer. He sold the bottle of Burton, for some reason I am not quite sure of. We ran through it once or twice, polishing the original improvisation each time, with such suggestions as: 'Yes, but let us feel something when you have come out of the wood and see

[146]

Above: relaxed movement. Adult Dance Group, Rea Street Drama Centre, Birmingham

Left: 'overcoming'. During dance drama. Educational Drama Association Summer Course, Saltley, Birmingham

Above left: young helper dusts crown before procession. Theatre for Children, Rea Street, Birmingham

Above right: three strong men help to carry a canoe. Theatre for Children, Rea Street, Birmingham

Below: important conversation with a totem pole and a bird. Rea Street Centre, Birmingham

that wonderful stretch of corn. Don't overact, just let us share a bright picture in your mind. No theatrical jerking-back in astonishment, or "leading man's" lift of the chin. Be real. *Work*. Recall some past experience or create a new one.'

And again: 'You know how peculiar it feels in real life when you talk to someone and they can't look you in the eye, well if someone speaks to you *look* at them, in this situation—even if the person is a tree. In arena work we are very close. We are intimate. Each detail can be noticed. When, you hold someone's eye with your own, some thought and understanding is caught. So, in acting, there is mental action of importance, and therefore logic and a purpose, therefore an 'accord' to be discovered. These things shared at close quarters give you the sort of electric truth, which is necessary.'

Later: 'Good. Now it has quite a different "feel". It is believable now. Now we want to add rhythm.' I explained how to fit in the rhythm of 'man's' slow footfalls and fade in the rustle of trees and the 'clapping of the corn' (rather as in a good radio production), then fitted lights to the production picking out the various areas of acting with spotlights as needed, and finally set

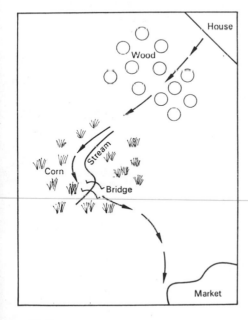

the show to music. We used pieces from 'The Planets' and 'Job', and added real drums and harmonium music to make a good strong climax at the end with the clapping and cheering in an attempt to make the very heavens rock. At least the school hall did.

COMMENT

It is a good thing to have some joy in life. 'We laughed for a bit about our story, then when I felt they were relaxed enough I started them off.' There is something important about intended timing. There is generally one moment when you ought to begin. It has something to do with experience and taste. Not always easy to find, it has a link with good theatre and good teaching and is absolutely necessary for good dance.

I often find that it is a good thing to use something with which a group is familiar and then mix it with imagination. It helps to keep their feet on the ground, take themselves less seriously as well as making them feel it all very much belongs to them—hence the theme on an actual tutor, in this case. The part about the trees was partly symbolic too, for we often have ambitions to teach someone or somewhere else, which may unduly pressurise us, when in fact there are lots of people already around us who may need our help.

The pleasure of working with this group was that it was a healthy mixture. Some teachers, perhaps, but also people from totally different walks of life. That always adds to the gaiety. We can become over serious and on our dignity if we only meet our own kind.

28. Ice Cream and Boiling Blood

Course for intending foster parents in Cottage Homes, Birmingham, 1948–9

MEN ONLY

IDEAS: *Singing   Cricket   Cry   Wet*

My story: A selfish young man would play *cricket*. He didn't like it really, but wanted to be Captain and go in first. He went in and was bowled first ball. He was very angry and retired to the pavilion and started to eat ice cream. While the others were still playing, he ate up all the ice cream. Then it suddenly started to

[148]

rain. It came down like the outpouring from giants' buckets and of course the players and pitch got very *wet* indeed. It was clear there would be no more play that day.

The players ran to the pavilion. When they got there they remembered the ices. But when they looked for them they found that the selfish young man had eaten them all up. At this a great annoyance fastened itself upon them, and they remembered all of one accord that there was one thing the young man couldn't abide. He hated *singing*. So just to punish him for being so selfish they made a ring round him and began to sing louder and louder and louder.

At this the young man became very angry indeed and got hotter and hotter. His blood boiled, and jets of steam shot off from the ends of his hair, till the whole place was in a cloud. His feet got hotter and hotter too, till they became red hot like electric irons left on too long. Then two little streams of smoke began to appear and his feet burnt right through the floor boards.

Suddenly there was a fearful *cry* that froze the singers to silence. The floor opened up, and the young man disappeared and was never seen again. So that, you might say, was the end of him. And you know you'd really be quite right.

NOTE: *The play took 6½ mins: and they sang D'ye Ken John Peel. It was splendidly intolerable.*

LADIES ONLY

Self: 'You are a woman making a decision. You walk round the room thinking "Will I do this or will I do that?" When you have walked once round you are influenced by evil. These three here are the evil ones.

'They get up and follow you but you give them a withering glance and they fall back, in these stylised steps (I show them).[1] Will everyone make percussion noises to accompany their feet please! You, the Woman, pass on, but of course you are not strong enough to stand up to Evil all alone. But you pass into the sphere of influence of Truth and Justice (two nuns took these parts sitting in chairs).

[1] I should not have shown them unless stylised.

'As you pass them we see you bear yourself more strongly. You are fortified. Yet even now you are not safe, though you pass the evil ones this time without being tempted, so the spirits of goodness come to your aid. As you pass them, they take flaming torches of righteousness from brackets in the walls of the Palace where they live and follow after you in solemn procession, step by step to the end of your journey.

'And will everyone else please accompany the solemn procession by making noises!' (Several of the students pulled out pipes from their music work, and we ended on a fine sort of dirge.)

We also had an improvisation about gangsters (men and women) and acted a story out of a newspaper.

COMMENT

There were to be many courses down the years for the Home Office and for intending parents in cottage homes. Not all of them would be able to take this sort of activity, but there is a desperate need for personal expression through Child Drama in cottage homes. Ordinary and more fortunate children have their games at home, and parental love, but the children in cottage homes have virtually nothing. However much we try, we can never quite make up for what they have lost. Nevertheless, I was trying to give these good folk an experience of being young again and of experiencing acting in the round as a preliminary to rediscovering what it is like to be young—a process I would strongly advocate for Colleges of Education—for we forget so quickly what it is like to be a child. Indeed, why should we not? It is very hard to break from unconscious childhood to conscious adulthood. The very process tends to let down a curtain behind us and we fumble to find the opening back, full knowing that even if successful we cannot stay, but must return again with wisdom to reality.

Nevertheless a number of staff in homes and schools of various kinds, for unhappy or deprived children, *have* succeeded in rediscovery and have since done splendid work in bringing some happiness and spontaneous outburst to those almost without hope.

In the section on 'Ladies only' in this report, the two nuns were turned into Truth and Justice because they were hesitant to take part. I know it will be forgiven if I say that nuns seem to be divided into two distinct kinds in their approach to this work, they either wish quite understandably not to take full part—and then one can nearly always include them as something 'abstract'—or they tuck up their skirts and become more active than anybody else and dash us practically off the floor with their gusto. Other people, though, and any children, even bombastic ones, can sometimes be helped by being something abstract or by turning into an inanimate object like a lamp-post. Regarding the footnote on stylised work, this may involve repeated and somewhat 'unreal' movements in which the pattern in your own mind *has* to be shown in order to be re-enacted at all. Unfortunately, many teachers demonstrate every movement as being the easiest way to obtain results but, of course, children only copy them, become lazy over imaginative work and less confident in creation altogether.

29. *Blue Glasses, Milk Churns and a Gramophone*

Notes on the first Educational Drama Association one-day Conference on Primary Education, Emergency Training College Hall, Birmingham, 1949

After lectures and a good deal of discussion, practical work started. We were suggesting that it was important to keep stories short for younger children. We asked teachers to begin to feel what it was like to act in three dimensions, as children do in their genuine Child Drama. They therefore tried stories of a Junior nature, themselves. We explained various ways of starting things and mentioned the Ideas Game.

Short story No. 1

IDEAS: *Full moon   Dinner time   Blue glasses*

Once upon a time there was a huge castle—made of lots of chairs—over there, and in it lived a kind wizard. He was at his best at the time of the *full moon*, and did good spells then, like making toys out of grass, banishing soap and water, or creating perpetual *dinner time*. But the magic and the moonlight were rather strong for him and he had to wear *blue glasses*. One night a big wind got up, so big that the trees found it very difficult to stay standing. One old fellow fell down. He tried to avoid the kind wizard but one of his hands slipped, and a branch broke the wizard's blue glasses. So the wizard couldn't see, and he went sadly back to his castle, had a big dinner and was never seen again.

A teacher: 'Why wasn't he seen again?'

Self: 'Isn't it *extraordinary!* I don't really know—perhaps he misunderstood, and was sad because he thought the tree hit him on purpose, some people are like that, you know.'

A teacher: 'Well *I* think the trees gathered a lot of leaves and covered up the wizard, and that's why he wasn't seen again.'

Self: 'You may be quite right. What does anyone else think?'

And so the discussion started. Finally we played the story. They were asked to make up their own words, and as a final accompaniment I invited everyone not actually playing parts to make a blue humming noise when the moon was switched on, and to fade when a cloud came over it. Such moonlight has never been heard before.

Short story No. 2

IDEAS: *Milkchurns   Gramophone*

A man wanted a *gramophone*, so he went to a shop. They sold special needles there, needles that could turn things into things. So he came out with some of these special gramophone needles and saw some *milkchurns*. He touched a churn very carefully with one of the needles—like that, 'tap, tap'. (Will everyone in the room do the 'tap' noise, please—a hundred or so people made a 'tap tap'. Yes, very lightly and all together, he only used one needle, you know—they did it more together then. That's better . . .) and immediately he tapped the churn, it turned into a gramophone and the lid became a record.

By this time things were beginning to move. The actors leapt to it. A shop was set up; a row of churns appeared (people); the churns danced a bit; the gramophone was created out of several human beings; it was wound up by an invisible handle in someone's tummy. The 'one churn' somehow became many and in the end, when the gramophone started to play, a remarkable sort of self-controlled rugger scrum waltzed round on a given centre. Everyone in the room invented and contributed to the music. I have an uneasy feeling that we ate the 'special needles' to finish up with and that an army of school doctors had to be called in to make us better. But, if that did happen, and I can't vouch for it now, they didn't succeed very well, for it is well known that many people suffer from indigestion to this day.

One extra thing I do remember about this meeting, though— our President at the time, the late Sir Wilfrid Martineau, was good enough to be present. In a typically kind flash of humour, he looked at me, early in the proceedings, from under his bushy eyebrows, and said in his deep voice: 'I think it would be more comfortable for everyone present, if I didn't take a very active part, Slade, I'll just be a *bulrush*.'

COMMENT

Again, in this course, one was attempting to give teachers a three-dimensional experience in imaginative work so as to get nearer to the child's mind. Some of the work seen in the city had been rather formal for younger children and I wanted to help rather than criticize. Some remarks in the discussion indicate that teachers were well able to think at an imaginative level. They became quite hot about it at times. Some of them needed to use a proscenium stage still, though flowing on and off for the first time in their lives, but the rest of the work was done on the floor. One Head, now retired, and not very sure of this work, used to question people round him, during the day, looking bewildered but trying very hard. Whilst climbing into a chariot he said on one occasion—'Ah, we're in. Now what do we do, shut the door, do I?' He reached for a handle but one of the horses said 'Heh, that's my ear, you fool.'

For those interested in the history of Creative Drama, this course would have been about a year after my being invited to become Director of the Educational Drama Association and to train people in my particular ways of doing things. It is interesting to think how many people present that day have since done work of distinction, a large number now being in important posts in colleges and other places.

30. *The Bird and the Orange Peel*

Notes on a course for teachers in junior schools by one who was present, Rea Street Drama Centre, Birmingham, 1949

Mr Slade was back, directing the course again this week. The class discussed the way in which their own school classes had reacted to this new kind of creative work.

[153]

A teacher: 'I find that, in music and movement, my children tend to use their feet only, to start with. What do I do about that?'
Slade: 'Don't be too worried. Using one's arms, hands and fingers to express properly takes time and practice. When children are first given permission to move about, they sometimes get excited over the sound of their feet—just as in street play—it is very exciting, after all. They concentrate rather on the lower part of the body, but when they are more used to moving about in space, they begin to express more carefully with other parts of their body. But in any session of music and movement, see that everyone really understands a purpose in what is being done. Is there a situation that can be believed? If not, there may be nothing for the child to express. Always be ready to allow speech. This often brings reality. It offers a more genuine way. And a story situation behind the movement generally brings purpose. It is the difference between Movement as the adult conceives it and genuine Child Drama.'[1]
Teacher: 'I think that's what I've been doing wrong in the past. I've been trying out an educational fashion in movement, instead of finding real Child Drama. I haven't got very far with either yet.'
Slade: 'Persevere. Know what you are looking for, and you are more likely to offer the right opportunities to your children. Their work will improve then.'

After giving advice on bringing teacher and children together in friendship, making suggestions about integrating the Arts with 3 Rs, explaining the use of polished improvisations between the age of nine years and eleven, Mr Slade asked for ideas. We gave him:

IDEAS: *Cat   Wall   Orange peel   Garden*

His story: A bird, who liked bright colours—and lived in a house over in that corner—flew over the market place flapping his wings and making a rushing noise, and he swooped on to the baskets of the market people and flew off with an orange, which he peeled, dropping the *peel* as he went. Then he noticed a *wall*

---

[1] Movement to music has changed somewhat down the years. In those days, work in schools was rather more rigid and there was not enough practice in informal speech.

and decided to drop peel right along the top of this wall, and after trying three times he managed to drop it along the top in a nice straight line. That night a *cat* and another cat came along the wall from opposite directions. Just when they met face to face, each hoping the other would give way, they slipped on a piece of peel and fell plop down into some prickly bushes that grew in a *garden* beneath. They pulled out the prickles, one by one with little popping noises, then put on their thinking caps (which they kept folded neatly in their hip pockets) very carefully. They did this to try and find out who had done this awful thing to them. After a few moments they realised it could only have been a bird. No one else would do such a thing. So they waited all night. But in the morning the bird came to see the orange peel again and the cats jumped up and spat at him rudely, such spitting as ne'er had been heard (every one in the room can make spitting noises here). And that bird was so frightened he flew away in a fuss and never came back any more.

We then tried out the story and used up everyone on the course. We were the wall, or bushes in the garden, people in charge of the market stalls. Four people were the prickly bushes that scratched. One fat man wanted to be an orange, but we decided the bird wouldn't be able to lift him, so he became a melon and lay on the floor. Our first attempt at spitting was weak, so we were asked to do it again and let ourselves go.

At the end Mr Slade said: 'Poor bird, he must be very sad after that big spitting, let's sing him to sleep.' So we all stood round the bird and sang a little, becoming quieter and quieter.

He was showing us what he meant by de-climax and how to establish discipline with large classes.

COMMENT

Courses of this kind were run in those days on one night a week for several weeks at a time. It made it possible for me to follow up some of the work in schools as we went along.

'Integrating the Arts with 3 Rs.' It is terribly discouraging for some children to fail in their lessons and the Arts can offer other channels of success. In spontaneous drama, we are concerned with the doing of life and the realm of personal play and this is a different kingdom in which to succeed and be happy. But anyway, some link with a dramatic approach can give many lessons an uplift in interest. Role playing can come into History, Geography and R.I. Now that the first two are considered Social Studies there is not much excuse for it not doing so in a junior school; and space and the physical feeling of plus and minus can come into the teaching of number. Drama situations for oral English and French are even more obvious. Although this particular comment is concerned with junior education, I might just mention that with older children and with adults in London, I have had successful dance sessions using atomic patterns, ending up with nuclear fission.

It will be noticed that the story of 'The Bird and the Orange Peel' is very short. One cannot repeat too often that stories for infants and young juniors *should* be very short. They cannot listen with all ears for long and can only do their best work in bursts. If asked to do longer stretches they will only 'fill in' and not put full energy into spontaneous work, thus chopping a log soon turns into what looks like leaning a fist on a jelly. This is very bad for them. The activity is of the emotions and they can catch the habit of doing everything at second best, lazy level or worse.

31. The Musician Who Smiled

At the Central Council of Physical Recreation, West Midland Region Day Rally, Birmingham Emergency Training College, 12 February 1950

I had been speaking on the link between Dance, Speech and Drama, and then we started practical work. I asked for ideas and was given:

IDEAS: *Piano playing   Open window   Brown bag*

My story: Once upon a time there was a musician, and he lived in that house over there. Over here was a peaceful village.

Now, the villagers used to get up early every morning and listen to the birds singing, before eating their breakfast. One morning a woman and her friends decided to go to market (there), so they set out down the path (across the hall there) and passed by the musician's house. But whenever they went that way, they would always hear the exquisite *piano playing*, which held them in the midst of their travel. This day they came

[156]

to the house, and again were enchanted by the lovely sounds, which flowed out to them through the *open window*. They peeped inside and there was the musician playing his piano, and smiling the smile of another world. Then he stopped, and the women retreated into the wood by the house, and remembered their marketing.

On they went by the zig-zag path and came in view of the stalls. Here they bought buns and biscuits and bread. But the woman who suggested coming had put all her purchases into a basket, and was about to pay, when suddenly she discovered she had no money. So great had been the beauty of the birds and their song that she had forgotten all about it. It was all at home in her little *brown bag*. But her friends said: 'We will lend you the money. We trust you. You are our friend.' So the money was paid and all was well.

The women returned by the zig-zag path through the wood. But when they came to the musician's house, they could hear no playing, all was silent. They tiptoed up to the window and peeped in. There was the musician sitting on his stool. But his hands were still. He sat there smiling, and his smile was like music from another world. His music was in his face, for he would not play again. He was dead. The women mourned for him, and passed sadly home. They slept a sad sleep. But, do you know, something very strange happened in the morning. When they opened their windows to hear the birds, the birds from the wood sang the same tune the musician always played, and they remembered it for ever.

In acting this piece we included people as birds.
Self to musician: 'Here is your house, you may play where you like. These people can be your piano if you wish.' (Ultimately she chose to sit alone.)

The birds used a selection of Laban movements. All onlookers were asked to chirrup, and then to try to feel with their neighbours so as to give one big clap in unison (group sensitivity training). The clap represented a window banging. The birds were to fly away frightened.

The villagers did a sort of naturalistic movement.

[157]

Self (*during play*) *to onlookers:* 'If you were taking this in a school, club or institute, you would sense that the shopping is going on rather long, and the birds may get a bit bored. All the movement is on one side of the arena too. This space is getting lonely, the pattern is weak in this area, so I'm going to suggest that the birds circle round and settle near the stall to try and pick up crumbs.'

After all was done, I commented on the type of movement shown, suggested how one could polish, and how at a certain point the birds distracted attention from the death of the musician by flying away too late.

Self: 'And now just to finish up, I think we had better have a big funeral. Would someone play music for the birds?—Then on into a steady slow march as the villagers get up and beckon to all those watching, so that all of us slowly become part of the procession. We are too big a crowd for the zig-zag path, so we go first to the wood, break off a branch, dip it in the burning bowl outside the musician's house, and walk steadily and with great dignity, torch in hand down the big S-shaped road to that corner of the room where the musician will lie in state.

'Children would probably hold a complete service, if doing this piece, and probably finish up singing "God Save the King" or something like that, but I want everyone in the room to experience something of the immense dignity of this last journey.'

Later we discussed many ways of moving to the same music, from sensitive small movements (like the flick of a finger) to wide stylised forms (associated with the sound of feet). The link was shown between children's innocent creation and adults' discovery of more polished imaginative theatre.

COMMENT

We have met this slow marching before, but on this day it was superb. It was a delightful opportunity to work with people interested in Physical Education. There has been a feeling for years now in that sphere that you should not show emotion and that 'pure movement' is more important than a dramatic situation and that you must not allow imagination to come into things. No wonder some of

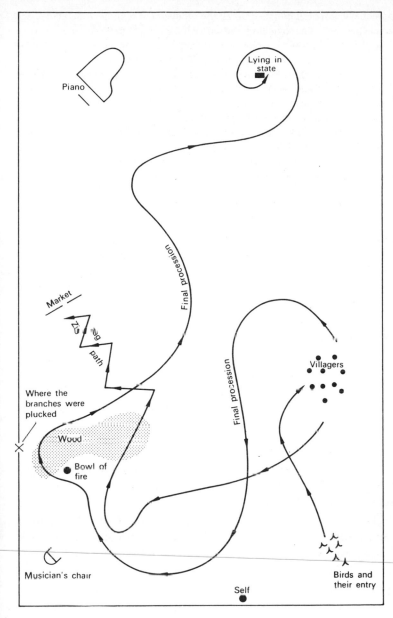

Outline of main positions during story of the musician at C.C.P.R. Rally, 1950.

our potentially ardent youngsters do all their movement with dead pan faces and repeat clichés with unconvincing self-consciousness in gravelike silence. How sad. The P.E. world should become our greatest allies. They are too often divided from the world of drama and life. They are the gods, we are the untouchables. Fortunately there are signs that the ice is cracking—certainly in particular places. I look forward to the time when it has cracked everywhere and a flood of reasoned friendship will unite the two worlds. Gone will be the days when you have to ring a cockerel's neck, to wash your hands with soap, or spear the next star with a 'thrust' when you are only expected to mime offering a cigarette. Fifty girls being grief. Why? A hall full of 'strong movement, isn't it'—Why? What *is* it all for? Even if it wasn't strong, you wouldn't dare say so because teacher is already showing you how to do it and you must catch up and copy the rest.

> Oh, why so strong
> at the sound of a gong?

This was the sort of discussion we had and thus we began to break the ice that day and thus one has been tempted into speaking sometimes since. If anyone is worried or offended, please try to forgive. The situation needs serious thought and because one has dared to say so, in the end I now count many P.E. specialists my allies and friends. From his last discussion with me, let all be comforted that Laban himself would have agreed also.

32. *Miracle for a Blind Girl*

Weekend school run by the Educational Drama Association, Barnsley, 1951[1]

The Educational Drama Association had been a national association for two and a half to three years and some of the main officers went to other places to help start the work.
Self: 'You are a blind girl. You move slowly down the room to this spot, about half way. You feel utterly alone and in the dark. You are sad because of some private misfortune—choose it in your mind. When you come to this spot, feel something unusual happening to you. You look slowly up, and suddenly a light pierces onto your face from up there in the dark. There is a

[1] The outline of this improvisation has been used by many people since, including Girls' Life Brigade Groups, Girls' Friendly Society, Teachers' Courses and Home Office Courses.

[160]

miracle, and all at once you can see. Two streams of companions come from these two corners facing you, converging in an arrow-head shape, and take you by the hand. They lead you forward, round, and away whence you came. But now when you reach that place, it is dark no more. Your eyes and heart are full of light and love.'

They did this slowly to the music of 'Paradise Garden'. We repeated it, and I suggested they should speak, if they wished to. The girl cried out 'I can *see*', after the miracle. And when the companions arrived they chatted a bit until music faded in for their general exit.

Self: 'Good, that was lovely. Now this time, think out more carefully what you would say, Companions. You have found and experienced a strong fine exit. But let us develop it a bit now in the middle. What would a blind girl want to do, if she could suddenly see? What would she say? What would you say to her?'

Answers: 'Look at those lovely things.' 'Pick flowers.' 'Want to go to shops.' 'Buy all sorts of things.' 'Find a boy friend.'

Self: 'Yes, I bet she'd buy a hat too.'

Answers: 'And gloves.' 'And a bag to match.'

Self: 'Grand. Yes, we'd better not let her buy too much, she might run out of money in her excitement. Right—the shops are over here.'

We had a nice walk through woods, picking flowers, and some very tender moments of the blind girl giving them to her companions, and some finding sudden sun flashes to 'The First Cuckoo in Spring' music. The girl bought lots of things in quick excited little movements—full of gay snatching. Each snatch accompanied by a light drum beat. Then at the end of the day the companions left her, to the sound of 'Paradise Garden'.

Self: 'Yes, I don't think I need to add anything. You all, obviously felt the sun die, and the slight sadness of the parting of the friends at eventide. Don't be afraid to put into it what you feel. Let it become the symbol of some of your own partings, your own suffering. In that way you throw off your burdens, and incidentally create beauty.'

The Blind Girl (to me later): 'I felt I hadn't finished. After my

[161]

companions had gone I felt I wanted to kneel down and thank God.'

Self: 'Well, why didn't you? It's always a very good thing to do.'

COMMENT

We outlined the sort of work which might be taken with children from five years of age to fifteen years, in some detail, as I do now with an assistant, on one-day schools. We also did a great deal of work at adult level with reference back to the needs of the child.

The exercise described took us fairly deeply into things near the end of the day. They were ready for it and I have seldom seen a miracle done so well. It had been started off by a question about whether you could use spontaneous creation in connection with religious teaching and training.

It will be noted that some questioning provides answers which lead on to the next part of the action or plot. Not too many questions or the session becomes boring. You yourself can add the occasional suggestion. Tone of voice, as you tell the story, is all important in building the atmosphere. Needless to say, you must be master of the music. If using a gramophone, there must be no scrape of the needle. Fade in smoothly and out at the end. Even pick up the tone arm to avoid a click from the brake or your whole creation built together may be ruined.

33. *Cold Beginnings Which Warmed Up*
At a Townswomen's Guild, North Worcestershire, 1952–3

When everyone else feels ghastly, I begin to get gay. It was a horrible cold night and if we did not have some robust sort of fun, I thought we would all die.

One sometimes feels, in a fit of exuberance, that the people who have kindly invited you are ready to share your own joy of life. This was one such occasion. They had asked me to talk on Arena Theatre and then do practical work. 'We want you to get us moving too,' said Madam Chairman.

Then they gave me these ideas: *Yellow bag   Big feet   Shut up   Cold feet*

My story: A lecturer came to Stourbridge. He was awful. He had enormous boots and huge *big feet*, and he made a noise like a traction engine, and broke the glass in the windows when he began to speak. A woman on his left said: 'I wish he'd *shut up*' (this caused some joy as, when we first got the idea out of this lady on the left, it referred to shutting up the yellow bag). And the cry was slowly caught together until half the room said 'shut up, shut up'. Then a counter chorus too—on this side of the room—on the words: 'Yes, I've got *cold feet*.' 'Cold feet, cold feet,' echoed the chorus. Then the Chairman thought to herself: 'I can't stand for this.' And she drew an ancient Mexican dagger out of her *yellow bag*, dipped the point in an ink bottle, where she kept poison for members of the Guild she didn't like, threw it deftly at the lecturer, and got him 'ping' in the middle of the back. He fell like a chain store, and, as a cloud of dust rose, so did the audience also—to their cold feet, and formed a horseshoe. But the poison was a magic poison, and as they watched, the lecturer's large feet began to get smaller and smaller. At the moment that his feet became normal size he died. There was a sound of distant bells, and all the feet of the women in the room became warm. Then they cried out in a loud voice: 'Oh he wasn't such a bad man after all', and they surged forward, lifted the late lecturer gently, carrying him three times round the hall and carefully out of the door, the Chairman bringing up the rear and the Hon. Secretary reading the minutes of the last meeting as a dirge.

COMMENT

The Townswomen's Guilds at that time were keen on choral speech (they may be still) and although invited to talk on Arena Theatre and do practical work, I thought It worth putting in some very simple chorus work. Loud speaking also helps you to get warm as well as stamping about. In choral speech it is important not to fall into a group whine, with up and down intonation not found in everyday life. This type of herd utterance (choral speech) is a very difficult form of art and I was a bit chary about the results. I need not have been. There was nothing of the self-conscious mannerisms sometimes to be found in choirs on Festival days. They were splendid and absolutely fresh. No doubt, it was the drama situation which lent reality as well as the actual coolth. Anyway their cry of 'cold feet' raised the roof and the forgiveness in '. . . wasn't such a bad man' was deep. We discussed the basic shapes of Child Drama particularly the S shape, which helps an actor to present himself to all parts of an audience in arena theatre. Then we practised the exit several times, for it was important to be outside the door—everyone—exactly on the last phrase of the music. This sort of tidiness is what gives polish to what may at first have been only spontaneous attempts. The art of polishing is to do just enough without destroying the feeling of freshness and life in the creation.

34. *Vienna and the Hungry Musician*

Dance drama, Adult Group, Rea Street Drama Centre, Birmingham, 1954

Self: 'You remember what we have been saying about the love of sound in words during the earlier part of the evening, and I related the drawn out sounds and the short sharp percussion sounds that we do in Infant Schools to the vowels and consonants, and you saw how this widening of the imaginative orchestration brought a new quality to our reading. Now I want you to do the same in our dance tonight. As we progress, try and pick out more carefully the soft and hard-sharp sounds. By taking more care we learn to love them more. They need a different sympathy, different interpretation.

'You remember in the past you were all doing the same sort of mimsy dreamy self-sentimental movements that are common when first personal release is established in free improvised dance. Now, what everyone else does is not good enough for work in this centre. We have worked long enough together for me to share any thought with you. If I'm outspoken, you know now that I'm not being unkind—that is a great release for me, because I don't have to be on guard. We are building a wisdom together. Anyway, improvised dance is so personal a thing at first that you don't know how you look until a sympathetic person tells you. We can easily fall into habits of expression too. That's why I continue to tell you. (One probably wouldn't with beginners.) Out of that telling has come the progress you have established. Right—now for it.

'Men, last week you were mimsy too, in some of your movements. You went on too long with the softer expression. You

[164]

can be virile when you want to. Be careful not to "catch" too much from the women. Don't be afraid to be different. Women's minds are very different from our own, as we know to our cost —and pleasure. I shall do more exercises for virility later. Men's work is going to be virile in this place or bust. You know now about Running Play in Child Drama, well think in terms of a further run at adult level. Jump onto things sometimes and jump off again, but mind you keep on the time beat *just the same as before*. Use bigger contrasts between relaxation and tension. But, all of you, girls too, relate the earlier part of the evening to the present. To start with, then, virility for the men; great attention to the sound; distinguish in your mind between soft and sharp sound; bear in mind the difference we have discussed between time beat and the magic life, which is rhythm. Ready to begin? Now—Sorry, there is one person moving, quite quiet please. Now—Someone moved a hand.—Now.'

When there had been complete stillness for several moments, I faded in a record of Mexican music.

Self: 'Not good enough. Five people started late. Now you have heard the opening bars try and begin all at once.'

We began again.

Self: 'No. Two people still not quite on beat. Look, in proscenium theatre a lot of people chatter, whisper or mess about in the wings before their cue, and scramble onstage when they hear it. That is not good enough. You should be thinking, and in your part *before* you go on, then you are more likely to keep the scene alive. Art has responsibilities. Now, be thinking and ready and more sensitive for your dance, too. Be quicker in your reaction. One of the differences between "any old dance group" and a good one is that you all start at once in the good one.'

We began again. Everyone was in time. I left them without further interruption because they were now keyed to the necessary pitch of discipline without loss of their original urge to create. One must judge carefully about this. Sometimes it is better to let them smooth into dance straight away and suggest (if necessary) later. But this group is advanced so I do not allow any slackness.

I wandered amongst them (they are trained not to bump into

[165]

me). I began to half dance in sympathy with one person so as to keep up with them and pass a message.

Self (*quietly*): 'Make your footfall firmer. Listen for the end of a sentence in the music.'

(*Later to another*): 'Try and relax your hands. They are stiff at the wrists. Loosen them first, then use your fingers more.'

(*To another*): 'Good; hands *much* better, now try bringing your message right off the finger tips more.'

During a sad piece in the middle of the music, I stopped by one person: 'I see you have begun to suffer; good. Be careful though. Suffering brings sympathy. But remember there is another step after that. Don't become top heavy or sentimental, there is a *mastery*, even of the suffering. That brings the final control and adds an indefinable sort of dignity to your art. You are going to be a professional. Your work is good now, so you will understand what I mean. Most of the dance one sees hasn't got the final quality. Work for it, and ask me questions *whenever you don't understand*. Don't let a single uncertainty stay in your mind, and don't allow any secondrate movement to slip through. *Master* it. This is the difference between the "wet" dancer and an artist. You'll get your chance to learn in this place as nowhere else perhaps. Don't waste it.'

Self (*to everyone*): 'Not quite satisfied with that ending. There wasn't a proper group agreement about the moment of finish. Therefore we didn't get the sort of electric excitement of the thing well "said". In a way—though you will understand that I don't mean it entirely in a literary sense—dance can be like writing. It needs purpose of idea and punctuation. Pause and clarity. Now, your dance has got to the stage when you have punctuation, logic and purpose in the message. But your paragraphs in sympathy with the musical phrase are not concise enough. At the end of that piece your movement showed no obvious paragraph and some of you forgot the full stop at the end. I think you can improve on that finish. Let's try again.'

We tried and this time it came off very well. They stayed in their positions without any wobble (one of their exercises). So I left them for a beat of 26 seconds on complete silence after the music had stopped. Then judging that the atmosphere would hold no more, said quietly, 'right', and they relaxed. *Self (after leaving them to chat quietly and judging the moment carefully):* 'Now, we'll try something where you are not just creating your own dream. We pass on to the greater discipline in improvised dance—of keeping your own creation fresh whilst beginning to accept a producer's dream. We won't discuss it and make it a group creation this time. There'll be a simple story and you'll be produced a bit. Just relax, close your eyes and listen.'

I put on a record and let it play for a bit.

Self (quietly): 'Right, now, you've just heard enough to get something of the mood. This is our story—At the beginning, where the sad part is, we are in Vienna. The sun climbs slowly up to slit the throat of clouds and break in day. A musician is asleep in a little top room, he lies for all the world like that famous picture of a dead poet, something grey and faintly moon-blue about the room—till the sun catches it. As the warmth moves in, stealthily, through a broken window pane, mothering him with kindness, he becomes aware, and wakes to a new hope.—Have any of you ever had any of this in your life? If you have, remember it *hard*, enjoy it again. Bring it alive. Be grateful. Repeat it. Act your thanks . . .

'The musician gets up slowly. He is weary and ill. He is starving. When you haven't eaten much for a long time, you come to a sort of new life of the half-dream. He has come to that. He gets off the bed and goes to his violin. The violin he thought he'd never play again. But music is with him, in his mind; or is it that the sun sings? Who can tell and who can care, for the music is *there*. So he plays it as his own. As he plays, visions of his old life come before him again. A girl moves towards him. He remembers his love in a flooding flash of pain. He passes forward, out of the window, over the roof tops, through a drifting of space as of damp clouds slowly wheeling, and approaches her. He looks his love, but she becomes embarrassed. He follows, but she avoids him. He becomes frantic, searching everywhere. But life crowds in on him. He is in the streets now. Vienna comes alive. Many people throng at him, all busy with their business. There are many smiles and laughter, but not for him. Every man has his girl but not he his. Occasionally he

[167]

sees his love in the crowd but always she is unobtainable, like some of our own deepest hopes, there is always some wall in the way, so he tries to forget her.

'Later in the record you will hear the main theme change, and more instruments come in. Here he decides to devote himself to his work again as in the years before, but instead of his failure, the crowd parts in two mountain waves, diagonal in un-dilemma, and motions him welcome with a great waving of oncoming hands, like Milton's hosts "horrid in arms", but in this case in wide open-palmed salute, at once both Fascist and face-saving, and he enters like a King into the great hall where the vast orchestra is playing, and the conductor waves him to the throne where leading players may sit between rehearsals. He starts to play, and such playing has never been heard. But as he plays he looks up and behold the conductor has changed. Instead of the bearded man, his girl-love is there conducting with accusing stabs. He cannot advance to her for he *must play*. As he plays, the other players rise up and get bigger; he crouches down, but they leer up larger than ever, till in a fleeting moment he sees his love's face once again. Now it is kind at last. But as so often in this life—it is too late. His heart breaks, and Music, symbolised by the efficient grotesque orchestra of time-beat mechanical giants, stands over him as he dies. Mechanical music has again killed art and the true artist—

'Now, I'm sorry, the actual music breaks off rather suddenly there, on the record, so you will have to make it very rigid and purposeful to carry it off. But we'll add a happy ending later. Let's use the stage for part of this, plus some rostrum blocks. Orchestra, Vienna and Girl on the whole stretch of the hall floor, and the tiny stage can be the musician's garret. He "passes forward" out of the proscenium arch onto the rostrum blocks to meet his love on the floor of the hall. We'll have Pippa for the poet—I mean the musician, because she'll do it so well. Nita, you be the girl, and Tom—will you be the Conductor, please. Jane, you deal with the dimmer board.

'Right now—orchestra, come to the centre—who shall we have? And doing what?'

A good short discussion ensued on the personalities of members

[168]

of the group and the instruments they should play. When this was over we were nearly ready to start.

Self: 'Musician—on the stage, please, on his bed. Let's start from darkness, then fade the light up just on the stage. A cold light, then gradually warm it. Take care to blend things so that music and light fade up as one. Pick up on spot bar No 1 as the musician moves forward, then use a flood and one spot for the centre of the arena, fading out at the end, leaving one spot on centre: Ready? Quite quiet—'

The music was slowly faded in and the light blended up with it, as if it were part of the sound. The warm of the sun moved in, 'stealthily through a broken window pane—'. The dance had begun.

Self (later): 'Good. Now, you know what a wonderful sight it is when for a moment or two the strings of a large orchestra move all their arms together. On the occasions when the light strikes their forearms in unison it gives me almost more joy than the sound they make. But together the two things are sort of intoxicating—do you know what I mean? Well, let's have our orchestra like that. Overstress it a bit too. Our orchestra would be more grotesque that way. It'll need practice.'

We practised the same short piece some fifteen times.

Self: 'Nearly got it. You know I never show you a movement if I can help it, but prefer you to find your own. You tend to get out of time because of the beginning bar of your phrase here. May I suggest you start like this. (I did show them this time.) The short sharp moves will get you strongly into the lilt. Get over that bit and the next is easy.'

When that had been improved, we played through the whole story without interruption.

Self (later): 'Good. Some beautiful moments. Now, just so we won't be too depressed by the poor man, let's say what happened after—this is what happened—when he died he found himself on a cloud and he felt full of good food. The sound of music came to him, music of the sun, his own music, the music of the grotesque orchestra, but grotesque no more. It was charged now with golden comfort and the breath of a holy wind. And there, coming towards him, and smiling true, was his girl-love.

She came to him slowly and raised him up. And he, taking her calm hand in his, walked off with her, slowly, across the clouds in a garden of bright light to some far safe place of their dreams, we know not where.'

This was played out to the last half of 'The Walk to Paradise Garden' (Delius).

Self (to end): 'Some of our work has been much better tonight. I felt we could really go on to more difficult stuff and more polished. It was a lovely fade of light and sound at the end of the lovers' walk. Now, just remember, if you can, what we've been exploring this evening. More conscious pleasure in vowel and consonant. Less fear of joy in simple beautiful things. How to let go and yet not be sentimental. Repose and its relation to sincerity; mental association of long and short sound to vowel and consonant; punctuation in dance. There are a lot of other things too, like precision of movement with music. But the most important is that I want you to remember the experience —which most of you clearly have had—of bringing polished improvisation to the point of conscious prepared dance drama. And lastly you will have felt the deep experience of moments of atmosphere which can only be described as "Good Theatre". You created that this evening, and I am very grateful to you. Good night.'

COMMENT

The first paragraph refers to a more imaginative approach to speech, also to the techniques of diction and what is called 'attack' in the theatre. Making the best of vowel sounds too, rather than shortening them.

'I began to half dance in sympathy'—this is a technique I use with adults in order to get the feel of how things are going. It helps me to decide on what are their needs. I often shadow dance behind them for short moments too, for a good dancer without knowing it, throws off personality, message, energy all round his body. It is similar to the process of acting in the round as mentioned in the comments on description No. 25. When not fully 'lit' by the fire of expression, this thrown-off message is weak in dance. Shadow dancing (dancing behind) also helps me to know whether a dancer is still in the personal dream stage, when much of the work is somewhat private and withdrawn and the courageous and vivid description by the mind and body in harmony is not yet fully established. But

[170]

anyway, if there is any question of self-consciousness because you suddenly dance with people in front and face to face, it is kinder sometimes to dance behind. This would, of course, apply more to beginners than to the group described here. I hope other comments in the report are enough to give a constructive indication of a way of going about things. 'Take care to blend things so that music and light fade up as one.' This is a form of aesthetic tidiness too often lacking. One can almost see a good fade of sound and hear a good fade with light. Combine the two and you have the best of both worlds.

35. *Putting Mike Together Again*

Social and imaginative drama at Bournville Day Continuation College, 1955

After preliminary simple movements to music, the teacher told a story about a person in a tunnel. There were moments of fear, then relief, at coming out into the open again. Everyone in the room acted in their own space as if they were the only hero there.

Teacher: 'Would you care to take on from there?'

Self: 'Right. (*To the class*): Now, some of your work in the middle became a bit untrue, though in general, it's starting all right. Some of the music went on too long and was of the wrong kind. Your invention gave out, so you were "filling in" to the sound. I suspect that the music and you were trying to accompany each other, and there was a misunderstanding, and no one knew when to stop. Well I'm going to pick out the piece which had most life—that part where you were treading carefully and with fear, and we'll start from there. Right, all the lads are under the sway of the gang leader—that's you, the tall one. You are Mike. Mike and gang, tiptoe into a room in exactly the same mood. But there's a bomb in the room. You can hear it ticking —rather like *The Crimson Coconut*. Anyone know that play? (*Some did.*) Well this bomb isn't a funny bomb quite like that. This is a real bomb. It's grim. Just as they find it, it bursts. The gang is blown to the side of the room, but Mike is blown to pieces. Now the girls—that's all the rest of you—you come in when you hear the explosion (grand explosion sounds on the piano, please, pianist), and you look round. Suddenly someone sees a bit of Mike in the corner. Now, you know how wonderful women are, they're always doing something to save the situation, aren't they? They've got a sort of magic, which makes things all right again, and they're always surprising us men. Well, so it is this time. They find all the pieces of Mike, and they put him together again. There you are then, that's your story.'

I repeated the main points quickly, and concisely, then added: 'Now, the first part is serious, the last is frankly silly. But it's part of an actor's task to make an unlikely situation believable and that's what you're going to do here. After all, we piece together memories and recreate people, don't we? I bet Mike's girl friend did that. So, make it true for us, if you can. Quite quiet. Ready? Now . . .'

They did it in mime, but again the music held things up.

Self: 'Right, it's still untrue in places, but the gang is coming on well. First entry good, and lovely piecing together of Mike by the girls—very calm and full of purpose, wasn't it, like building a snowman. Now this time, men, we'll have music just for your tiptoe entry, then silence and see what happens, and only music for the remaking of Mike by the girls.'

They started. They looked for the bomb. Music finished. I watched carefully and judged the moment.

Self: 'Speak, if you want to.'

Immediately speech began, and the scene became real. Tension built up at once. This helped the pianist to follow what was happening, and 'explosion music' came at exactly the right time. There was a terrific moment as all the boys flung themselves about the room and lay flat. The girls entered and Mike was re-made again.

Self: 'Yes. That's good. But just at the end it seems a bit weak, and theatrically there is no finish. I think when Mike's "moll" had recreated him in her mind, she would see herself marrying him in wishful-thinking. So let's go on from there and see them happily spliced, shall we? *Luckily*, one of the gang happened to be a parson or a ship's captain before he went wrong, so he marries them, in a quick dreamlike way, and everyone marches round and makes a good strong finish. Make sure you draw

[172]

a nice movement with the path of the journey of your feet in that final exit.'

They did it well, but enjoyed the marriage so much that they forgot their grand finale.

Self: 'Yes, but you're still in church or something. You can't stay there for ever. Don't forget the march out.'

Music struck up and they made a good exit.

The teacher then took on again, and the class became seaweed in calm sea, then seaweed in a storm. After that they became divers, moving slowly against the pressure of deep water. Fish swam by, and finally they all had a fight with a shark. Then there was a good movement when they were 'hauled up' out of the water.

Teacher: 'Do you want to say anything more about that?'

Self: 'Oh well, it seemed to me that the music again went on too long, and that at one time there was a "fill in", actors only acting because the music was there, rather than because they were emotionally inspired *with* it, and because of it. It came during the time they were fighting their shark with slow movements. Instead of helping the idea of underwater pressure impeding their purpose as divers, the enforced slow movement seemed to impede their determination as actors, so that if you were doing that again you might try: "But when the diver went to sleep that night he had a dream. And he dreamed that he was fighting the shark again. But this time there were no diver's clothes and no underwater pressure. He fought as he liked with swift sharp movements." That would bring life to the whole thing.

'You must keep a strong purpose in this work otherwise it goes flat. Go back to your original idea later, if you like, to see if it has improved. But be ready to change the plan in order to help your actors find truth, in the early stages.'

(*Later to teacher*): 'It's going very well, particularly as that is only their second time of doing the work. Remarkable that you have got the boys and girls working so well together. Your music is a bit drawnout still. You must keep the acting vital, and if you think it better, don't use music all the time. You saw how it came together and became true when we stopped the music

[173]

and the boys talked, in the bomb scene. Music is really a sort of incidental sound, and your task is to watch for the moments when the drama dies, and cut at that point.'

(*To the pianist*): 'You find it difficult to accompany? You are trying to do too much "fill in". You can't follow *everything* or everybody. Choose your moments and be concise. A few strong chords at the right time are much more effective than a lot of strum. Think how well you got the explosion. Don't forget, music, in this work, is divided into two classes. It is either the main theme, a straight piece from which the actor draws inspiration *or* you allow the actor to really act, and accompany, in sound, certain movements.'

Pianist: 'Yes, I see, I've been worried about "time" and haven't known what to accompany.'

Self: 'Time comes in when you are playing the straight piece. In accompanying the sort of acting we've seen today, try to think purely in terms of sound. You become sensitive after a bit, to making a sound, which is concise and appropriate. The piano can't do everything. Some scenes need the drawnout agony of strings. Don't fluff about and try and imitate that on the piano. Can't be done. But light sounds for tiptoe, good chords for heavy steps, watery sounds and so on, *can*. If you are in doubt about what to accompany, follow the playing carefully with your eye and pick out something, which becomes obvious. Often a leader arises, at a certain point, and if you accompany the leader, the drama often begins to centre round him and the whole has unity. At other times there may be lovely unconscious group agreement and then it is possible to accompany and add something to *all* of it. Most important of all, stop being uncertain. Decide what you will do. Do *less* and do it well. "Uncertain" music is no inspiration to anybody, nor is it a dignified accompaniment to good acting.'

 Pianist: 'Yes, I see, it's all rather new to me. I have been waiting for them, and they have been waiting for me. I've been used to playing for ballet and formal mime.'

Self: 'Ah, *then* you have more set pieces perhaps. But even then in the best work there should be an accord between music and the movement—no undue *reliance* where fine Art is made.'

[174]

Pianist: 'I wish we were taught more of this. I would love to see more of it.'

Self: 'I'm afraid a lot of music training is rather unimaginative. A lot of people learn to understand notation, time beat and rules and this is good, but they don't seem to learn enough about the sheer love of sound. It is the same problem as in the teaching of literature.'

The teacher then asked, 'Well, where would you go from there?'

Self: 'With young people of this age, and seeing that it is a Day Continuation College, I should fasten on at once to the feeling of cooperation and team spirit that one espied in the nature of these actors. The very form of the group work helps here too. I should play hard on realisation of the needs of other people than oneself and then relate that to their daily life. Each person is necessary to this scene, the *whole group* produces the drama. So it is in their daily life at the factory. A factory is like a ship. Each person is of supreme importance from the captain downwards and from the work bench upwards. Each person owes a loyalty to the other and the *whole group* produces the factory article. A wealth of training (through discussion of situations) in relationship of boy to girl, attitude to superiors, possibly marriage and "walking-out" guidance would be added. Leadership and wise management is learned by the producer in modern drama training, foremanship and shop management by the stage-manager. Public relations and sales management by proper training of actors and programme sellers and by "front of house" management's attitude to audience or visitors.'

The polite welcome is what young people are not being taught enough of, for use in shops, factories or public services. Drama is not only an immense personal release for young and old alike, but by a proper stress on group work the student can discover an active experience of 'loyalty' and 'team spirit', which often brings a vivid realisation that these things are not mere words but social facts, and that they, in turn, bring with them happiness and understanding. The continual reversal of rôles too is of extreme importance, just as in the deeper forms of Psychodrama and Dramatherapy, so in Social Drama.

Example: 'Right, you have been the boss for a bit. Did you notice how you behaved to so and so? Would that irritate him? Was it just?' Discussion follows, then: 'Now Boss, you are the Worker. If you were really that man in that position what would you think, what would you say?' Now we go back to the boss again. 'What has the boss the right to expect? Remember we have thought out his attitude now. He is a good boss, behaves justly and fairly. He expects loyalty and a fair return of labour for a decent wage. So does the community.'

So we turn to the customer and the well-produced article upon which we can depend. There might be a scene about a housewife's joy at a new article. The joy dies as the article breaks in first use. Thus can the imaginative be slowly brought to bear upon reality. Young people can be led to appreciate a wider view. Those, who do not develop the inner person too, are only half living and unlikely to be fully balanced.

Our constructive energies, as well as our grouses, well up inside, though the immediate apparent cause may be in exterior circumstances or our interpretation of them. It is most important that the inner man shall have developed enough to judge the daily round aright.

Our society and particularly our industry, suffers from sickness of many kinds, and many mistaken attitudes arising out of lack of thought for others. Imaginative Drama, properly taught, is not merely a vague fanciful extra. By training in depth, and by incorporating at once the inner person in this pleasant activity, it is easier than any other way to win general confidence, so that deep behaviour traits can be discussed, openly and without too much grudge or fear. Everyone who has done work in youth clubs, will know what a help this sort of discussion can be. A wider application of Imaginative and Social Drama could do a great deal for straight living and for decent cooperation in industry. Perhaps one day it will be realised, and will be used on a large scale. The tendency towards 'music while you work' and 'canteen concerts' shows a slow (almost unconscious) appreciation of some need, but is only a hovering around the fringe of the problem. Perhaps no one so far has put forward so unusual a proposition as a bald statement of sociological fact. I put it now: Drama the Dream is a natural way of incorporating the

[176]

whole person and of leading man to face the true facts of Drama
the Doing of Life.

COMMENT

Numbers of teachers in technical schools and further education have asked me to
write more about personality development and social drama. In this description
the teacher is beginning with Imaginative Drama and I am pushing on towards
Social Drama. But often with youngsters in secondary schools and young adults
on day release, it is better to start with Social and move to Imaginative afterwards.
In this way you deal at once with *life* at a time when they are desperately anxious
to be grown-up and it finds its own way to more imaginative situations.

Much of the personality training I have done since the day described here, with
factory workers and those from commerce and the retail trades started with life
situations, but not always. I think you have to see how they reveal themselves. On
one course, a film was made of their very first entrance into the hall and we carried
on with movement, then getting out of a chair and finally not knocking into
people during sales, all in the first session, to hot jazz.

My direct and somewhat outspoken words to the pianist were because I had
been asked to speak to her. They told me, before starting that she would like some
advice. Perhaps it may help other pianists who do this particular work in schools,
clubs or institutions.

36. Codfish and the Chicken in Striped Pyjamas

N.U.T. Refresher Course, Somerset, 1956

For a number of years now, it has been my pleasure to give
lectures, run dance courses or practical demonstrations of drama
in various parts of the country. Just such a one was this. An
invitation came to direct the Drama in Education section of
the N.U.T. Refresher Course in Somerset. Accordingly, having
decided who should help, Phyl Lutley and I set off for a physically cold but heart-warming weekend.

'Cold,' I said to the shopkeeper who sold us a morning paper.
'Ah,' he said, 'but we get used to it down 'ere. You from these
parts?' 'Well, yes and no,' I answered, 'but at the moment I
come from Birmingham.' 'Oh, I coom from Birminggham too.'

'*Do* you,' I said, attempting to be amazed despite those give-away g's. 'Oh yes. There's a lot uz down 'ere. They call it Bir-minggham-super-Mare, you know. Them as don't like uz sez that's the cause of all the mud 'ere. But I don't think we're so bud. Not reely.' I agreed and made off to start the course.

There were a large number of enthusiastic members but some, who, no doubt, wondered what they had got themselves mixed up with. There were the five large gentlemen who sat in a row at the back, taciturn, terrifying, yet somehow exuding a thousand years or more of wisdom from some far Somerset salt flat below the Tor at Glaston. My thought must have been caught by the Chairman's intuition. 'Don't worry about those five men at the back, who won't join in,' she hissed. 'They're awful good fellows really. They look as if they can't understand a word you say, but they mean to get hold of this stuff, if it's the last thing they do.' So I took hope and got braver. The scene was changed and I put on a bit of 'La Mer' music and explained that we were at the bottom of the ocean. Most of the people moving about became prawns and odd swimming things and then a bright thought came. We turned the five quiet gentlemen into cod-fish and the smoke from their pipes could be the bubbles coming up from the dark bed of the sea. Whereupon they all rose to their feet as if this were the task of their life, yea, the very reason of their being, and began to march up and down the hall in a solid cinq, shaped like the dots on a domino. Woe betide any small fish or weed-urchin who got in their way! Not only had their steadfast progress something of the feeling of unavoidable fate to be found in Greek tragedy, but the puffing of their pipes made a haze of blue terror. Then the record came to an end. But did the codfish stop? No. They were so absorbed that they neither saw nor heard. All of their five-ishness was centred on the common plunder of their task. All the 'small fry' melted back to their seats, but the cod-fish carried on. I was fascinated. I wanted to see how long they *would* go on—just those rhythmic footsteps and the blue smoke churning. But the Chairman brought us to order with a bang and five cods became becalmed. There was a moment's deep silence, then a burst of clapping! The ice was truly broken. Our five were beaming at their achieve-

Left: some of the audience become magnets to draw the young hunter down from a cloud. Theatre for Children, Rea Street Drama Centre, Birmingham

Centre: the whole audience is involved in a last salute. Theatre for Children, Rea Street Drama Centre, Birmingham

Bottom: audience helps to open windows. Theatre for Children, Rea Street Drama Centre, Birmingham

Group isolated in light during a silence in Theatre for Children, Rea Street
Drama Centre, Birmingham

Parable Players performing 'The Interlude of Youth' at St Andrews by the
Wardrobe, London, about 1935–6. Caryl Jenner on left as Youth. Production
Peter Slade

ment and I knew that for the rest of the period it would be possible to bring them in in any way one liked. So far, the imaginative exercises had all been for general thawing and loosening up. Now the time had come for a story to be acted through, something not too serious, rather light, a bit wistful perhaps, but with a touch of poetic quality to give them the experience of mood.

I did not quite know what would come out of it, but the very end of that session, despite the oddness of the tale, had a moving quality of atmosphere—a feeling of deep symbolic 'goodbye' in the midst of humour, like the end of a Charlie Chaplin film, when he either skips or walks off—into the sun—alone. They gave me:

IDEAS: *Bag   Chicken   Striped pyjamas*
My story: Over there in a little house all alone lived a chicken. Sometimes he would stroll down by the shops over there, where the five men are sitting, sometimes he would pass down the road here in the centre of the room, between the trees. One day he was looking at the shops when he saw in the window, on one of the five dummy men sitting there,[1] a wonderful pair of striped pyjama trousers—oh yes, you see one of them *has* got pin stripes on (they really had)—and he looked in his little bag and counted his pennies, but there weren't enough to buy the trousers. So he walked away sadly amongst the trees till he met a wizard. And the wizard asked what was the matter. 'Well, it's about a pair of pyjama trousers I'm keen on,' said the chicken, and he took the wizard and showed him the very pair, gleaming in the window. The wizard didn't think there'd be any difficulty at all about this little matter. He did a spell, and when it was over the chicken saw that he'd got beautiful stripes on his legs and his feathers were just the colour he wanted. Away he went with a smile on his beak, the proudest bird in Somerset, to live happily in his little house in the corner. Now, we haven't got time on this course to go into all the details, but, as a matter of fact, by a most *interesting* and cunning arrangement of cross-breeding, that's how we got the Wessex Saddleback pig. Yes, yes, it's all very scientific. But there's one more thing—sometimes on a late

[1] The five again.

ES–G

summer evening, when the gold is just turning to deep blue, a faint squawk is heard high up. And away from the trees on the hill above Weston-super-Mare, a strange bird is seen to fly out over the Bristol Channel. And people say that it has *extraordinary* legs. You'd think, for all the world, it was wearing *striped pyjamas*.

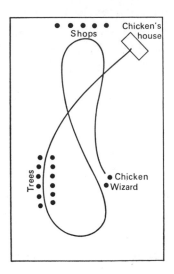

COMMENT

Organisations of various kinds ask for courses including practical work. This was one of them. Perhaps one of the lessons to learn from the description is that many of us are shy. Sometimes we fear the reactions of other people, but it is always worth remembering that if you are shy, probably other people are too. In this case the cod-fish looked forbidding but they thawed all right. I do not want to imply that we always succeed. We can fail all the time, or nine times out of ten, but do remember again and again that sometimes it is not you who have failed, those you are taking have merely revealed by your type of test or suggestion 'Where they really are in life'.

37. Youth and his Dream of the Future
A University Theatre Course, 1957

An invitation had come to take a post-graduate Theatre Course

[180]

at a university and it sounded as if it would do me good. But it turned out to be very different from the expected. Most of the students were from grammar school and delightful people, but they seemed to be very tied up inside. They had terrific frontal lobes, so to speak, but their imaginative and philosophic outlook had not been developed. Apart from their own subject, they found it difficult to discuss anything that was going on in the world. Many of them were over grave. The child inside had been squashed and it was difficult to find evidence of genuine maturity beneath the grown-up exterior. Their education seemed to have turned them into clever shells. As some of them were going to teach in state schools and knew themselves to be totally unprepared for the task, they begged me to speak about Child Drama. The rest were quite prepared to join in for their own sake. So we talked and they could understand a concept quickly, but to enlarge upon it and bring it to life defeated them. We accordingly went right back to young secondary modern work and started on improvisation exercises that one might do with twelve year olds. It is not their fault, I kept saying to myself. This is what we have done to them. It is almost as if they have been deprived of their childhood.

We tried five-minute speeches, and in time these improved. We tried working in pairs and reading a book that wasn't there. We tried to buy and sell from each other. It was very bad, they had no language flow. We tried scripts but they couldn't get inside their parts. They read clearly but it didn't mean anything. We tried 'living newspaper' but they hadn't had the time or taken interest to think out world events. Finally I gave them a modern play to study and *The Interlude of Youth*[1] and by way of contrast we built a sort of oblong market place to do it in.

Self: 'Riot, be a bit more riotous, can you?'

He became a bit louder. Pride kept interrupting over some intellectual unnecessity, Finally we got Riot going, by making him go outside the room, burst into it and by letting everyone

---

[1] I have produced this many times now; once at Coventry in the cathedral ruins for the Festival of Britain. I remember a wonderful rehearsal when characters loomed out of the mist like mediæval ghosts.

else shout rude things at him. He had to be loud to answer, so at last we arrived at a bit of 'attack', theatrically speaking. Humility entered to a nice bit of Debussy. It seemed time to infuse more life, though, so I tried putting in an improvised dance in the tavern. This they found impossible. Some of them raised good arguments for not doing it, but they did not deceive the others, who knew they just couldn't. So we worked through being knights in armour, stamping round and hitting each other with imaginary swords, then doing the same in a more stylised way, so that the footwork was almost a dance, to a drum. Then we tried a bit of jazz and that foxed them, they returned to very formal steps, but most of them gave up. I tried a period piece of music but they really missed not knowing the steps. They were almost unable to move, with 'life', to any sound at all. At last we got somewhere by going right back to clapping rhythms, question and answer and statement in sound, whilst working with a partner, then tapping the toes. Then heel and toe and twist. In the end, some steps emerged and they developed these in their own way.

Ultimately we got around to discussing whether the moral of the play had any meaning today. Some of them thought it had, so we evolved a sort of Dunn's parallel in time and Youth had a dream after he had been to the tavern and woke up many years later to find himself as President Nasser. We had done some 'living newspaper' on the Suez crisis, so we relived this bit and brought in a number of the others, who had no part in the play, to be members of the United Nations. Quite a reasonable documentary was built up. I chiefly remember that 'Mr Dulles' kept changing his mind, whatever the British suggested, and was apt to shout from the top of a gym horse: 'You have no legal justification', when anyone was late with their line. This made some of them angry, which really delighted me, for at last they were showing some emotion. In the end, a very reasonable and just discourse was produced, with people entering the arena in diagonals from all sorts of directions. I remember a quavering voice saying, '—but there's only a dozen years to run, only a dozen—'. 'Anthony Eden' would exclaim 'but you can't just annex things'. Finally it built to a climax on 'We must nationalise' (one voice), to which the crowd added, 'seize it, seize it, *seize* it'. Finally, Humility came in and brought peace, allowing Charity to say some of his last lines. I don't remember, though, whether this went straight on or whether Youth woke up and returned to his own period. What matter? Youth belongs to all periods.

Let no one think that my description here is in any way a criticism of the students themselves. No one could have been more delightful in many ways. They were so humble and so keen to learn. They seemed aware of certain things lacking in themselves. I should have liked them to have had more fun at school and more 'all round' education, so as to prepare them better for being our future leaders.

An example of intellectualisation always comes to mind in a quite different set of students. As their President, I had been invited in to help them in certain scenes for a production of their theatre group and we had spent a long time building up a believable relationship in a difficult scene. At last it was in that stage between very good and wonderful, a golden silence and then someone asked 'Mr Slade, what age do you think this woman is?' I have to admit that I was amazed and think my answer was, 'I don't know. Does it matter? At this moment, does it *matter?*—If you must know, it is probably in some description at the beginning of the script. But don't try to overact yourself into a character you cannot play. What you had just achieved is far more important. You had built a situation where love no longer remembers age. Isn't this one of the wonderful things that, in a perfect moment of relationship, we release the whole symbol of woman and of man? At that moment you had created something where the audience would entirely forget age, their own age even. We had arrived at last at a moment of instruction, of aesthetic and emotional experience. Now we are back at numbers.'

These are remarks from another University Course. They are selected as an example of Group Playmaking and were written down during a discussion on why students thought they were at a University. They were for making into a documentary programme, so the way in which each voice should be spoken—according to decision of our group—is put in brackets after each one.

'So I thought about teaching. Was it a calling? It was full of ideas and theories. Are they ideals or can they be carried out?' (to be said in a vague voice, woman's with a lot of eye-lash flicking).

'Learn to live, I say' (straight and hearty).

'Relevance of Values. It's all relevance of values' (very pedantic with mouth like a prune).

'Join societies. Widen yourself. Become more tolerant. Work *and* play, I say' (jolly, sporting and breezy).

'The best degree, the best job' (matter of fact; hard).

'But my dear, you can't drink your coffee *and* be at a lecture' (very blah).

'As to marriage at University, I want to keep myself alive by reducing home life to the minimum' (professor-like; scientific).

'By drama, people become more sociable. You can sell yourself' (explanatory, with hand movements).

'Work at some schools is valuable, because it is an attempt to make something out of nothing' (very earnest and highbrow or, we decided, could be pompous and slightly sarcastic).

'Don't mistake frivolity for lack of serious interests' (avuncular but dictatorial).

I always enjoy this list. It is worth reading when depressed. The last remark might even refer to this book.

COMMENT

This description is an exact example of finding to one's surprise 'where they really are in life'. These young folk, clever as they were, had not had the chance of developing the child inside them. A frequent question is—How do you start spontaneous work with people who have never had it before? Hence this description. We did not go back to babyhood, but, it will be noted, we did go back to early adolescence and do exercises appropriate for that age. There were plenty of trials and failures in trying to get them to express themselves but it all improved and drew eventually nearer to their mental level. It was nothing for them to be ashamed of that part of their personality had not been developed, that the child in each of us had not lived fully in them but had been starved. It was the type of one-sided education they had received. They had had noses kept to the grindstone for years with no let up, which can, in extreme cases, make people in the realm of philosophy, and morals even, dangerously immature.

One always hopes that one day all universities will have some sort of cross-fertilisation of the arts as a matter of course and not too closely tied to academic attainment nor imprisoned by factual and numerical research either. Students often need just those sides of themselves developed which are the least easy in cold blood to assess.

Even in the description of theatre, here, over-intellectualisation takes place in a most insensitive way, which exhausted the patience of all of us for the moment.

Fortunately there are now courses of preparation to help graduates to fit into 'ordinary' education. A bridge is being built, particularly where they are to fit into junior schools. Whenever they come my way, I am delighted to work with them, for they can understand a *concept*, which is so rare and marvellous these days; and all they need is a little help in remembering (or learning almost for the first time) what it is like to be a child. In other words, one is dealing with the phenomenon of underfunctioning fun. To see it function again is fascinating and a wonderful reward.

38. A Hazardous Adventure

Morning, at a centre for those hard to educate, Birmingham, undated

In my notes I found the following undated details, not fully written up. They may have been waiting for another book altogether: at last found the place. How cross one gets at being baulked, particularly when in hurry. Thought of keeping people waiting turns tummy over. Entered portals in seething upset, quieted at once by sight. Strange people in world; some there. Some very quiet. Some soon prove affectionate.

A smiling hostess: 'Well, here we are, Mr Slade. What are you going to do? I don't know what you will be *able* to do with us, but here we are.' She took me round and told some young people I was a visitor. Some able to take a little notice, some not at all, some too much.

One lad (fair sized) very affectionate, followed hostess round —like a pony. Sometimes she turned and gave an affectionate,

[185]

gentle tug at his tuft of hair. He loved this and gurgled laughter. After inspection and careful 'take-in', with every kind of group, always start: 'Where are these people in life?'

Self: (*suddenly*): 'Can they cross a road?'

Answer: 'Sometimes, not always.'

Self: 'Well, let's practise, then.'

With help of staff, all lined up.

From now on, I can write things up more fully from the notes, for the experience is strongly in my memory.

Patiently, we got them all in a row and then patiently, all holding hands. This was to stop some of them turning round the wrong way. I and the staff were dispersed along the row. I extricated myself and joined two other hands together behind me.

Self: 'THIS IS A ROAD.

'THIS—FROM HERE (pause for slow walk) TO HERE—IS A ROAD.

'A ROAD.

'THIS IS A PAVEMENT. PAVEMENT. (I walked along the row smiling). PAVEMENT.

'YOU ARE ON THE PAVEMENT (I showed a crack on the edge of a floor board for the curb).

'WE WILL CROSS THE ROAD (some hunched their shoulders, excited).

'LOOK RIGHT—THAT WAY. ALL—THAT WAY. (It took a bit of time. The staff were very helpful.)

'NOW—THAT WAY (the other, it also took time).

'NOW—THAT WAY AGAIN—THAT WAY (gently again).

'THAT WAY. That way. That way. Good.

'NOW WE WILL CROSS. I CLAP AND WE CROSS. (I clapped): WE CROSS

A slow surge forward with staff and everybody. One or two members of the centre were lame so we went slow, partly for them.

We did this several times. Then we came back. Then we tried a few people doing it alone, in a row still, but not all with hands clasped, though some still were. We did it several times. By now people began to chant on the footsteps. One counted, singing out loud. Discussing quickly with staff, I judged some

[186]

had had enough and they went back to other tasks, but the others had not. In fact they didn't want to stop. So we went on and on over the same few boards, from 'pavement' to 'pavement', very sincere, very absorbed at times, occasionally laughing at our own mistakes, but able now not to hold hands, any of us, though occasionally we forgot and turned left or right instead of facing over the road. Then finally, the climax I had been working up to—one of the staff became a bus—A BUS— and drove slowly and gently along the road. We had to judge when to go across the road. We had to let it pass first, then go.

'IT GOES FIRST. THEN WE GO.

'IT GOES. WE GO.

'Look, there it goes. Slowly past. IT GOES.

'NOW. WE GO. WE GO—NOW.'

(We surged over—triumphant.)

Just one or two finally did it all. They waited for the bus, let it pass and 'went over the road', without me and without clasping hands. Once the bus honked and one or two people echoed it. Then everyone honked, it seemed. The whole room shook with joyous honking. My smiling hostess calmed them down.

One tall girl looked at me a long time and came forward. The lad mentioned before came over.

The girl said: 'I crossed the road.'

'Yes,' I said, terribly moved, 'you crossed the road.'

In my mind a famous last line kept paraphrasing itself—'and the crossing shall never be done'. So ended our great adventure. For some of us a small thing is a great thing. Achievement is a question of degree.

It was time for lunch, I looked at my watch. We had taken the whole morning.

COMMENT

I find it rather touching that this report should come next to the university one. It is rather representative of the whole book, which tends to show that some spontaneous work can be done with almost anyone. The reader will guess that this group was actually labelled ineducable. Yet they did actually progress, though there is no means of knowing whether they retained the ability they had won. However it made me change their description to 'hard to educate', rather than the final label. At a totally different and more advanced level, it is worth noting that the various stages of development are built up slowly and gradually so that in personality development in day release or in general therapy work, for instance, one would make the exercises a little tougher each time so as to stretch the ability to face shy-making situations and thus strengthen the inner person. Here we are attempting very elementary acts in a simple situation, but the method is the same. First we hold hands and do things altogether, then some try alone, we all turn round together, then some alone. Finally we wait for a bus *then* go over the road. Note the triumph of the girl who said 'I crossed the *road*'. Yes, in her mind she did, not just a yard or two of the room.

Many years ago now, I conceived a deep compassion for those who cannot do the ordinary things of life. Oh, all you who live everyday life with such ease, catching buses, writing letters, buying things in shops, washing yourself, counting your money and able to make decisions, how lucky you are! There are many living who can do only some of these things and some none. They desperately need help and hope. But hope only comes by help, though triumphs may be of the simplest kind.

It is very much hoped that this report may be of some service to those working with E.S.N., physically handicapped or older mental patients.

39. Golden Moments

Theatre for children and how some things began, but centring round 1960

'Don't provoke Peter, he's been behaving very well so far.'

John Allen was chairman of a session at a conference on Children's Theatre at the British Drama League in March 1960. The British Children's Theatre Association had expressed some misgivings about a Drama League statement, in that the work might overlap, and I had said that the policy of the Educational Drama Association was to work with anyone who cared to work with them. Rather a mixed situation, really, as I was a member of British Children's Theatre Association national committee, as well as Director of the E.D.A. John English had strongly defended the B.C.T.A. and was just starting to ask me some question across the floor when Mr Allen interrupted him and the rest of his remark was lost in a gale of laughter. I hope they will not mind my mentioning this, as it is really such a gorgeous joke against myself. I have often felt a bit of an outlaw. Not wanting to be, but being made to feel 'it is too early to have said that yet', and I had better just go away and get on with my own work and not bother other people till they approach me for themselves. But at conferences I do tend to speak my mind, it is one of the things you go for. So this was an entirely new situation—something like 'coming out' or being accepted at the Athenaeum. One was almost respectable and I treasure the moment.

People often ask me now, 'How did all this begin with you? What influenced you to start thinking the way you do?' Well, this book would not be complete without some mention of Children's Theatre or Theatre for Children, as perhaps it should be called, though the latter does not trip so lightly off the tongue, and it makes me consider carefully how my own interest in it arose. For the Theatre for Children I now do arises out of a life time of spontaneous experience infused by some knowledge of theatre itself. I have already described how theatre engulfed me at the age of six, apart from many spontaneous experiences. In a way, one was 'producing' without knowing it, in the section describing life at preparatory school. There were other similar experiences. Apart from a terrible year with T.B. glands spent almost entirely alone, going for a brief spell to another school and returning to my own, then suffering the humility of being moved lower and lower in form till finding a decent level, I was happy at this time and moderately prospering. I had my own jazz band by the age of eleven and a half and was able to improvise harmony; and by twelve years was being allowed occasionally to produce grown-ups in plays. These very seldom stuck entirely to a proscenium shape. I played the Cabby in *Vice Versa* at school, which did my acting more harm than ever because the master, who produced it, taught me to pull funny faces till the audience laughed. They laughed all right, but it must have been an outrageous and disgusting performance by any decent standard, but again bringing with it an intoxicating feeling of power and excitement at being able to sway a crowd.

It took me years to get over that performance, though the change at leaving preparatory school, where there had been success, where one was trusted, where one was offered the mental stimulation of adult discussion and friendship—the change took me down a peg.

My shop girls in the personality courses for retail trades, in recent years, have sometimes talked of being degraded. This is what happened to me when I first went to public school and it was typical of my whole time there that, although acting a great deal in the holidays, my interest was entirely undiscovered until my last term, when they gave me two parts, one amongst the Headmaster's chosen favourites—by mistake, for I certainly wasn't one—and the other part by acceptable recognition. After the terrible experience of that school, I was sent to Germany to keep me apart from another innocent lady love who had been sent to France, and there I produced the arena play with children in the woods (before mentioned) and the feature programme with adults in a swimming bath. Then—return to England, the depression, no jobs for anyone.

Although at Ely and already interested in fluid forms of stage production, I never really knew the work of Gray at Cambridge, during some of the years I was so close. I was too young.

To London again, to work for the examinations I did not get at school. I gave myself a sort of advanced university education instead of attending very badly taught classes at a cramming school, reading everything I could on art, poetry, psychology and theatre, and did manage to pass an examination for advertising! Almost at once life brought me in contact with theatre and I built a group out of students mostly from a Polytechnic and toured them in what was more or less Theatre for Children (about 1931 or so). After this followed the joining of numerous groups of professional or semi-professional, little theatre, stuck-in-a-corner type of studio around the West End, which were thick on the ground at that time, and several ventures into running my own companies for playing to children. I was still playing 'to' rather than 'amongst' at this period.

Then happened one of those things that can have such unexpected effects. I had a row with my father (after a former row with my mother) mostly over a red tie, packed my weekend bag and never went home again—though my parents did make it up with me later, on coming to London themselves.

It was one of those ordinary adolescent battles for freedom and it had been brewing a long time. The more you are tied, the harder you must kick to get free. I think it really started (justly or unjustly, for one sees my parents' point of view) with the little girl in the bicycle shop, was followed by having to put up with an untrained nurse (an earlier 'very good one', I do not really remember); it continued with being constantly stopped from making friends with boys at the grammar school (my brief temporary school); then with the continual and growing consternation over servants. We had so many of them and I could never bear it. I always thought it was wrong and felt ashamed of being served. Not that I disapprove of service as such, it can be a noble thing. But often one wasn't even served properly, and this was as humiliating as it was stupid, for then there was no excuse for the whole thing. I was always tripping over servants rubbing at something. It was undignified. In the end, there was never a room where they weren't. I felt deeply guilty about them and after being deprived of companions, who were supposed to be socially inferior, I could stand the starchy nightmare no longer and left.

This was my enlightenment about class and our whole social structure and from that moment I saw with vivid reality that somehow, sometime, this would all pass. It could not last. And I started to readapt to life, but the leap into reality was a very cold douche in the deep end and it left me very uncertain for a number of years. I went to live in an attic over Royal Oak Station and finally went on the stage. I trained my own students from time to time, started the Parable Players to keep alive the old morality plays, with a backbone of former Central School students, touring mostly in schools and in between times, having used up all the money, I starved. I would sometimes manage a penny bun and take a shilling seat at the pictures. The rest of the time I tramped the streets, and it was then that my knowledge of children began to deepen, for during these periods I spent hours and days just standing and observing play. Never was there such an education in the ways of the child. There comes a time when hunger makes one more perceptive too.

The wonder and beauty of what I saw are embodied in my first book, and it was the fact that children play so often in a circular form that made me start to break consciously away from proscenium presentations, in the early 1930s. And it was because of watching the use of higher and lower levels in pavement play that I first advocated the use of rostrum blocks to the schools my companies visited. It is faintly amusing sometimes to hear the proud assertions of later enthusiasts on blocks and arena work. I often smile quietly somewhere inside (but not in the least in a disparaging or supercilious way) on thinking of those tough early days, completely retraining my actors for work with children. For even sixteen years ago, to talk of acting in the round meant probably to face a hostile audience.

At one time I had a flat almost in Red Lion Square and there was supposed to be a communist centre opposite. I always wondered, why 'the leader' came in such an expensive car and had the only big radiogram in the street. Occasionally I earned something and would buy a coffee and a bun for down-and-outs, and once or twice shared a biscuit on a cold floor, beneath the communist's warm flat, with the first batches of refugees from Europe. I remember a publisher (whom I met again years later) giving his last coffee away. What could my parents have said to see me now? I kept the flat for a bit, as a base somehow, until the window fell out into Red Lion Square and it became too cold to stay. Then my parents came to Town and I came together with them again a bit. I would dress up all clean for their benefit and oh how good occasional meals with them tasted! One lunch I remember, too, at a hotel with my beloved grandmother Franks. Unused to such luxury as a midday meal, I was sick for hours afterwards. They never knew.

Then came the Christmas party when I sat next to my father, to make him feel less lonely, and I felt him dying. A little later, I watched him die of cancer, through some long terrible hours, just after leaving a North London Repertory and watching the audience go, with the marks of my gold-painted seats on their backs. My father seemed to turn to paper and his soul flew

[192]

out of the window. I left to join the B.B.C. in Birmingham.

A manager continued my companies for a time. But it wasn't the same and I closed them down. Occasionally I got to London and was greatly cheered by my cousin Roy de Maistre, who kept me amused, taught me about Picasso and gave me heart at this time. I shall always be grateful to him.

Despite running sort of Garcia Lorca groups round villages, starting non competitive festivals with youth groups in 1937 or so, producing odd shows in the Army and odder ones in munitions factories, after being blown up, I was not concerned with a professional company again until 1945, when I originated and trained the Pear Tree Players. This, I am told, was probably the first professional company entirely devoted to education.[1] They trained more or less on dance and improvisation for two years or so before producing a show. Then they had to present plays in any shape, in any place, to any audience large or small (once to thirteen people only in a W.E.A. group, for they had been taught how to believe in the thing created without relying too much on audience). They did script plays from the Youth Library, three-act plays from the West End or improvised on ideas given by the audience. 'Imaginative Shakespeare' and mime were also part of their repertoire. 'A burglary to drum beats', says one programme. Needless to say they did a lot of theatre-in-the-round like all my earlier companies. They also had to take work in youth clubs and some of them finally taught in schools. It was a new profession—Actor-Teacher—or rather, the resurrection of a very old one. I shall never know a team like that again.

It was, like so many of my other experiments, all too early. There was no money to be had. When all my small savings were exhausted, it was the end of the group. But I think it formed a pattern, at least in the subconscious. Professional groups at the present time are doing what we did and always hoped to continue, both in Children's Theatre and theatre with and for youth; some of the work today is almost of the Pear Tree pattern. I am glad—so long as they do it well.

There followed a period of sadness after the Pear Tree Players.

[1] See Coggin, *Drama and Education;* also my *Child Drama.*

[193]

Though one thing cheered me—some of them did film work afterwards and said the training we had done together helped them to get into the part quicker. Hardly any retakes.

But there was soon plenty to do and we were very comfortable in our large white house on the crest of the hill at Swynnerton, rented to us by Lord Stafford. (His late brother became godfather to my second daughter soon after.)

Mostly, the work was still with youth, but increasingly it was to be established in industry, and one was beginning to develop ideas in schools. My advice was sought on a new technical college in Stafford, what to do in drama in a new training college and also on plans for a North Staffordshire University. With members of a munitions factory, I produced the first amateur presentation of Duncan's *This Way to the Tomb*.[1] (The leading man even obtained permission, somehow, to play whilst the London production was still running) and I took sessions of improvised dance in masks to break down any strain over status relationships.

There was a lot going on nationally too, with the Advisory Committee on Drama in Education of Theatre News Service, in London, of which I was a member. The Service ran some of the most influential conferences of their kind.

In the hard winter of 1946–7, we were snowed up for several weeks, but had obtained a crate of gin for some reason—perhaps to celebrate being able to get it at all, just after the war. It was the happiest time in my life.

But I remember managing to dig myself out of several feet of snow in order to get to London for the exhibition at Heal's of *Penny Plain, Twopence Coloured*, and obtained the signature of George Speaight in my copy of his excellent book *The Juvenile Theatre* and of Sir Ralph Richardson on a Pollock's Toy Theatre Sheet.

Soon afterwards, a remarkable post in the City of Birmingham was advertised, quite the outstanding one of its kind in the country at that time and I was lucky enough to get it.

1 I was to produce this again in 1952 as an arena production in my Birmingham back street, with Brian Way as Antony. Information on other arena productions of this play would be welcome.

After a christening party at the house and a dinner from Lord Stafford, I came to work in Birmingham for the hottest summer I ever remember, though we kept on the house for a time whilst finishing outstanding engagements, one of which is described in Report No 24.

After the historical conference at the Bonnington Hotel, London, in 1948,[1] the Educational Drama Association, based in Birmingham invited me to become their Director and it became a national body almost overnight. Very soon I became involved with training the Birmingham Children's Theatre Players and it is due to their patience and forbearance that the present company evolved and has formed a pattern for numerous other amateur companies in various parts of the world, and some professional ones.

Briefly, adults present plays in the sort of shapes to be observed in children's play—a sort of fluid arena shape. Children usually join in at certain points and one American book[2] reproduced a picture of when my audience, having been 'watered', with a green can, all got up and danced as dandelions.

But although we produce in the manner—almost the 'coin-age'—of children's play, so as to touch their emotional level, we attempt to add a certain sophistication and aesthetic polish, which we hope is a sort of crowning experience to their own efforts. This I believe to be the true purpose of genuine Theatre for Children, anyway for young children—to be like their creation but different and, in one sense, better. There must be an emotional and aesthetic experience for the audience and it should be a step ahead of them, to lead them on to fresh fields. Some Theatre for Children is too many steps ahead. It is too different, too sentimental perhaps, too adult. This does not always lead children to fresh fields. It *can* lead to destruction and lack of confidence in their own type of creating, and to somewhat sterile copying. It will not necessarily be found to encourage future theatre-going in the least, which is one avowed purpose of such enterprises.

As usual there was a dearth of money, and for ten to twelve

[1] See Coggin, *Drama and Education.*
[2] Geraldine Brain Siks, *Creative Dramatics, an Art for Children.*

years I had to keep the group going, often out of my own pocket. Some of the players contributed too. It is not pretended that the expense was great, but it was inconvenient, and the whole situation was unworthy of our children.

One ought to be present to see and feel this sort of work, particularly as our own group has been rather concentrating lately on little batches of children that no one else might consider much. We have welcomed little groups of thirty, fifty, or a hundred, sometimes of rather neglected children, backward or emotionally disturbed. They do not pay. For there is some aid from the local authority now. We run it as a service and are touched to do so.

Here is my description of one such performance that appeared in *Creative Drama*.[1] Although it had been prepared for presentation, with the grouping and lighting and the cue sentences involving plot being set, the rest of the words were improvised, which is why it belongs to this book.

THEATRE FOR TOP INFANTS TO MIDDLE JUNIORS

As I sit here writing, there is a sound of cows in the main hall at Rea Street. It is nothing to be alarmed about, because they are there every Wednesday just now. The Children's Theatre is in progress and the cow voices made by the children are caught in a bottle and sold to unsuspecting customers from a wheelbarrow 'in the Bull Ring'. I don't quite know how this story evolved, but we always make up our plays for Juniors by group discussion. The present story is this:

An oldish King enters with his young daughter. They talk about a beautiful garden and walk all round the hall, discussing flowers and fountains, occasionally testing the children for shyness or 'open-ness' by the odd remark. (The audience is seated on three sides of the hall, leaving the whole of the middle and small stage free.) Finally the King leaves his daughter singing on a rostrum block in a pool of golden light.

The Prince of the Moon enters (from the stage) and is en-

---

[1] The Magazine of the Educational Drama Association (Vol. 2, No. 11). By courtesy, reprinted. Mr A. E. Thomas is to be particularly thanked for his hard work as editor, apart from his tact as Chairman.

chanted by the Princess's voice. He passes down on to the floor and listens, then falls asleep. Very tiring work travelling on moonbeams. The Princess goes away and the Palace Cook comes in from the far end of the hall. She collects herbs for the soup, then suddenly notices the Moon Prince. As he has taken off his magic travelling mask with tall feelers, she is quite able to catch him in a blue strawberry net. He is hauled off calling for help. Sometimes his cries are a little too loud and the younger ones go through it a bit. Sometimes one or two children get up as if to try and help him, but he calls the Moonmen and, at this stage in the play, most of the children do not yet feel they are Moonmen. The Princess enters singing. Then some Moonmen enter at the opposite end of the hall, through arches on either side of the stage. They crouch and listen. Then they steal the Voice by hauling on sort of cobwebs at it. They break it up and take a bit each. The Voice wavers, so they decided to put it together again and pop it in a pot. They then bear this off to the Moon by climbing (to music) up steps and through a slit of curtain onto the stage.

The Princess meets the King, who asks the audience what to do. He finally says he'll get the police to help and the audience generally roars at him for being so stupid.

I am not always there for all of the performances because there are sometimes people to see me, but I think what happens next is that a woman suddenly appears, for no good reason, pushing a wheelbarrow. She sort of waltzes along to music and calls 'Voices for sale'. When she stops, the music fades out. She talks to the audience. Finally she gets to the Bull Ring and sets up her stall. She shows all the bottles with corks out, and with labels on. The audience is invited to make the voices of cows, a cat and a donkey. She runs about catching each Voice, which as a rule is a mighty roar. The roar cuts off as the cork jams home. I should have said earlier that there are members of the Court who enter from the arches near-stage and the King pops back once or twice, to royal music, and processes with his dumb Princess to the throne. Everyone is asked to help find the Voice.

Then an English Me-lord enters. He is something of a clown

and offers to find the Voice. Nobody wants him to, least of all the King, who says so in a charming quiet way to one or two children as he goes out. The Me-Lord has funny music which he walks to. Now he is coming back and asking the way to the Bull Ring. He goes amongst the audience and they joyfully shout the way. He is very silly at finding it and whenever he stops the music stops. Finally he sees the woman with her barrow and, coming up behind her quietly, touches her on the head with his gold-knobbed stick. The music stops bonk. On some nights there are one or two children nearly sick with laughter at this moment. I have nearly fallen off my chair too on occasions. Then the bartering begins. All of us present help to make the Voices, but finally the Me-lord buys one in a yellow bottle. It is ghastly—(a woman pop singer supposed to be singing at speed 45 but revved up to 78 and at full volume). Me-lord is delighted though, and goes off to present his find to the Palace. Some nice things happen during the bartering. The Me-lord hasn't got quite enough money, but each evening the audience forgives him his stupidity and urges the voice seller to 'let 'im 'ave it. Gor on.' One night a little boy ran out and pressed two pennies into his hand to make up the required sum.

Of course the whole Court is fascinated when the bottle arrives and the suspense builds up. It is a vile moment when the Princess pulls the cork from the yellow bottle and the ghastly voice comes out. The King is furious and asks the whole room to help him decide the penalty for such wickedness.

This is where I went back into the hall this evening. The voices of the mob were pouring forth: ''ang 'im; knock 'is 'ead orf; chop 'im up'. 'Ah,' said the King—'chop him up, eh?— and put *salt* on. Yes, we could do that.' Finally the noise abated and as usual he said 'No. I know what we'll do. We'll hang him up by the big toe and tickle him to death.' Everyone roared 'Yes' and a guard tickled the bad Me-lord all over the room to very ticklish music, then finally out and to his death. The King sadly bade everyone look again. The Cook then had a go, in the hope of obtaining the hand of the Princess in marriage for her son. Back came the voice-seller, to her lilting music, but rather than finding the right Voice something went wrong and the cat voice went into the Cook, who was chased behind the stage by the barrow and its owner.

We had a new noise this night. The voice-seller happened to thank the children for helping her so well. At this praise a great sucking-in noise came from a number of children. At first I couldn't quite make it out. Then they started to rub their finger nails hard on their lapels, then regarded them carefully and finally[1] blew out in unison like a Yoga cleansing breath. A sudden roar of joy followed. Then the Moon Prince came in. He was very happy that the Cook had disappeared. He'd got his flying mask on again and asked the children to help him escape and fly back to the moon. He couldn't remember how to fly, so everyone made suggestions. Finally he said 'I know. Count one, two, three, then *blow*. Blow as hard as you can. Perhaps that'll get me there.' So they did and it did. Away soared the Prince on a puff and Vaughan Williams, flying down the length of the hall and up onto the stage. (There is always a lovely cross fade here from puff to music, but Vaughan Williams always wins and the Prince is away on up his moonbeam before we know where we are.)

As we were now on the Moon, the Moonmen entered slowly from the arches, walked all down the hall and turned back to the stage, whence appeared suddenly the Prince. They bowed. The Prince told of his capture and a few children called out in assent and added a bit to the story. Then the Moonmen offered their Prince a gift. He discovered it was the lost Voice. Of course he could not stay on the Moon now, the Voice must be returned. So, the slow walk to music began again—up on to the stage, round the back and down and out through one of the arches into the hall.

I always love this bit. The Prince enters bearing aloft a silver cup with the Voice in it. He and his 'men' are all in shining white with 'feelers' on silver masks. The King and daughter come back from the opposite end of the hall and they walk diagonally towards the Moonmen and meet. This moment always makes history for me—it is 'Mr Livingstone, I presume' all over

[1] An 'act silly' mannerism that became the vogue at that time when anyone praised you. Comedians sometimes do it.

again. It is Milton and his hordes. No, it is greater. It is, after all, Royalty meeting Royalty. The Man in the Moon meets Childhood. It is Innocence incarnate. I cannot properly describe what this double entrance means to me. On the best nights it can only be understood by such trite, if accurate, description as a true moment of good theatre. Because of its quality it is intensely moving.

Well, the Prince handed the cup back, the Princess lifted the lid. Out came the Voice and she drank it—all, to the bottom of the cup. Then, of course, she had her voice again and could sing and finally speak. The King didn't want to lose his daughter, but the Moon Prince was adamant. The King tried every way to get out of his promise that whoever found the Princess's voice should have the dearest wish of his heart—'I know. Sweets. What kind of sweets?' 'Jelly babies?', called one little voice. 'But I don't like sweets,' persisted the Moon Prince. Finally, after some pathetic argument the King agreed that the Princess should go to the Moon for Six Months every year, and come back to Earth for six, and that there would be feasting and strawberries and cream to welcome her. This night someone wanted her to have porridge too, for some reason. 'But I must go, at least for six months,' said the Princess, 'you see, he's so handsome.' The King looked at the Moon Prince in his silver mask and feelers. After a long pause he said: 'Oh well, there's no accounting for taste.' They hugged farewell and the music began to swell, as the Moon Prince and Princess walked slowly up a moonbeam on to the stage. The Moonmen fell in behind. At the slit in the curtain the Prince and Princess turned to wave—a sort of 'dance' wave, exactly in unison and to the music. (I enjoyed producing this bit. It has a moment of deep sadness somehow, akin in theatre quality to the grandeur of the great meeting as described above.)

The Moon party passed on and up, then disappeared in darkness. The King hurried after them a few paces but they were lost to view. The music dropped down to a quieter mood and he was left standing alone in a pool of light from one 'spot'. Finally he gave up and walked slowly away down the hall and out. The lights accompanied his journey and by the time he

[200]

had gone we were in darkness. There was not a sound in the hall. Then quietly stealing, like a memory on a cool wind, came the recurring phrase of the Princess singing, singing from the Moon, so that we shall always remember her.

For yet another evening our story was done. It is always a little bit different. The actors are trained to let it flow the way the children take it by their participation. (In some of our plays, children actively join in and walk about. They don't happen to in this one. It isn't arranged like that.) On one recent performance it nearly flowed away, as some of the children recognised their headmaster in the clown. They did not want him to be punished, but finally the thought of his being hung up by the big toe and tickled to death was too much for them and they decided not to banish the Prince to the Moon for ever after all.

Each time I see this simple story it gets better and I wonder why it succeeds. I think the answer is that it is presented in the sort of shapes that children use in their own play, it is played absolutely 'straight', there is a lot of cross-chat and it moves one, in places, because interesting grouping and journeys are blended with a deep sincerity of acting. If we did not achieve this, we should not think the presentation of Children's Theatre worth while.

———

There are so many moments in the last thirty-five years that spring to mind in this sort of drama and many, many more forgotten. But a few years back, I recall the energy of a certain Humbug Factory and the strange sweets that came out of it; a Spirit of the Well, who first came to us, sent by a clinic, because he had had an accident and was unable to use his legs properly. He became one of our best dancers and could leap several feet high from a standing position into his well, during one show —bang in the hole every time; the grand march round of a Prince, who had turned to stone and turned back again, with trainbearers from the audience; the child who came out each night to dust away funny named dust on a clock, that could do terrible harm; my personal joy in accompanying this action

[201]

with music, slightly different at each performance, because of the personality of the child involved; an Indian warrior on a cloud (a metal bar on the roof) watching the Morning Star go by to faint music and the only way to get him down was for some of the audience to get magnets and pull him down. One night they became magnets themselves. And the magic drumming at the end when everyone joined in; (this play was produced by an American visitor). At one time Birmingham College of Education started the work well[1] and asked me in to help where I could.

I was fascinated at their washing machine that churned a gentleman up, though overawed too. So was the audience for a moment, until real bubbles arose from the machine. This broke the tension and there was a roar of joy; finally, the family of Green People, Father and Mother and the Littlun. They had 'no fumbs', so never could do their bootlaces up until the hero came and did it for them.

What is it that makes this work so marvellous to do? Perhaps it is the weaving in of all the best of theatre (some of which one has learned by slow degrees) together with an intense and unashamed adventure into the world of imagination. It employs fantasy but demands believability. The actors must be deeply absorbed in the task and deeply sincere about the way they do it—as children themselves are. I once wrote: 'Children's Theatre is a LAND that you go to.' Each piece of action must be established slowly, so that a young mind can follow; theatre is often too fast and much of the message is lost. With children, one must not be afraid to have occasional moments of complete silence. They cannot find peace without our aid. But the rhythm and timing must be right. Sometimes these silences are the golden moments when everyone present is spell bound. This is a mixture of the best of adult artistry with the heart beat of the child. At such moments in time, we build *Wisdom*—out of innocence.

[1] Under Miss Audrey Stanley.

COMMENT

There is considerable and growing interest now in Theatre for Children, and fortunately older attitudes are dying—that of gripping children almost by the throat in the hope that they would become audiences of the future, or shoving any old theatre at them and ordering them to like it. This will never succeed, nor is it even right. Children must be allowed their own choice of whether they wish to go to the theatre or not, without being made to feel guilty or immoral. If the theatre isn't good enough, they won't go. If it isn't of the kind they understand, they won't go. They can be made interested by actually creating drama themselves and then seeing theatre of carefully prepared kind, which considers the steps in their development without shattering their own creation. Fortunately many professionals now see this, they are quicker to appreciate the needs of children as witnessed by fascinating recent discussions with members of the Royal Shakespeare Theatre Company at Stratford-upon-Avon.

'Golden Moments' gives a rather personal history of my own experience in Theatre for Children because so many people write to me now about it and almost every week students ask how I became involved, how I formed my opinions, what was my own personal background, what made me think that way, did I do it in my own childhood? In a way this whole book is an answer to that question but in this report I have tried to collect events and influences into a short history. I have done this again in Nos. 41 and 44 and in the Appendices, for students to pick out quickly from the rest of the writing. I hope this will help them in their interests or in their theses.

One can hardly make too much of the Golden Moments, they are an intentional magic built up out of rhythm. They are a climax held in great quietness for several seconds, as when a spotlight shines on a bowl or the sun comes out—a dawning slow realisation. 'There is no hurry, here,' I am always saying during production. 'Just relax, create the magic, enjoy the beauty yourself and don't move till the music stops.' It is part of the poetic eye, the way children see things and are fascinated by very simple and wonderful experiences in everyday life that we adults often now disdain, have forgotten or take for granted—as sun coming through water when you pour it into a glass.

In this description the entry of the Prince bearing the silver cup is one such moment and even more so when the Princess lifts the lid and her own voice that she had lost comes out. Such Golden Moments can be a heightened experience, arrived at on purpose.

To give another example—in a professional performance of Theatre for Children a few years back, in the Midlands, a hero came on and made a good entrance. Then he suddenly said 'Ah, we want some sun. Mr Electrician, will you give us some more sun, please. The theatre is so wonderful you can do anything you like in it.' Crash went the whole scene. It was not a funny play nor one of the sort of extravert convention. It was a legend, a fairy story. This crude sort of propaganda will not bring children to the theatre. It is no good *saying* theatre is wonderful in the wrong way and at the wrong time, it must *be* wonderful, then we shall believe it.

[203]

Another way of presenting this scene would have been to allow a breathtaking suspense, let the hero suddenly and quietly enter, then let him stand quite still. The sun could then have come up on him *because* of the magic of the theatre. The whole stage could be bathed in light and the sun would be believable, true, fully joyously experienced, perhaps never to be forgotten.

Golden Moments are a secret which must be learned by anyone contemplating presentation of Theatre for Children.

40. *Interpol and the Electric Roller Skates*
Unusual happenings at a sclerosis club, 1961

Group Captain Cheshire had been a Patron of the Educational Drama Association for some time but now my wife and I had been up to see him at Market Mews in London and had also met Sue Ryder, his charming and energetic wife. A committee had been formed, with the intention of investigating how to use drama for the physically handicapped and for providing such activity for those interested. Some had already written in to say that they would like to join a group, and a hall had been discovered across the way from the Court Theatre. The committee did not feel able to go ahead, however, with taking the hall. My wife and I were determined not to let down those physically handicapped who had applied. We could not bear to think of those lonely people at home, with some faint hope of new interest and opportunity for meeting others, being disappointed. The upshot of it was that Group Captain Cheshire asked us to undertake the job. On the understanding that I could only do it in the holidays and occasional free time, so as not to interfere with my main work, I agreed.

We were invited to Cavendish during one holiday to meet some of those staying there. We walked round the charming garden, saw the new building that was being done, and were taken to meet a blind man who had suffered terrible things in his life. I told him about my geese and about Albert (so called, because he had a grey waistcoat and a curious 'chain' mark across his tummy) who would stand by me and allow me to put the palm of my hand on his head. We would then, both of us, adopt a sort of Victorian stance, as if being photographed at that period. Albert also had about five wives and was very happy. Suddenly one of the helpers entered the room to bring the blind man some tea, I think it was. He turned to me with a delightful smile and said in a deep foreign voice: 'You see, I am Albert. I also have many kind and pretty girls to look after me. I am happy too.' After learning more about the problems we must face if determined to carry out our task, we went on towards home via Cambridge, where a Professor had asked to talk things over with me. On the way I was delighted to pass the Gog Magog hills, for there the 'family horse' is buried. This is a sort of family joke-saying, because of Godolphin ancestry. The 'horse' alluded to is the Godolphin Arabian, given by the Bey of Tunis to Louis XV in 1731. After various adventures it came into the hands of the second Earl of Godolphin and, after first being spurned, for being too delicate and too small, became one of three famous sires from whom all present British thoroughbreds are believed to be descended. Curiously enough, a high officer of the American Educational Theatre Association had recently sent me a present of a book on this animal, and a picture of it hangs in the study of my Cotswold home today. Unfortunately, it is after the one painted by Stubbs, who did his best, after the death of the Arabian. But the head is too big, not at all like descriptions, nor like an Arab (the face should be 'dished' with large mysterious eyes), the only picture presumed to be a good likeness being the one painted in lifetime by Wootton.[1]

Ultimately we took on the job of investigation, a hall was found, transport arranged and a studio in Hampstead was extablished to give a home to my club for the handicapped. Our thanks must go to members of the Rotary movement, who provided free transport for members living as far apart as Roehampton and Potters Bar.

When time would permit, we visited other clubs too, of various kinds and in various parts, to discover, to learn and to hope to help. This is the sort of thing that happened:

[1] See also Lady Wentworth, *British Horses and Ponies*, Collins 1937.

I went in and fixed the gramophone in a socket at the far end of the hall opposite the stage. There were six tables of people, approximately seven at each, and the club leader suddenly announced that I would entertain the company. I had to begin by explaining that it was not quite entertainment, and that my wife and our assistant and myself were not going to perform a play, that we hoped the people there were going to take part *themselves* (amazed murmurs). I explained that one of the things that Drama could do was to offer us the possibility of being imaginative, or even slightly silly, if we wanted to be. So would they all start by imagining they were conductors in charge of a huge orchestra but playing a very simple tune. I then faded up a record of 'Among my souvenirs' and encouraged them to wave their wands as wildly as possible. When the music stopped and they had become loosened, they naturally broke off and began to chat and laugh between each other, and they were then asked to pair off, St John Ambulance attendants being brought into the game to make the numbers equal where necessary. Then, in each pair, one became the buyer and one the seller of any goods that they wished. Some of the things sold were: stockings, hats, newspapers, tobacco, gin and orange, and double Scotch. One woman wore a marvellous 'hat'.

In order that people at different tables should keep a sort of link with each other and find out what everyone was doing, I stopped the proceedings temporarily, after they'd had a good go and quickly went round the tables asking a few people for a brief explanation of what they had been doing. I then repeated this loudly after each statement so that everybody could be sure of hearing, giving encouragement to the ideas wherever possible. One woman, who looked rather forthcoming, on being asked about her partner, said: 'She wanted to buy the clothes off me back. Good thing she didn't want to buy *me*, wasn't it?' (This is the sort of brave joke people sometimes make about a helpless condition.)

We had now been at it something like twenty or twenty-five minutes and it was all going very cheerfully and they were cooperating beautifully. I felt that I had thoroughly broken the ice, and then asked my wife whether she felt able to have a go. She did so and started a piece of 'living newspaper', which we had tried at our first meeting of disabled in the Peter Slade Studio at Hampstead. It was a story of a burglar who had pinched a lot of birds, including a parrot, and the parrot finally gives away the fact that he doesn't belong in this house, when the police come, because he automatically gives his real home address and it is obvious he doesn't belong to the man who says the bird is his. We found in this club that almost everybody knew the story. They had seen it in the paper, so it was quite easy to build it up. But it seemed to get rather 'sticky' near the end and I could see that my wife was getting into difficulties a little, so I jumped in there to say that 'The thief escaped again, and let's imagine that, because he couldn't be caught in England, we turn each table into a different country, with people ringing each other up in an excited manner, as if they are Interpol'. I rushed round, stirring up enthusiasm about which country it should be, and asked them to choose. One table had already chosen Spain, and another very delightful character at his table, when asked what he would be, not having heard that another table was Spain, also tried to say 'Spain', but, partly because his speech was already affected, in fact said 'space'. He was rather embarrassed about this, though he needn't have been. To help him I pretended not to notice and accepted 'space' as his idea and it proved extremely useful in the end. I suggested Interpol got so hot on the trail, on the telephone, that in fact the thief had to take to a space rocket. 'He took all the money he got for the birds and some of the birds with him into space, but he couldn't get back again, because nobody knew how to control the thing, so there he was flying round and round the world with all his money, but it would *never* be any good to him again.' There was a spontaneous burst of joyful remarks at the end of this story and everybody was now looking extremely cheerful and pleased with themselves.

The club leader then began to thank us and to say that he had no idea what was going to happen when we came, and that he had been very delighted by everything and could see that people were obviously pleased. We thought we were going to get a rest then—but no!—we had to take round cups of tea to various people and only just managed to get one ourselves in time, before the pot emptied. That awful moment! There were one or two extremely intelligent helpers at the club, who came up to talk about this work, and also about Child Drama and about our hopes for a proper centre.

The leader then suddenly announced that we would do some more. I said that we would be willing to, though we wondered whether people hadn't had enough for a first attempt. However we were cajoled into it, though hesitant, as we were desperately tired, having rushed all over the country in order to get to the club in time at all. I finally agreed and started an 'ideas game'.

HAPPENING NO 2: THE ELECTRIC ROLLER SKATES
IDEAS: *A fishing rod   A cigarette lighter   Roller skates*
A man at, say, table 1 (if you imagine the tables to have been placed in almost a domino pattern of six) was living in his house *there* and the different tables are different houses in the village. Everybody watched this man because he used to come out into the village square and play cards with some rowdy companions, and he smoked a lot. (There was a lot of laughter here because one man had been smoking a pipe all the evening.) And to light up his dreadful cigars and pipe (I smiled at him during this to show it was only fun and he beamed back) he used a huge cigarette lighter that had a large hooked handle. The people, who looked out of the other houses, were always gossiping about this and objecting to the noise, and a man living in *that* house (we had invited volunteers for this and I pointed to them)—that would be table 3 on the same side of the aisle —tried to get the cigarette lighter by casting a line on a fishing rod, as if he were pretending to do trout fishing, in the hope that he would be able to get the hook under the large handle of the cigarette lighter. (At this point that particular man did some wonderful fly-throwing across the room, and I then went swiftly over to another table—which would be table 5, the middle of the other three and the other side of the aisle)—and somebody there had a big walking-stick to help them. And I suggested

[208]

that he pretend to be using a long pole, which was leaning against a wall to help open the top windows with. (They seemed to like this geographical touch.) He turned the crook of his handle up so that it looked like a hook on the end of this pole, and, from the window in his house, encouraged by his family, he tried also to hook the large cigarette lighter. His family, just next door to 'the card players'—that would be table 6 in the pattern —were, I think, 'washing clothes' or 'mending' and jabbering about the card players, but at table 4 was an ingenious family who talked about how to be sure of getting the lighter, and they decided to send two members on electric roller skates, dashing at ninety miles an hour, and all that family would make the noise of the roller skates going fast. This was splendid imagination for a first try at this sort of creative doing! My wife and the attendant helped two people in wheelchairs to get their feet comfortably settled up on the rest for this, and then (partly by my help and partly by another person's aid) we whizzed them fairly gently across the floor while they smiled and burred hard as if they were on roller skates, supported by the others who had decided to make this noise. They rushed up to table 1, pretended to snatch the lighter and made off round the room. They told me they wanted to go much faster than that. 'We can stand it.' 'Oh fine,' I said and we did. I think I then finished by suggesting that 'the card players broke up because the leader refused to do any more without his lighter, because nobody had any matches and so he couldn't smoke. Therefore there was general rejoicing in the village'. And I think we put on a record for that, for terrific 'rejoicing', which started up, though I can't quite remember. Anyway it finished in joyous uproar and a spontaneous burst of clapping, and we were then asked if we would like to talk about a central hall we had obtained for this work and a possible future Peter Slade Centre for training other leaders.

I outlined the scheme and invited people to come, either separately, if any were particularly interested, or all of them if they wished, though again, if preferred, I would be pleased to come another time to their own club. They all said that certainly they would like us to come again to their club; they were worried about how to get to the other hall. But the club leader said there would be no difficulty in getting ambulances and taking the whole club to the other Centre on an outing for fun, also to meet other people. The chief organiser of the Clubs for Sclerosis, came up and thanked us; she said she had never before seen anything like what we had done and in her opinion it had been a quite wonderful success, and she hoped we would go to other clubs. The club leader said: 'My job is going to be very much more difficult now, and I really mean that, because I don't know how to carry on after this wonderful evening. We shall be hard put to it to make such another exciting one again.' A young assistant very kindly helped me out with the gramophone to my car, and we finally sank exhausted into the seat, quite unable to drive anywhere for several moments.

Several things we had noticed so far in our investigation into drama with disabled were outstanding. Those whose voice is beginning to be affected always choose to play the parrot, in the particular story outlined. So we may use this, or something like it, fairly often, so as to give them a chance of joining in. In the case of a member in my own club for disabled, I suddenly thought of putting a microphone closer than usual and by turning up the level whilst tape recording made the voice sound equal in strength to the others when played back. This gave enormous confidence to *try* and speak. Where it is possible to give a special job or rôle to those in wheelchairs, as long as they are not extra shy—and one never presses them, if so—they seem to enjoy the fun of joining in and are delighted at feeling they are not bound to one spot. They obviously (and actually) have a special contribution. We had not always been very impressed, though, by their ability to guide their chairs, and wondered whether there ought not to be more simple instruction lessons given. It is not always a question of their arms not being strong enough; it is that they have not quite grasped yet how the business functions. One might consider doing some of this for fun, as a pretence of rowing a boat, for the oars do rather the same thing to a boat, even to one 'oar' going forward and another backward, for turning the conveyance round. This would not apply, of course, to those more fortunate ones—if one can call any of

A 'golden moment' of repose when the scene is held only with the eyes. Slow entry during Adult Theatre, Rea Street, Birmingham. Left to right · Michael Hall, Sylvia Demmery, and Charles Adams

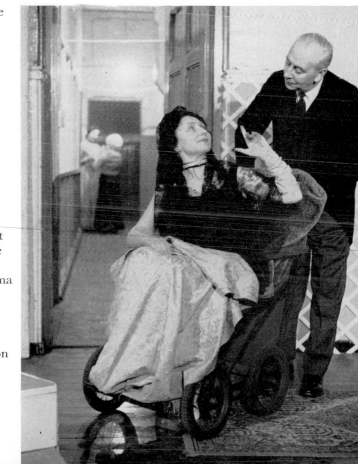

Actors living well in the part and continuing to improvise down far end of corridor. Adult Theatre Group, Drama Centre, Rea Street, Birmingham. Menna Coupland and Charles Adams in foreground. Phyl Lutley and Miriam Cameron in distance

Above: moving fast, swinging scarves, carrying parcels, yet not bumping into customers (the chairs). Long personality course. YWCA, Birmingham

Centre: clearing away golden cobwebs (first time out of chairs). Personality course. YWCA, Dinton Park, near Salisbury. Exercise set by author

Bottom: 'threading a needle' to music. Starting exercise (still in chairs). Exercise set by Sylvia Demmery. Personality course with YWCA, Dinton Park, near Salisbury

them more fortunate—with modern electric sort of Rolls Royces.

One member suggested that, for the first time, people had moved from table to table and not stayed dumped with one lot. Though liking their 'lot' it had proved wonderful to meet others. (This is not unlike the tyranny of the gang with Junior Children, mentioned in my book, *Child Drama*.) 'What very useful information,' said the club secretary, 'another good thing coming out of your evening with us!'

The last thing is that in every club visit there has been a pathetic gratitude that anyone should bother to come and do this work with them, and in every case we have been asked to come again, and whether it was enjoyment of the actual drama or not is of little importance. The point is that in this work, everybody can join in; that all feel part of the party; and we try to ensure that for one short space of time, *all* have forgotten their problems, have had sincere moments, but have laughed and built real joy between us. One person told me later that the joy had lasted her all one week—'Me, what thought I'd never know what happiness was again.'

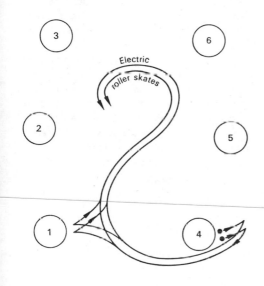

'I jumped in there to say . . .' This is an example of team teaching or team social work, one senses things are going down or need a new mind at certain moments and it is possible to take over from another person without an obvious break and share with them the responsibility for sustaining spontaneous creation. It is a technique I have used for years in personality training and even longer in schools. Children and adolescents often make a special relationship with their teacher or youth leader and an outside adviser coming in ought not to break this down for lack of care or thought. The outsider may not make a quick relationship, or he (or she) may be very successful and 'show how', then march smugly off and leave things rather unhappy afterwards. So at schools I like a teacher to start, then perhaps I take over for a time, if it seems right to do so, then be quite sure to hand back to the teacher so that their relationship with the children is less likely to be impaired.

Teachers from special schools often ask me to talk on work with handicapped children, and readers wishing to study further would find my talks at conferences published in the past in copies of the Special Schools Association *Journal* and also in *Creative Drama*, published by The Educational Drama Association. The ideas of other speakers and writers appear in this magazine too, especially on maladjusted children and E.S.N.

I would add, though it may seem obvious, that each physically handicapped patient is still a person, not a case. Their minds and their emotions work. They are often sad, and the older ones terribly lonely, so they need to be helped out of themselves by going to private houses as well as to clubs; and having ordinary conversation about anything other than their illness, and by having fun. Spontaneous creation can be very valuable here. One woman in a Paddington Club had looked so sad when I first went in but on doing some 'buying and selling' she started to roar with laughter. I asked what it was all about. 'Cor,' she said, 'this is a rotten shop, I was asking my partner to sell me red flannel bloomers and she said she hadn't had any in for twenty years!' I had the feeling it was a good thing the shopkeeper didn't add 'there's no call for it' or she would have had a jovially rough time. Could I make a special plea here, following on the question of theatre-goers from the last comment. It is that in the building of all new theatres consideration be given to special places for some wheelchair users to 'park' and see the show.

41. *Street Gangs and Bombs in the Garden*

The history of an experimental centre and events in 1958–9

The years 1957, 1958 and 1959 seem to have been very much concerned with theatre, apart from helping with numerous plays in schools. For some years I had been developing intimate theatre at very close quarters, feeling that a vast new audience was concerned with enacted story on television and, if ever they turned to theatre as a change, they would want something like that. I felt someone ought to be creating it. Accordingly, a keen group of adults had been working with me in placing plays in one corner or so of a small hall and letting the audience live right on top of the action. We had done *Strange Orchestra* in this way, also *Living Room*, *The Old Ladies* and *Private Lives*, sometimes bringing out particular attitudes in the play, especially if inviting adolescents and providing Theatre for Youth. There were many more of these plays, but the period also seems to have been much concerned with the educationally subnormal, the maladjusted and with delinquents.

My diaries tell me that I was taking a Theatre Course for a university and also speaking at South Wales University in 1956, speaking at Birmingham University and Bristol in 1957 and at Stratford Theatre hall in 1958, speaking at Reading University and attending the birth of the British Children's Theatre Association at Leicester in 1959, and was also dealing with other categories in parallel: 1957—lecturing to the E.S.N. Course at Birmingham University; March—organising a Drama in Education Conference (slant on prevention of delinquency); May—organising a conference on the Disturbed Child; later—a conference on the Child at Play (they had roped me in on Adventure Playgrounds). 1958—Birmingham E.S.N. Course again, also speaking at Liverpool and Hull University. In the summer, speaking at Cambridge University to a conference of Psychologists, and at the Ministry of Education Summer Course on work with the educationally subnormal; September, speaking in London on 'Dramatherapy as an Aid to becoming a Person'.

In 1959 I was lecturing at a London Clinic; speaking on prevention of delinquency to the National Playing Fields Association; to Birmingham University Summer School on the Value of the Arts in a scientific age (slant on emotional balance); and at Birmingham University on delinquency and what we had tried to do in this line at my own Centre. I still have a wonderful picture that they drew, to advertise the talk, of a 'teddy boy',

[213]

chained by one leg. 1958 had also seen the publication of my second book, *An Introduction to Child Drama*, with its stress on Social Drama and by 1959 my London speech on Dramatherapy had been published by The Guild of Pastoral Psychology. Added to this I had been lecturing for Home Office courses regularly for about fifteen years. My helper, during some of this time, at the Rea Street Centre, had been Jack Beckett, who had done sterling work in handling unhappy and difficult children. I had also taken Child Drama with children at the Birmingham University Clinic, helped a bit at Uffculme Clinic and directed a course, including the medical staff, at a mental institution.

As well as seeing the sad side of other lives through some of this work, 1958 had brought a sad misunderstanding with old friends of my own; and because it distressed me so, I tried to take some personal therapy away from most humans,[1] outside work, and did some investigation into the ways of animals. My wife had done some splendid research into virus pneumonia with our herd of pigs and learned how to deal with it, and now we were building up what was to become one of the biggest herds of Dartmoor ponies in the Midlands. Our ways went together for once during the aforementioned Reading University course, for I left my production of *The Beautiful Spirit of the Fireplace* for a few hours to join her at Ascot, just down the road, where we were showing my little colt too. We went far enough to investigate the reactions of chickens to light, I learned the Head of the herd's warning note in pigs and could alert or 'O.K.' them again at will and was later to learn how to talk to a pony by breathing into its nose. Incidentally, pigs are very sensitive creatures and show many of the qualities of children. But that would take a separate book on its own.

'Wot 'e needs is the birch,' a grown-up had said to me. But the young man in question had said, 'If she beats me agen, I'll knife 'er.' Well, I suppose people don't like being beaten. My mind went back to my own earlier times. We were beaten at one of my schools by twigs across our bare legs, when very

[1] Those few who helped me through this period can never be properly thanked.

young (our Latin master), with a riding crop on our hands (by the Greek master, for fun and to get us through common entrance), with a ruler on our heads (by the Maths master), our knuckles were cracked with a cane (our Music mistress). Our Head only used a thick stick on the backside and occasionally string with lead at the end, if the argument needed stressing. At my next school one was beaten by prefects with a walking stick, I personally was birched for having a cocktail bar in my study and then sent to the sanatorium for five days, as being unfit to mix with my fellow men. Why five days, one wonders? And why, if one's father tries to teach one to take and judge a good wine from eleven years of age, is it so wicked to continue to like it at eighteen, particularly at a school where foundation ruling is said to state that scholars shall be entitled to free beer at breakfast? Alas, we were only allowed into a town once a year. It was a strange place.

There was a public parade when birching was to happen, rather like a public hanging, except that the end was private. The Head would walk across grass most people must not cross, next came the culprit and last, the school steward, carrying the birch. All across the quadrangle, down the steps towards the sea and freedom, then suddenly off to the private den. I thought—'Ah, I've never been allowed here before. Big brother has marched over this grass, pounding a tenor drum in band practice, but I never have.' I walked over the same trail again with my wife many years later and we shamelessly pushed our way into an empty dormitory, during the holidays, to see where young men used to break ice in the hand bowls. The Execution March was all an experience and had its moments. Prefect beatings were sometimes deserved, as when flicking salt across great hall or butter balls onto kings' faces in the roof; one knew the penalty and took the risk. But I did take exception to being thrashed with a rhinoceros hide whip, almost on my last night. I had a headache and one or two of us stayed in the House room instead of singing the school song in the end of term concert. We were showing each other card tricks and playing patience. A master, we none of us liked, looked in and five minutes later I was being thrashed for gambling. Rather sad really. I don't gamble and have never liked cards. I'm not clever enough. More unjust than my little affray was the case of a boy in another House, who had been induced by a low church clergyman housemaster, practising being high church, to make a confession. He did so, much against his will, whereupon the little man blew up and shouted, 'I never want to hear such a disgraceful story again,' and gave him six of the best.

Choirs sang somewhere, for some of us, the day we left that place. So my friend of the knife had my sympathy, but on the whole I was a little inclined to think him fussy. He did bash people, he did steal, he did set things on fire and pull younger boys' hair till they screamed and some of us don't like this sort of thing. Sometimes we react. But one couldn't reason with him then. One of the things that got him was that he was being beaten by a woman and young men don't like this. His persona was impaired, his pride was bent.

We used to get our difficult ones jumping from rostrum block to rostrum block for twenty minutes to hot jazz, and when they were exhausted, we thought we could handle them.

Once or twice a lady in a fur coat drove a sort of lorry up and deposited a bunch of teddy boys on our door step. Later she drove up and took them all away again.

We evolved a sort of technique I called 'fielding'. A ring of grown-ups—certainly the three of us—Jack Beckett, Phyl Lutley and I, would try tentatively to give a suggestion about what to do. At this, a difficult one would start to shoot out from the centre towards the boundary, 'to not be' where he'd been asked to be. One night a very tough customer came like a cricket ball towards me. We fielders closed in a bit. I remembered all they say about lions and looked him full in the eye, wondering *who* would win. Suddenly he wavered and turned back to the centre. Now, this was a very important moment for him. He had tried to disobey by refusing to take the faint suggestion of staying in the middle of the room. He wanted to reach the wall of the room, but in failing to do so, what did he do? He obeyed by mistake, and so, not to lose face, just like a cat, he pretended he was going to stay in the middle of the room all the time. I think at that moment he knew he had had to cooperate and possibly

[216]

found it wasn't so bad after all, for to my mind, he began to get better from that night on.

There were three lads, who had a peculiar relationship. One poor little one, often being set upon by two older ones. He would ingratiate himself often, but the strain of his fear was written all over his face.

One night, the three of them had been playing about very roughly, but settled down, more or less, to a simple piece of drama. Even so I got tired of their behaviour and felt intuitively it was time to win. I very seldom raise my voice, so it is a sudden shock, if I suddenly do it and this is reserved intentionally for very rare occasions. I roared out: '*Sit down*, Claude, and play it properly.' He sat down on some rostrum blocks and was busy 'murdering' the younger boy. He clutched at the smaller one's hair, forgot the play and tugged hard. I went forward at speed and caught Claude's wrist.

Claude: 'Sir, wotcher doin' that for? I wasn't doin' nuffin'.'
Self: 'You're pulling his hair out.'
Claude: 'That's what it's for.'
Self: 'Well I think he looks better with his hair *in*.'
Claude: 'Looks —— silly to me anyway.'
Self: 'Never mind what you think. We'll play the scene this way, if you don't mind.'
Claude: ''Ark at 'im—if you don't mind.'
Self (shouting again on purpose): 'Claude, shut up and get *on* with it.'

Now an extraordinary thing happened. He suddenly went quiet and played through the whole scene with me holding his wrist all the time, so the younger boy didn't get hurt. I give this example, because it shows part of my method. I think, for the first time then, he discovered how to play a situation through emotionally without actually using physical violence. It is a process I call 'experience without sin'. It is one thing that the drama can offer, in a way that few other things can.

There were tall ones and fat ones, jolly bullies and lean-faced sneaks. There were the ones that tried to set fire to the place, the ones that would catch a pretty girl, get two other boys to hold her down and burn patterns on her face, till we

[217]

were afraid a lot of young women might be walking about the city looking like dominoes.

There was the mild one, who was dressed all in yellow—not a bad lad, I judged. Wanting to make him feel at home, I wondered what on earth to say. Suddenly it came to me. I walked past this canary and whispered 'what a *remarkable suit*'. His face lit up, it was sheer luck—just the right thing to say. He never made any fuss, just generally looked lost and wistful. He probably had to feel he belonged to some group.

There were girls on probation and one lad who hated grown-ups so much that he intended to tear the guts out of all of them, so, for practice, in the meantime, he was tearing the guts out of horses in a knacker's yard. But this was the one, who much later came back 'to give sweets to the kids'. I didn't like to ask where he had got them from, but the point is he had at last thought of someone other than *himself*. I bring this idea into play therapy from time to time, as it is an attitude that must burst through into consciousness. But, fortunately for mankind, the giving of sweets in play is anyway a recurring symbol in that realm. I treat it as a sign of recovery. This lad had brought it to actuality. He became a successful lorry driver and, as far as I know, hasn't run over anybody on purpose yet.

One thing one would like to bring more into the light, after our years of investigation. It is the burden that some young people live with, being of actual age so-and-so, but when induced to act spontaneously, show the play patterns normally associated with a much younger child. This one expects, to some extent. But I have known numbers of fourteen- and fifteen-year-olds—even eighteen-year-olds—liberated successfully enough to play as eight- and nine-year-olds. Going back to the 'cathartic years'? Going back to the last time they were allowed to play? Going back to safety or the last time they were happy? In any case, for a fifteen-year-old to play like an eight-year-old is a great unbalance. In the Personal Play realm, their emotional maturity, so to speak, is halfway behind actual age. For them it is an unbalance of half a life time. Do we realise what a strain that must be to live with?

I seriously wish many more people did this work. It is desperately needed. People need training and there should be many such places where the young can blow off steam, so they don't need to actually 'do the deed' in real life. They have to be helped to see the difference between dream and reality. Even punishment might be more justly assessed, if something like these methods were used; for a fifteen-year-old, seen to play consistently in, say, the pattern of a fourteen-year-old (and if this is compared with other tests) probably needs a smart smack in the pants, but a fourteen-year-old consistently playing as an eight-year-old needs treatment. We can be pretty sure that, as things are, the wrong child gets the wrong sentence, for their behaviour is not properly tested, one suspects, before sentence. I have talked with a previous Home Secretary about this and got as far as speaking to the officers of a special committee in the House of Commons, for it appears to me to be a matter of great importance and of human justice.

Superficial investigation of these points might end in the notion that group therapy is superseding attempts at using spontaneous drama, for some drama methods are considered only as a form of structured grouping. But this is a very inaccurate calculation if applied to proper dramatherapy, and entirely leaves out the actual nature of young people, their power of using constructive (and destructive) imagination, the manner in which they can be guided through personal dream play to conscious expression, from selfish personal expression to work in pairs and then the group, watching continually for ways in which to offer them opportunities of working off aggression, until harmony and cooperation are established. But even then, catharsis is not enough and this, one suspects, is where most methods fail; there must be an added hope process. I have written about this in *Dramatherapy as an Aid to Becoming a Person*, giving as an example some play on the theme of a dog that has been feared. The fear begins to evaporate through play, but there must *then* be the 'hope process', i.e. a strong visual image established of your *own* future dog, and this dog does not bite; or passing a gate with no dog, etc.

Moreover, in all this work one has the added yardstick of Child Drama, the child's own way of creating. Those that have taken the trouble to know it and love it well, know also by a thousand and more examples what is expected as normal patterns in play, round about a given age. Only by knowing the normal can you more truly judge the abnormal and lead it to the imprisoned normality that lies at the back of many a hardened case. Mere group therapy, compared with this depth of treatment is, in some instances (forgive the pun) mere child's play. One group of toughs we aided through to cooperation was finally allowed to play in a room by themselves. We were able to trust them not to smash up quite valuable equipment and eventually only had to glance occasionally through a glass window at them. They were fourteen- and fifteen-year-olds. What were they playing when we glanced through at them?—fairies, wizards and knights in armour, dressed up like little children in rags and scarves and fighting with wooden swords; the little gang play of the seven- to nine-year-old. Fighting, in play, is not of itself a sign of delinquency. It is normal, even important, though it worries many adults, because it is inconvenient, particularly in school. It is St George and the Dragon, the symbol of overcoming—overcoming evil, or difficulties, or the enemy in yourself. The normal child uses it often but can be weaned away from it. But many who are really mentally ill have lost even the will to overcome. One girl, who was sent to me by a psychologist from another area, could not show anything much in play. Miss Sylvia Demmery (who was helping me in this case) and I tried everything we knew for some weeks to obtain a psychic effort. Finally the girl killed her first creature to drums, in the jungle. It was a snake—the symbol of evil. We knew we had begun. Most of our tough cases found an anchor in life at the Centre. They were not 'judged' there. It was not a court room.[1]

We do not have delinquents these days, but often those who are sent for one purpose or another—being backward or finding adjustments difficult or because they want to go on the stage, or merely because they are highly intelligent. Some pass on from the Junior Group to the Theatre for Children Section.

[1] See Michael Burn, *Mr Lyward's Answer*.

Many students and visitors ask—how did you ever get this idea? How did it start? What is the history of it?

Well, you may judge that some of the earlier part of this book is the history of it. The beginnings are in the story of my own life. But the recent and immediate history is as follows.

Soon after coming to Birmingham in 1947, I became rather ill for a number of years, which made work very difficult, but I was determined not to give up, for this was my life. One day the telephone rang. It was Andrew Campbell speaking from the first British Theatre Conference, which he had organised. 'Peter, the Education Section is in a mess: can you come up?' With the extreme generosity of my own Education Committee, though wondering what on earth I could do, I left at once and was there in under three hours. I did my stuff but I felt that only about one person really knew what I meant and that was Dame Sybil Thorndike. At another section of the conference, I made the plea that we should not rush into Children's Theatre without consulting the Ministry of Education. After this, the Ministry of Education National Drama Working Party came into being and a number of us, who had been on the Advisory Committee set up by Theatre News Service, were invited to join it. We met often for about two years, so far as I remember, but unfortunately our report was not published. It would have saved a great deal of sticking out of necks in later lectures down the years. But the Welsh Ministry beat us to it and published a very good report.

There was less agreement on general principles than there is now and putting across one's views then was like a crucifixion. But good support came from a certain lady architect and from Andrew Campbell.

Following up these exciting discussions often meant going away and just getting on with what you knew to be right, and from that moment began the serious collection of data (such as watching 3,000 and later 30,000 children doing certain things and collecting their sayings before writing anything) that was later to be published.

In our road was a lad, who shall be called Geoffrey. He threw 'bombs' at windows and, as the children in the street were rather under his sway, we feared that our elder daughter might end up in one cell and we should separately inhabit others—magistrates being prone to astonishing statements about the deserts of already suffering parents. So we decided to take the whole gang into our house. And the garage and newly painted front room (oh, those dirty little hands!) became their H.Q. Some short accounts from this period went into the out-of-school section of *Child Drama*, but briefly what happened was that we weaned them from throwing actual stones against windows in the street to throwing imaginary bombs in the garden, to Count Basie music. A bomb to each bonk of the double-bass, thence to imagined bows and arrows and to fearful hospital operations. They learned how to blow off steam without actually doing harm. They had a place to go to where they could use their emotions under guidance and have our old friend 'experience without sin'. They all became manageable, though Geoffrey was tough. Some I could help further, by getting Child Drama started in their schools, but I don't know what happened to Geoffrey, because we moved.

Then there was Pete's Kitchen, a place where a few children came to cook spells with me and hardly any adults were allowed.

After these two final experiences, I was determined to have one place in the world, other than a clinic, where children could come and do their own Child Drama under trained and sympathetic guidance. There should be hundreds of such places but at least there would be one. I wanted also to run Theatre for Children, adult experimental theatre, dance; and let all ages meet when possible, and see each other at work, so as to help break down the barrier between youth and age and to remember again what it is like to be someone else—to build interest and sympathy and tolerance. It would also be a basic training place for the work. The local authority finally provided me with simple premises, in part of a bombed out school. The Head of the re-established school, Charles Adams, was enthusiastic over a sort of drama playground outside and already a member of the Birmingham Children's Theatre Players (he still is to date).[1] His cooperation was won and that is how the Rea Street Centre

[1] Just retired now, before this publication.

[222]

came into being. The first course advertised brought 400 enquiries and I accepted the lot. For the children's evening we had open doors at first and we used to get anything up to a hundred or more a night. Later it settled down to eighty to a hundred. It was very hard work and I would like to record my praise for the helpers. One teacher came every Tuesday evening in term for at least eight years, with hardly a single break, for not a penny extra pay. Others since have done the same.[1] In recent years, drama has developed in schools. There are plenty of flourishing after-school drama clubs now, so much more careful selection can take place and Rea Street is not so overrun. University courses come regularly to observe, students from training colleges come and work, and visitors have come from all over the world. At the height of our difficulties some one once said: 'You have no money, very little help and the children you work with at this time are grim. How *do* you manage it?' I answered: 'You have to love your fellow man.' My answer would be the same today.

COMMENT

This is another history, put together because so many inquiries have come for it not only from this country but from abroad too, that it has become almost impossible to keep writing the same sort of letter in answer, with small changes to suit the particular need. In recent years the following sort of remark has nearly always accompanied the request for information: ' —and please be sure to give some personal description of your own life leading up to the work, so as to form a background to why and how you started'. General questions are always: How did your Centre begin ? Can we start one like it ? What do you advise on delinquency ? etc. Well, this is my attempt at an answer. I have put in some private experiences of my own, here and in other parts of the book, in so far as they seem to affect the work, and why I gained my first sympathy for the outlaw or the chap in trouble. I hope they read as fairly objective reporting without sounding like a chip on the shoulder, for I don't really think I have one. I hope not. You can't help other people so well, if you have. It is very important to be more concerned with other people than yourself, but I have hinted at the opposition that one had to overcome at times, on occasion almost entirely alone, which once or twice nearly beat me to the ground.

A close colleague, on reading this book, whilst being kindly encouraging over

[1] Particular praise must go to Phyllis Lutley, who has almost made the work her life.

the general value of the text said: 'What I miss, in this book, is your struggle.' Well, maybe, but this is not a side upon which one wants to dwell. In the last twenty years, many battles in convincing and persuading have been won. I judged it unwise to risk unnecessary opening of old wounds, deeming it more tasteful as well as kinder to rejoice at any new friends won and to try to be constructive, giving the history in as honest a way as possible as it seemed to concern only the subject of spontaneous experience or the immediate personal events that appear to have led to the shaping of my feelings, attitudes, sympathies and determinations.

Apart from the many inquiries from abroad, from universities, social workers, Mental Health departments, doctors, teachers and those dealing with special branches of work with difficult children, I hope this section may be of some value to students of delinquency in this country, our own social workers, mental health officials and Home Office staff, as well as providing some bare bones for long essays and theses, which are the cause of so many inquiries from our own universities and colleges of education.

I would also like to encourage as many people as possible to start drama centres and arts centres, even quite small ones, for people to develop themselves, old and young, in their various ways, under trained and sympathetic guidance, also as places for constructive leisure time pursuit.

42. Grace and Outburst

Social drama with adolescents and personality training with shop girls, 1962–4

For some time now I had had a blitz on general manners and having been disappointed rather often over politeness in buses, on the roads and particularly in shops, when some pin-heeled damsel would go on talking to her companion about the dance that night instead of noticing your existence, I urged the development of Social Drama in secondary schools even more strongly and some tutors, who had been training with me, began to take it in teachers' training colleges in various parts of the country also.

In one secondary school for girls, in a fairly tough area, we had been going at it pretty hard. The social side of this was particularly for better relationships with parents. We had been creating scenes about getting into trouble for staying out late and the television people were interested. They took quite a lot of film of the girls and of myself creating various situations

with them. After one particularly violent outburst against her
'mother', one girl admitted that she thought eleven o'clock
was about right for girls of her age to be expected in. I generally
like to reverse rôles a bit and give a chance for the person, who
has 'burst out', to play their own mother or father afterwards,
so as to begin to build up sympathy with the parent and thereby possibly improve relationships by easing the strain. Playing
the other part helps a young person at least to consider another
view and you can help them with such questions as 'Why do
you think your parents said that?' 'Have you ever thought why
your parents want you in at night?' 'Did you consider that it
might really be their love for you that made them seem over
concerned? With this in mind, now try being them.' We then
had a splendid piece and the 'telly' men took that, though I'm
not sure that they showed it in the final programme. There
were some frightening pieces of me looking even more ugly
than usual and this was a pity, because we had just moved
from Whitmore House near the celebrated sign of 'Pink Green
only', divided our pony herd and gone to make our main home
nearer Chastleton in the Cotswolds, a former ancestral house of
my Whitmore forebears, and at least one member of our new
village had been put off.

After reversal of rôles, to my mind there should be a further
process, something which in general psychology I call 'the
hope process'. The hope process relevant to this school's work
was to play the *perfect* family with ideal parents. This bit was
splendid, but the television men did not use it. One of the girls
seemed to go even further at one point and become the ideal
child, for she rang up her father and asked to be picked up by
car at about 10.45 p.m. at the house where a boy had asked her
out. In discussion afterwards I asked whether she thought the
boy friend would mind father coming into it like that. 'Ah well,'
was the answer, 'ah well, see, I didn't know cem very well. First
night out.'

The school was visited again later, when the first students of
Newcastle University diploma course for Drama in Education
came to me for part of their training.

'—The project of a full time course was triggered off in

correspondence begun by Mr Peter Slade,' Professor Brian Stanley had written to Sir Lionel Russell in January 1963, and a little earlier, to myself: 'If we could refer to the time spent with you, that will show to those interested that you are our patron.' Now they were here and on this occasion a lot of real Child Art make-up had been used in lines and spots for men's faces and one story was about a jilted young man. The school attendance officer was also in it somehow. The Headmistress leaned over and said 'This is really true. It's him. I mean it's ours. It's him to the life.' Then one of those almost too perfect things happened. The school attendance officer walked in. It stopped the show for a minute but he was so beaming and delightful that all soon continued. What is more he had his own part of a play in his pocket that he was hoping to learn.

Still on the subject of social training, a request had come for me to pioneer some work on personality training in industry, in the Birmingham area, particularly with the retail trades and particularly bringing in my own methods. This was very dear to me, from my own earlier experiences and from working on it with medical men more and more, expecially after about 1937, when the results of my work in Worcestershire had been taken to London.

The Birmingham courses attracted a certain amount of attention. The *Guardian* gave an interesting write-up. They had also been the subject of a television programme and, earlier still, the studios had given me the honour of an invitation to appear in the series 'Midland Profile', but that was mostly to do with my ideas for centres, my dance work and the investigation I was making into drama with physically handicapped, for and in association with, Sue Ryder and Group Captain Cheshire. The 'personality' work is very difficult to talk about. In putting it over to firms, and after speaking to personnel officers, I wondered what on earth they would say, and how they would describe my efforts? Well, for the record, this is part of what they did say, in the official handout.

'The central core of the day's curriculum is a period of expression through movement . . . Through his philosophy that drama is a vital social force, he presents opportunities for the "playing-out" of situations involving antisocial feelings and builds up better relationships by practice in actual situations in daily life. By developing group sensitivity, his work aims also at a better understanding of other people. As far as industry is concerned, this may mean, not only between employees themselves but also between staff and public. Here the training is essentially practical. He has proved that his methods (which are used by psychologists and social workers here and abroad) can help to form balanced personalities, which make the best of their potential powers. He points out that never before has there been so much opportunity for young people, and that this brings with it an obligation for us to provide adequate emotional training.'

There followed some embarrassing words about international recognition, but I am glad they put in the last bit quoted, because in accepting equal opportunity in education we are at once concerned with a social situation, and unlike the old education, fighting bravely and well to teach subjects, we must now be concerned with total preparation for life. So, apart from schools, day release and further education must also be based on this premise.

Many people have asked me to write about the personality training, but so much of it is intuitive that one almost has to be there at the time; and it is very hard to make conscious afterwards what one thought and did. However, the best thing may be to include here parts of my report, in the hope that it may have some significance:

'My aim was to develop the students as much as one could in the time—helping them to be able to express themselves more adequately in movement and in speech, and to be less self-conscious, to wear clothes better, to appreciate being clean, to make better relationships, to know themselves better (the inner self as well as the more obvious outer one) to mature a little more quickly and surely, to notice everyday things with more of a poet's eye and to be unashamed of beauty. It is so sad that so many people are. But it always seemed to me that there were two sides to the training and other aspects within those two. I wanted the students, not only to get on better with each other and to be more attractive to their boy friends, to have, perhaps, easier relationships with parents, but to be useful and attractive personalities in their every day work—the Retail Trades—for their own happiness, for the pleasure of customers and (not at all to be forgotten) in order to do their best for their employer and the firm they served; the firm that had, after all, sent them on the course.

'My basic method would be along the lines of preparation for life, based on Social Drama in secondary schools, as many good teachers now take it. I have written on this at some length in my books *Child Drama* and *An Introduction to Child Drama*, so do not need to do so here.

'The next part of the method would be along the lines of my *Dramatherapy as an aid to becoming a Person;* certainly of one or two of the selected cases mentioned there, but only the very simplest, those most concerned with building confidence.

'Finally, something special for the Retail Trades. "What is it that a customer most wants when entering a good shop?"; I pondered long and long. "What is it that a good sales-woman should put over first of all? What do I often miss?" The word that came back at me from almost every angle was the word "Welcome". So "Welcome" became the keynote of my course. I suspect that every facet of daily life or industry has some psychological key word of this kind, but "welcome" must, or should be common to many. In other facets of life I use key words too—in schools, "happiness"; in dealing with delinquents, "non-judgment"; in psychological cases, "hope" and so on.

'Just as in life there are two main activities of personal and projected play, so in the personality there are the upper and outer qualities and the inner and deeper ones. Both are linked and to some extent interdependent. In other words, there is the practical every day life on the one side and the inner dream world on the other. I did not attempt to explain the detail of my process to any of those aiding, or administering the course, though they were at all times understanding and helpful. I undertook to develop the inner dream world side by side with the outer. Developing the outer consisted of graded situations of Social Drama based on good salesmanship through the welcoming of customers, the inner was concerned with developing themes of welcome for friends, visitors, someone loved, in dance drama or with words—situations that had an emotional quality and choice of appropriate behaviour. "Appropriate behaviour in a given situation" that I am always talking about. One example, I remember, concerned a girl who put an arm round the waist of, and squeezed, the "Lady Mayoress" in the same way as she would a friend coming to a Youth Club for the first time. She just had not thought out the difference. There are many kinds of welcome!

'Then there was the inner dream symbolism relating to service to others. For development in this, we had the giving of presents in dance, finding beloved objects and giving them away. Then slap back to intensely practical everyday situations again to make the thing real. The dance is of a special kind, which I have developed down the years, and used for training my professional actors years ago. It springs from improvisation, but differs from most other methods in that it sets out to develop the individual style that is noticeable in each person, first. When this has been opened up and established, techniques and vocabulary training are added at the personal pace of the individuals concerned. People need to be allowed at least a period to "scribble" in movement, to find themselves. Most other forms of dance training are applied the other way round—vocabulary and techniques first—but personal style so often suffers in the process. As one is concerned in this Day Release Course with personality, personal style is more important than technique, but this has its place also. Personal style is a thing of interest and beauty and, to my mind, should be preserved. Why all this? Well it looks a bit slick just in plain print but in actual fact, if you develop the inner dream in the correct way, as well as everyday efficiency, you get a sudden fusing of the inner and outer parts of yourself. It is this that brings a successful flowering of the personality. I have watched this happen time and time again during thirty-five years of work on it. Here is a list of a few other things included, besides dream-welcome and actual welcome. Learning to be calm. Learning not to fidget. Things about being clean. Repose at difficult moments. Consideration for customers' needs.

Putting up with rudeness and being polite back. Learning to hurry through crowds, carrying things without knocking into anyone. Quick response to questions. Learning to walk and move gracefully. Learning to speak unselfconsciously. . . .'

As a result of objective assessment and of Ministry Inspection I was told that, on the whole, it was felt that my part of the course was the part that should be developed.

In the next course there would be a few less sessions but closer together with shorter breaks and not beginning until after the January sales. The course would finish before the end of School Summer Term. Also it was to be less than a full day, if no academic subject and only 'emotional' ones were to be included. You can't stay stretched for too long at a time.

It was a difficult but exciting course in the end. Bad weather plagued us, but did not subdue. One of the complications was that Sylvia Demmery[1] had to leave for several weeks to represent me in Canada (where they have started a Canadian Child and Youth Drama Association), to lecture all over the country and appear on television, so I had to swing back into full action for the weeks that she was away, though I had managed previously to look in, or take some part, on most days.

Here are some notes of what Sylvia Demmery did on the first day with the Second Course, just to give an indication. I have expanded them a little where explanation seemed necessary.

'Start with short speeches from each girl on "What I do at work". Followed by dancing "any way you like to this music". Jazz. "Avoid knocking into each other". Sitting on chairs— Typing (mime to music). Collect typed papers together. Put them into files. Type letter to customer saying you have the things she ordered at your shop now (all of these mimed to music).

[1] One of my chief assistants and the person I had put as tutor in charge of the course. As interest in the work grows abroad, it becomes rather difficult to supply the tutors. After he had worked closely with me for several years, I had previously asked Brian Way if he would care to represent me which he kindly did, going twice to Canada and to Stockholm. He also went to the West Indies and South Africa. Miss Demmery has represented me lately in Germany also. I am grateful for her talented help, though her absence greatly affects the close teamwork we have tried to build.

[230]

"Read your replies to me" (actual words to be spoken in improvised dialogue).

'Movement again—painting, cleaning windows (for wide gestures). Then dancing in their own way again to see if gestures remained wide. As girls get bolder, expand distance. Relieve tension by suggesting: "Everybody near each other, chatting about the course in couples". Sensitivity exercise—In line, lifting one arm up with eyes closed, kneeling on one knee (trying to arrive at the same gesture).

'Finish with bringing beautiful gifts to goddess (dance drama to music). "Slowly. Think how to finish it off properly—Still".'

Excerpt from notes of my own work with them much later on in the course (May 21st 1963):

Self: 'A harder task now, Group work again. Five minutes only to make up a story and be ready to act it—this time your own and no help with ideas from me.'

Group 1, of Main Group A

'Here comes Caesar.' 'Oh, Caesar, help me over my brother.' Caesar refuses and gets stabbed (very good sincere acting and slow dignified walking).

Group 2

Baby pulls boiling water over itself.

Group 3

In a cafe ordering tea and cream cakes. (We had already done Social Drama on this theme.)

Man: 'Can you lend me a pound?'

Girl: 'I told you not to order all those things. I haven't got any money.' (It worked into a very good little plot and good speech by the least able group and by very shy individual speakers, which led me to ask: 'Is it easier to speak separately or in groups?')

Answer: 'In groups.'

Self: 'What does it do for you?'

Answer: 'Makes you more sensitive. Teaches you to cooperate better.'

Self: 'Yes, particularly, perhaps, if you are in a group you might not have chosen to join. More of a test then.'

Answers on same question from Main Group.

B: 'Group work makes you get to know people better.' 'Helps you to be less shy.' 'Helps you not to be afraid of speaking out like we was at school.' 'Helps you to think of the needs of other people.'

Whole group together

Self: 'Dance in your own way. Now two groups go through each other. Don't touch. Four groups through each other. Faster. Don't touch, think how maddening it is when people push you in Sales and in queues. Faster. Two groups and two other groups dance through each other from four corners of room. Somebody touched. Start again. Well done.'

I walk round being rude about dresses, hair, make-up or expression. Girls are expected to give clear, crisp, polite, quick replies. Suddenly when tension is almost unbearable, I change and give a compliment (laughter).

Self: 'Oh well done. That was very nicely answered. So few people can take a compliment gracefully. I have stretched you on purpose by becoming progressively more rude, so that you can put up with difficult customers or even (perhaps just) criticism of superiors. Don't go off into a sulk. Don't take umbrage. For compliments, think out little sentences to begin with. If you are shy, have some little answer ready. Certainly don't snub a man, he might not do it again, then the whole level of thought, of living relationship slides down a peg and life is all grey again.'

These are only very small glimpses of a long graded development based on where the girls 'appear to be in life', i.e. what is their stage of maturity, and where one hoped to get them to. It will be seen that speech and movement alternate: reality and dream go side by side and the whole goes forward by progressive stages. I have taken a big chance in writing down somewhat tender things, which sound all right when you are talking straight, very sincerely and honestly and quietly, and I apologise if they look a bit 'itsy' in cold print. One word I would like to say again. To take this work successfully you need a lot of training and experience.

In fact, one should avoid trying to be too clever, but for those not experienced, merely . . . 'Help young people not to sulk or

[232]

moon too much over the past, but to look forward and to prepare for the future. It is much more healthy.'

As for our own type of personality courses, are we succeeding?[1] We hope so, in some cases, perhaps in most; but one learns all the time. One thing is clear—judging from girls on both courses and from a fairly wide range of schools. We need much more practice in communication in the early years. But the words of one girl from the first course always remain with me as an expressive comment: 'At first I thought it was all rather silly, but then I was all tied in a knot and now I am not.' This is as good when said as read.

The reason why I started personality training many years ago, to help other people, is that I am appallingly shy myself.

COMMENT

Again, this is a specialised report for those interested, but many of us should be, for what these young people lacked in confidence and ability to express shows the serious need for more experience of spontaneity in secondary schooling—in movement, development of imagination and in speech.

In some places we had mixed groups to deal with and the young men admitted even more than the girls how they suffered from shyness of various kinds. Most of their remarks after the course showed a touching gratitude.

To my mind the success of this work lies largely in one's sensitivity in inventing the right amount of 'stretch' for personal courage in each little exercise becoming harder and more daring. Make one slip and an individual, or your whole group, can go right back and you have to start all over again.

I have taken many people in this work, down the years, from Directors of Industry, to salesmen representatives and from workers on the bench to teachers and parents who were under-functioning. A number of teachers built up well and were able to pass interviews and become Heads. I arranged a cruel test with one teacher, of a particularly formidable mock committee. He came out sweating and said: 'My goodness, Mr Slade, if I can get through that I can get through anything I should think. All that shouting in a funny accent from you, I couldn't have stood it a few weeks back.' We must have judged it right. He got through his next interview and has been a successful Head ever since.

There is great need for much more thought and development in this subject, for there are still some courses going under the heading of personality training

---

[1] Similar courses have been started in other places, but those which include my own method have been run at Week-ends—several in London, at Brighton, at Aylesbury and near Salisbury.

which are rather old-fashioned and offer little more than an opportunity to try a five-minute speech and discuss a little. Good though this may be, it is not nearly enough and is never likely to come anywhere *near* the necessary training for serious promotion of sales abroad or even for good relations in home industry. I think firms will have to have their own trainers in this work, and pay them well. I often wish I could be part of a national scheme for its development.

Meanwhile, some advantage is being taken of courses run at technical colleges. But the best colleges are aware of the necessity of much deeper thinking, which sections under Communication and Liberal Studies reveal by their high standard of observation and investigation. I was invited to describe some of the techniques of what I had been doing, and Miss Sylvia Demmery and I took an exhibition session of team teaching at the first National Conference Course on this subject, for tutors in technical colleges, which was held at Huddersfield. This kind of work could also be used with advantage in Secondary Education for Girls in connection with suggestions in the Newsom report. The comment on No. 43 contains somewhat similar advice for boys.

43. *Theatre-in-the-Round; Monsters and Atomic Treacle*

Unexpected dance session with apprentices in the Electrical Industry, Summer Course, 1964[1]

For fifteen years now, there has been an invitation to direct a National Summer School on drama. From time to time, it has had a fairly international flavour too. We have had numbers of people from abroad, including some of the first to start drama in Education in Sweden. We have moved round England quite a lot, having started at Wentworth Castle in Yorkshire, then gone to Abingdon and to Roehampton, but for several years now have been at Keele University. The course has had a good influence in bringing teachers to Birmingham.

As a number of colleges are becoming interested in Child Drama and tutors are asking what to do about it, it was proposed to try out a special Leaders Course from 1965 onwards.

It is a particular pleasure for me to have been directing courses at Keele after hearing the early proposals for the creation of the University, before leaving Staffordshire, and being now on a sub-committee is a matter for further interest.

[1] This report is reproduced as recorded at the time.

[234]

Sometimes there are other courses on at the same time as our own. We stare at each other a lot and the elders on each side exchange occasional pleasantries. Sometimes it is a warming sensation to have other courses there, but with proper English reserve, we do not often mix. They occasionally peer in at us, mostly at the dance work but, occasionally, at rehearsals, for mighty are the feature programme creations that we have done in the past, with sixty people or so charging in at the great doors of the hall and eighty people marching out to *El Cid* music, or *Henry IV* to the Planets. God has shouted from the balcony and Faustus faced Hell on the floor, Aeneas has sighted land at a black spot on the wall, we have danced on the lawn outside and waited for Godot in vain. Although these concoctions have been fun to build up at Keele, particular experiences for me were the first arena production of my radio play *St Patrick* and my arena production of *Our Town*, when the whole hall became the street, but both these were at Wentworth Castle.

Some years afterwards someone, whose face I knew, met me in the London office of Longmans Green. 'You won't remember me,' he said. True his name had gone but, 'Of course I do,' I said, it was bright as yesterday, 'You are "Father" in *Our Town*.' Some of his intonations are with me yet, particularly 'Where's my girl, where's my birthday girl?' The music we used at each repetition of the word 'star' is also with me. Strange how music stays—music and music of the tongue. I can still hear 'Up the rebels' in *The Moon and the Yellow River* and distinguish between Malvern Festival and Westminster, 'there's pennies on the floor' from *Strange Orchestra*, different at Q from the West End, Henry Oscar saying '. . . bear our fortunes in our own *strong arms*' and Sir George Robey's '. . . have ye levers to lift me being down?', the jibbering of Robert Speaight in *Journey's End*, the slow footsteps of W. B. Yeats when I found him, long overdue on stage, deep in contemplation in the gentleman's cloakroom at Nancy Price's Theatre, the other slow footsteps of the lover going actually downstairs banging the door at the bottom and walking away, away across the courtyard, in my own production of *The Living Room* in a Birmingham back street. Oh, the dagger of sound and its loved, clutched wound. Less loved is the sound of a distant train, as it came to me when a little boy prisoner at boarding school, the train to freedom. How well I understand this symbol in the Negro Blues. And finally the sizzle of the bomb burning holes in my face.

But tonight it is the fine summer of 1964 and the Course has been invited to the Theatre-in-the-Round in Newcastle-under-Lyme. The show was a feature programme, much like some of our own, but a terrifying indictment against early conditions in the Potteries. My partner[1] and I were sought out afterwards and treated almost like royalty. It was quite unexpected and generous in the extreme. One or two of the actors knew me, it seemed, or had heard me speak, and I remembered that, about four years earlier, another group of Theatre-in-the-Round had visited Birmingham and all of them, except one, had trained under me at one time or another. I suddenly felt very old. They looked so young and so healthy, like a young policeman who once stopped me with an unusually bad hand sign, and I was tired and unwisely said that it would do some of them good to come and do some movement. He started jumping up and down like a stag in the street and shouting 'what did you say?' Finally he calmed down, threatened me, uttered some unprintable remark and ended up with: 'I'd have you know I've been on a course for thirteen weeks'. I just looked at him, feeling deep compassion. Thirteen weeks. I had been doing movement for forty years and one learns every hour. I did not say that the Chief Constable in a nearby county had once been one of my strongest supporters, nor that I was on a committee at the time with his own Deputy Chief, where we had discussed such things as delinquency, politeness and better relationships with the public. Perhaps I looked a hundred-years-old, aged and hopeless, for he suddenly let me pass. I do not infer that the Theatre-in-the-Round people were anything like this. It was only energy and youth they shared with my clowning constable.

At last we got back to Keele and had promised to lay on a dance session. Although it was very late, some of our game young ones turned up. Towards the end of it, some young lads began to filter in and sat respectfully round the hall. They

[1] Miss Sylvia Demmery, who had been taking Dance for me at the Course that year.

were apprentices in the Electrical Industry on a course of their own. One of them said, 'Can we have a go?' I sighed inwardly a bit, as it was midnight already: 'Yes, all right.'

'We've been here before and joined in, another year. We're interested.'

'Oh good.'

'It's sort of free expression isn't it? We want to know how to do it, 'cos we've all been invited later in the week.'

'All?' I said slightly appalled, for it was a very big course. There must have been some chat in the bar.

'Yeah.'

Then they crowded round, about ten or fifteen perhaps, asking questions: 'Do you do what you like?' 'It's free expression, aint it?' 'I don't know what to do. How d'you know what ter do, like?'

Self: 'Well no. It's not quite free expression. There is a way of going about it. There is a technique, but you build it up slowly. It is based on the individual style of movement. Everyone has a style of their own. It is this that we build on. I may suggest *what* to do, this helps when you are unsure at the beginning, but I hardly ever show *how* to do it. That is left to you (except in certain exercises); that is your chance for individual style. During actual dance itself, you will have longish periods of doing things entirely by yourself, discovering how your body works and using your imagination.'

They began to undress a bit, coats came off, shoes came off, ties were thrown aside. It reminded me rather of preparing to enter a swimming bath and, for them, I suppose it was something like it. I noticed two members of B.B.C. Staff enter the gallery. They may remember better than I exactly what happened, but I think it was something like this:

Self: 'Now, we'll just make this a short burst, as it's pretty late and I shall go rather faster than usual. That is, I shall take the progress in quicker stages than one would normally. We shall do what might be covered in a much longer period, in a short burst, rather like a potted course.'

They laughed a bit and one or two nudged each other.

Self: 'Righto—now come on out onto the floor. Spread out.'

They dived into the swimming bath. No, they lowered themselves carefully into the water.

Self: 'Now, the first thing I want you to notice is the difference between men's work and girls'. You have seen the girls work and how they can become smooth and graceful and flowing. Don't copy that. To start with, think of yourselves as men. Try not to do any meaningless, wet sort of movements. Think of your muscles up from the tummy, over your chest and neck and along your arms and make them work. Just to get this right, pick up a chair.' (I picked one up myself.) 'You will notice, I am showing you this, because it is an elementary exercise and we are not beginning to create yet.'

(I raised the chair with my arms parallel to the ground and spread my feet wider.)

'Now, you do that. Now, take steps forward and throw the chair from side to side a bit to the extent of your arm, but still holding on with both hands. Good. Do you feel the pull all up the front of you and on the biceps and spine? (one or two slight gasps). Notice also how you are using the muscles above the knee. Right. Now the next step—walk forward like that, stamping a bit as you go. The upper muscles of the leg must take quite a lot of the strain.' (I showed them.) 'Now, I'm going to stop showing you. You do it by yourselves and try and find a group agreement in the stamping sound. Yes. Now, try moving about the room more. Don't all go round in a circle with your hearts to the centre, nearly everyone does that at first, carve a journey out for yourself and *go* there.'

After a short rest, I asked them to do the same again to the sound of my hand beating on a chair, a straight, slow bang in measured time beat. After this I began to turn it into a proper drumming rhythm and they began to move about in quite an interesting way. After a second or two—'good, now use the chairs in any way you like'. I complicated the rhythm further and made it louder. The building of the climax, of course, induced more exciting action. 'Splendid. Well done. All right still? Sure? Don't strain yourself at the beginning. You don't want to do this for too long. All right, one more burst. You've done this to

[238]

stamping and knocking, now to music.' I put a fast version of 'Honeysuckle Rose' on the gramophone and they fairly threw themselves about.

Self: 'There, see? You are dancing already. Fine, now get rid of your chairs, but don't just put them away. Dance them away; start to be neat about all action, involve it with the sound of the music. Ow! Horrible noise. Pick up chairs again and this time, put them down quietly, dead on the beat of the music.' (They did it well.) 'Dance on without them.' (The record ended.)

'Imagine there are apples on a high tree. You have to jump and get them off the topmost branches.' (I made a bang on a chair seat for each jump.) 'So far you have moved to my sounds. Now, you do it in your own time and I will try to accompany you. The feeling and process is different. Notice it.'

We went on then to the use of various weapons. We fought with imagined axes, and lances. It is useful, with lads, to have 'weapons of air', then they can't hurt each other so easily! But they *can* be energetic. Finally, we did sword play, (two of them had heard of the Three Musketeers). This was to Count Basie music. Now I wanted to work backwards to see 'Where they were in life'.

Self: 'Do you enjoy Christmas parties?'

Answer: 'Yes; sometimes; Yeah, on the whole; well, you know.'

Self: 'Well, you've got funny noses on. March about the place with them on. (The Golden Bullet—Count Basie.) You've got tall hats on; large tummies; you're skating; you're carrying hampers on your heads; you're juggling, like on telly. You're very clever jugglers, you can dance about too. Don't just stay in one spot. Now, throw clubs up and across the floor to a partner on the other side of the room.' (The record ended.) 'Now a bit of balancing. I'll put on slow music and I want you to move around; then lift up a leg in a difficult position and hold it there, pass a leg over the top of a chair but go on dancing as if it *isn't* difficult. Master yourselves.' (This to 'A Closed Walk' —Pete Fountain.)

After this we went on to some exercises that are 'old friends' that one has used down the years—exploring under the sea to 'Daphnis and Chloe' by Ravel, also a slow motion film of

[239]

overcoming a sea monster; meeting other monsters on other planets; coming more up to date by walking in atomic treacle. Pressing buttons that are difficult in space craft. Then pressing buttons quickly ('Honeysuckle Rose' again). 'Pressing buttons everywhere, all round you and above your head. Must get the spacecraft away somehow and back to earth. 'Quick, the monsters are coming.' (Time was then left for them to think out and feel the action.)

Self: 'Well done. Now a slow piece. ('Stranger on the Shore'—Acker Bilk). Try to get the feeling of it. You are carrying something. Not just keeping it for yourself. You are going to *give* it to someone you like.'

I think this symbol is very important to suggest to young people in these days of affluent materialism and, with delinquents, I go on to press home the idea of ultimately giving a beloved object to someone they *don't* like or even hate. For they hate nearly everyone, not knowing that it is their own image.

We also had a nightmare, rose up gracefully from being tied in a knot, explored the moon rather quickly (as it was nearly one in the morning) to 'Electronic Movements', by Dissevelt and Balton; then finally:

Self: 'Well, by now, you should have some ideas about what you might do and where to put the various bits of yourselves. Dance in any way you like. Use some of these ideas that we have tried or some of your own. Do anything you like.' ('Say it with Music', Les Brown version.) I stopped them once to make them aware that their wrists were a bit stiff. 'We all tend to be like hams from the elbow down, to start with. Try to use your wrists more. Make them more flexible. Fine. Now, the last bit, *Anything* you like to this, but really *work*.'

And they really did, to 'Honeysuckle Rose' again (Joe Turner and Albert Nicholas quartet). It is often interesting to use the same music again at the end, it gives an even clearer indication of any development or improvement that might have taken place during the session. 'Phew, Sir, I'm about dead.' 'Thank you very much, Sir.' 'That was terrific.'

Then one lad said very seriously and formally after some whispering: 'Sir, me and my mates want to thank you very

[240]

much. It was fabulous. Absolutely fab.' I said 'Oh good. It would be better if only a small number came again, but, if the whole course does finally come, at least you people will have some idea of what you might like to do. You won't be fumbling for ideas. I hope you won't feel shy any more, anyway. And don't forget, use your muscles. To dance well is very hard work. It's not a bit wet.'

One boy said: 'What I want to know is, why wasn't we taught this at school?' Another said: 'Yeah. It's, well, you know—it's geometric really, I mean.'

If that is their standard of what is good, what makes purpose for them, so be it. What was so exciting was that they had wanted to do it and had worked so well. It reminded me somehow of the old miner. If one can only find a way to show apparent purpose in the discovery or rediscovery of fun or of things beautiful, I believe there is a lot of hidden longing for it in people of every kind. Let no one think that any one kind of person is necessarily outside the pale.

COMMENT

For those interested in movement work, this description should be taken in conjunction with 'Dance Drama on the Downs' (No. 7) and 'Vienna and the Hungry Musician' (No. 34). It might be of value to those in further education, day release and technical colleges, but also to teachers in secondary modern and comprehensive schools. Personal experience also shows that the parts of the Newsom report suggesting so incontestably that young people should grow upwards and outwards from school and make contact with different environments are concerned here. I have had wonderful movement sessions and imaginative spontaneous experience for years with groups, including 'difficult' ones, by taking them just down the road to a hall or to my own Centre,[1] when they were not always very inspired or cooperative at school. This is sometimes (but not always) the easy way and is not in the least intended as criticism of many wonderful teachers who succeed also in the school environment.

A frequent question is: How do you start things off when your group has had hardly any or even no experience before?

Be absolutely clear about the fact that this evening is described at the outset as a potted course, there are then clear indications of how to start things off.

In general: 'Don't all go round in a circle with your hearts to the centre'—

[1] See 'Comparisons with Newsom', *Creative Drama*, vol. 3, no. 5.

nearly everyone of any age does this to start with.[1] At the time of writing this comment, I have very recently drawn attention to this at Hereford College of Education and at the University of York by letting people do things in their own way and then making it conscious for them and then referring to the ways and needs of children. I generally let people go round the room in their own way for quite a time before pointing it out, so that they get used to just moving first. But we are considering a shortened version of training in description No. 43, and the fact is therefore made conscious earlier than usual—'we shall do what might be covered in a much longer period'—'the progress in quicker stages than one would normally'.

In more precise answer to the question 'How do you start things off when . . ., it will be noticed that I use time beat, rhythm and climax in the way that children use it, or rather I offer the experience of childhood to those that have not quite had it like that or not enough of it. They do not of course, know this unless you tell them.

'Weapons of air', often used in exercises in secondary schools, particularly with lads. Going back further towards childhood: 'Well, you've got funny noses on'—this paragraph describes almost exactly what one would do for quick stimulation of the imagination in junior schools. Quick contrasts and change of ideas for swift adaptation tests.

As to 'exercises that are old friends', these are suggestions to aid spontaneous creation that one has used every now and again for years and years. Sometimes it brings a warm feeling of surprise to hear them re-enacted on radio now—or to see them on television, used by people who have either been trained in this work with me at one time or by the many that have been influenced in some distant way. I also think that people travelling along similar lines of discovery tend to find similar kinds of exercise for themselves. This is very exciting, for in a way they too then become friends without knowing it, discovering a similar truth about a larger truth of life itself.

44. Television, Ghosts and the City Council

A very mixed group of officials, students, approved school teachers, a nun and a diploma course, Martineau Centre, Birmingham, 1965

The characters in the spontaneous episode recorded here are purely imaginary and it is very unlikely that they will bear any likeness to living persons. The coincidence would be too astonishing and they are not intended to do so.

About this time I had been working very hard in my own

[1] See descriptions of shapes in my *Child Drama, An Introduction to Child Drama, Child Drama and its Value in Education* and *A Chance for Everyone* written with John Hudson.

Learning to walk downstairs without looking down. Personality course session with author, YWCA, Dinton Park, 1964

Above: the author deep
in discussion with a pony
by breathing into its nose

Left: welcome to new
and old friends from
abroad with Miss P
Lutley, first
International Children's
Theatre Conference,
London, 1964

city, visiting schools, virtually running an evening institute at the Drama Centre, having my Children's Theatre production filmed, starting and directing a new theatre training course for adults, advising on a new personality training course for school leavers and undertaking the training of students from the second Newcastle University Diploma Course for 'Drama in Education', who were visiting for their period of several weeks. I had also been granted leave to lecture at Oxford and Northampton, had visited Coventry on the way home to discuss their Belgrade scheme and had had an exciting reception at an evening run by Keele University, when a hundred were first expected and over five hundred turned up for my talk, sitting all over the hall and all over the stage so that one almost had to hang like a battered Christmas decoration from a nail on one side of the proscenium arch in order to speak at all. But this was after a splendid dinner and nothing like that mattered.

I was also starting a new series on Monday afternoons in which two Home Office courses were joining, and a description of one of these occasions has been chosen, first so that it can be written now and finished, whilst fresh in mind, second because it seems to round off the book, lastly and perhaps most important of all, it includes so many different types of people and a number of different professions, all of whom happened to come together on that afternoon. It is symbolic somehow of the whole book, which indicates a surprising number of different people, sometimes those one would never have expected, who have tried out, been cajoled into, or voluntarily flung themselves into spontaneous experiences. My mind immediately sees groups of students in innumerable training colleges, women's clubs, a group of police, service units, monks, many nuns, old men's clubs, mental patients, sad withered little children in hospitals, gay brave people 'dancing' in wheel chairs, blind people 'seeing' gardens to Debussy, deaf people 'hearing' jazz to their finger beats and footsteps, people with no arms 'juggling' with clubs, a particular bunch of directors of industry, young actors, young outlaws, nurses, groups in community centres, many teachers from different lands and of course, many many children—they pass in a sort of filmic cavalcade as I write.

This afternoon there were Home Office staff, students from many walks of life preparing for residential child care, teachers, special schools representatives, teachers of E.S.N. and approved schools, a nun; and I had invited students from the second Newcastle Diploma Course for 'Drama in Education' to join us also. There may have been others, that have not been mentioned. There were over forty in all.

Notes kindly taken by one of the Diploma Group say that I started by outlining general attitudes of children to life, some aspects of their emotional need, the situation of the outlaw in life and his reactions to normality, and the general patterns of man's behaviour as evidenced in Child Drama.

I gave simple examples of therapy through drama and outlined my own experience in this line, for people often ask me about it—how it started by my having to overcome my own problems and background, the development of my drama-athletic-movement, it's testing abroad, the remarkable fortune of meeting certain minds and learning from them at Bonn University, further testing with backward children in England, working as a lay therapist with doctors and analysts, speaking on dramatherapy at the British Medical Institute, becoming a founder member of a Jungian Society in London, being invited to take courses for medical staff, having speeches published and finally having cases sent to me.

I played a record of children acting out fear of the dentist.

Then we started practical work. I asked each one of them to imagine they were a conductor and that the Birmingham Orchestra was in the middle of the room. 'Wonderful Orchestra, wonderful conductor. Conduct!' I put on some music. Most of them waved a bit and talked to a neighbour or laughed a bit.

Self: 'Good. Notice how you all suddenly wanted to talk, on having an unusual experience. The children in your charge will do the same. Now you understand how it feels, don't be angry with them, will you. You can get them quiet again.'

The next exercise was buying and selling in pairs. I went round asking what they were selling—it was mostly pens. The imagination was not moving very fast yet. They had used pens to conduct the orchestra, so pens they were selling: example of what I mean about discovering 'where they are in life'. I made it conscious for them and told them of it kindly, then said: 'Remember this, for children do the same thing. If one had the idea of food, others will hear it and have chops, pudding, jelly babies etc.—all eats, they tend to seize on the nearest and easiest ideas at first, just as you did. If you are actually asking for ideas and get copying, it is worth going close to some children and letting them whisper it. The others can't copy then.[1] Now—swap round; other person buy, other sell—and no pens!' I questioned some of the pairs, after a time, so that we could all hear what had been done. One was dealing with a child buying sweets. We went into the shopman's behaviour and discussed it. Others were asked. One demonstrated a watch, another a bracelet. I asked them questions about these to develop their flow of words in an imagined situation. Another was making a big land deal. We discussed that and then I said: 'All right, what will we do with such a man?' Some one called out 'bump him off.'

Self: 'Yes. We could do that. If you were developing this play in your own homes or groups, you could allow that, to play out telly. Or you could lead them *away* from bumping off, according to your judgment of their present needs. But just to let off steam, let's "bump off" in groups. Then in one large one. Don't actually touch the victim.'

Some good strong semi-stylised death blows began to form up. Later, I said: 'Notice that, when allowed to go on with bigger numbers than pairs, you fell into groups of about half a dozen. Children do just the same. What was the shape of that group I joined—Yes, a circle. Why? Because that is the shape, which humans make when cooperating and absorbed in play. They didn't even notice me joining them, did they? They were so absorbed. Children can be the same. Notice that they spoke so low, we couldn't hear them. Children at first are just the same. Now I am going to make the process conscious for you. Open out the circle, speak up across the wider space, half remember us watching. We want to share the ideas. With children say "Share the ideas"; they get less self-conscious that way. For us, as adults, note at the same time that this louder talking is to

[1] This suggestion was first contributed by Jack Beckett.

do with "attack", it is now more acceptable, more like theatre-in-the-round, less like just any old group activity or improvisation.'

We practised that a bit, then one gang, it turned out, was asking to buy ties for a pop group called 'The Gall Stones'. I made a mental note of it. After this I asked them to sit and allowed a good declimax; then asked them to pick up a musical instrument and play it (to St Louis Blues). They mimed this fairly well.

Self: 'Fine. Now exchange with someone across the room and see they know how to play your instrument!'

We then chose a band leader and they marched round after him.

Self: 'Now it just happens that it is the Lord Mayor's birthday (an imaginary Lord Mayor, of course, not the real one), and I heard at lunch time that the City Council is going to be televised. This is rather like Living Newspaper, but we are doing it even before it gets into the papers, perhaps. First of all—will *you* bunch go up onto the stage and start a discussion about it in the Council House. (A throng of men leaped forward.) Oh and one or two lady councillors—thank you. Must keep your end up you know.'

A quite good discussion followed but developed quite away from the subject.

Self: 'Good. Then the TV men came.'

A wonderful gang started to function. One man used a chair as a camera in a most serious and delightful way, doing a thoroughly professional job, wheeling in for a close-up.

Self: 'Fine. Now let's just repeat a little of that and to end up with, let's have the television interrupted by the rest of you being the band again and playing in Victoria Square, holding up all the traffic, but determined to pay respects for the Lord Mayor's birthday—er, My Lord Mayor, could you keep quiet a second —thanks. Band, don't come up New Street and across the square from the Post Office until you hear me fade in the music softly —and *don't* bump into Queen Victoria's statue, will you! Mayor! Where is he? Oh, there you are. My Lord Mayor, when you hear the band, go out onto the balcony, will you, and say something really nice to them? They are risking death, even imprisonment and endorsement of pedestrian licences, standing there playing like that, I should think.'

Off went the discussion in Council again, everything was tense and set; the noise mounted; one lady was thumping on the Council House table; the telly men moved slowly in; I faded in St Louis Blues softly, up, up; the band appeared up New Street, all right, wheeled from the south, northwards to the Council House, they were brilliant and very absorbed. No one disturbed them. 'Now, my Lord Mayor,' I cried, for he was so engrossed in Council House matters that the band was quite unheard. He looked up astonished, rose, turned magnificently, and tottered out of the windows, through the proscenium arch and on to the balcony on a rather shaky table. The band stopped. There was a terrible silence. So I said '. . . and the Lord Mayor wanted to thank them, so he said . . .'. Still a silence.

The Lord Mayor (suddenly): 'Oh heck, I've completely dried up—er—thank you.' (Then, coming out of character and as himself, to Band): 'Go away.'

There was a roar of joy and I faded up Band Music loud. They retired abashed but unbroken and dispersed as it were towards Paradise Street.

Self: 'All right. Bad luck. Rather a short speech, Lord Mayor, but sincere wasn't it! Council, come out into the Square a moment. Some of it was very good.'

Lord Mayor: 'I say. If it's my birthday, can't we have a sherry or something?'

Self: 'Yes, good idea, come down off the steps, across there and over to the bar—there.'

I asked the Principal in charge of the course to pour out drinks, which she did in a most charming manner. We found one phrase of music, which sounded like elbows going up higher by jerks, so we followed sherry by everyone drinking beer, to polish the mime and try to 'feel' what the sound suggested. Many good pints were swallowed that day.

Self: 'Oh fine. Well done. Now—the "Gall Stones". (I wanted to bring this idea in again.) You can come and play to us a bit in the Square. It is evening and we need different music.' (They did, to 'I get around'.)

[247]

I faded down the music and we had a wonderful declimax, about half a minute of complete silence (to show them how to induce moments of emotional peace for unhappy children).

Self (very quietly): 'Right. . . . Now something a little different. We might want to push home a message about not drinking before driving and so—it was very sad that some motorists, who had been drinking all those beers, drove too fast past the Museum and into some people in the Square.'

They were well in it now; some 'cars' immediately rushed forward without further direction and pedestrians toppled. We repeated this a bit and got another good declimax on leaving the bodies in the Square. A giggle or two at first, but we went on until it became sincere.

Self: 'The ghosts of the dead people got up and tried to drink beer, but the motorists had done their job and they weren't very successful—(a 45 speed record played at 33 gave the right feeling for this)—Poor ghosts, they were probably trying to help the anti-litter campaign too, by getting up off the ground—you're doing a nice dance though—and the ghosts faded away.'

Music was faded slowly. Complete silence again after the ghosts had backed to their chairs.

Self (picking up the scene): 'Good. Now, everyone enjoyed living in Birmingham so much, because of the Orchestra, the theatres and the wonderful *courses* (laughter) we run, that they all danced in the Square to show how happy they were—yes—everyone.' I faded up 'I get around' loud.

'Fine. But I think you could do even better. I want you to use arms and hands, but, notice, I don't shout at you in an old fashioned way "no, no, that's all wrong wrong, your hand movements are rotten" (very loud). (There was laughter.) You see that is not exactly inspiring. (More laughter. They obviously saw the point.) But I will ask you to hold up large footballs and jugs in each hand and juggle a bit with them—(Music again)—lovely, now you are all using your arms, and hands, because there is a *purpose* in it. (I stopped the music.) This would be just the same for children too. It all develops slowly. There is no hurry, when taking this work, don't try to get in too much at a time. Take development step by step. Don't show off to

[248]

anyone inspecting the work. The greatest temptation is to try and get quick results. Don't rush on to a full story too quickly. Even experienced tutors often make this mistake. They do it to get quick results, often without thinking, and leave out many steps necessary to the child. Don't forget—for a child, there is *no hurry*. For a disturbed, unhappy or delinquent child you *can't* hurry. If you are taking the work right, giving them opportunity for expression, they won't let you hurry. You can sometimes take the work at a fast rate. That is different. That is a matter of handling. It may help discipline. It is quite different from hurrying over separate steps in development of the individual. Fine. Now, we have come through a number of exercises. First you were selfconscious; then more absorbed; then sometimes quite unconscious of being watched; then I slowly made you conscious again, for we are not here just to help ourselves —though partly—but to prepare to help other people. We must experience it ourselves but also become aware of the processes, so as to be able to use this work wisely too. Now, just to finish —forget all about me, if you can. No directions from "teacher". And just enjoy yourselves in any way you like. If you succeed think how you can bring that joy to other people.' I faded in 'I get around' at normal speed and left it up high until the end, while they danced hard, improvising in various ways, then faded down for a long declimax and pin drop silence.

Self (very quietly): 'Right. . . . Well thank you very much. Thank you for your cooperation. Thank you for this afternoon. Thank you all for a gay, wonderful time.'

The Lord Mayor and some councillors rushed up: 'That was terrific', 'That declimax business is wonderful. It was a real experience. It gives a complete feeling of discipline, doesn't it.' A lady councillor thanked me. A robust gentleman beamed (surely an Alderman); 'I thoroughly enjoyed that.'

Lord Mayor: 'It was grand. I've never done anything like this before in my life. You know, I completely dried up on the balcony.'

Self: 'Never mind, you were going hot stuff in the Council House and that's where you need to talk your best!'

Lord Mayor: 'Oh. Was I all right, then?'

[249]

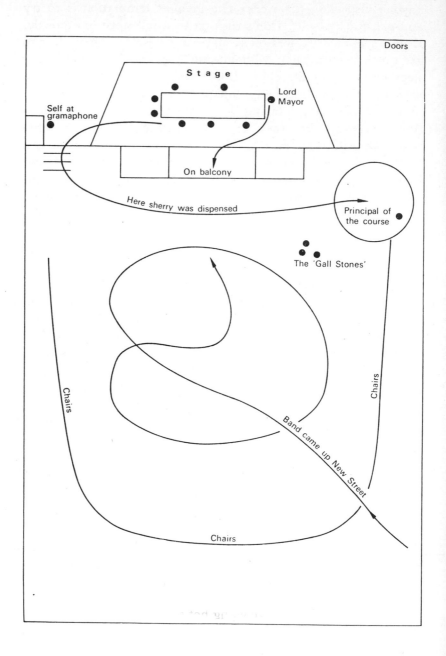

Self: 'My Lord Mayor, I feel sure the real City Fathers would have been proud of you.'

COMMENT

This description also gives part of the answer to questions about drama used as therapy or prevention of unhappiness and delinquency.

It may also help over 'How do you start things off?' At times, it will be noticed that I am keeping a firm hand and taking things at a fair pace in order to obtain first discipline, but also using things as they arise.

The methods used in general would be appropriate for visiting certain clubs too and also colleges of education.

'Buying and selling in pairs' can be used at almost any age with any group, so it is appropriate to find it again, as one exercise, in this last report. 'Remember this, for children do the same thing' is an example of reference back to the needs of the child after taking exercises at adult level, most important for nurses, teachers and Home Office staff. I always use something of this technique on courses at universities and colleges of education. It helps to give personal living experience and the detail of approach is more precise. I think people often need this help. They are generally grateful for it. 'There was a terrible silence, so I said . . . — and the Lord Mayor wanted to thank them, so he said . . .': this is the sort of way you can often help a thing along, by keeping in tune and in sympathy with the creation but adding just the right remark. Don't stop everything, try to keep things going. However, on this occasion it didn't work and I thought the reader, if only for encouragement, would like me to record in this last report a crashing failure. However, the atmosphere was not spoiled. By treating the situation as 'where he was in life' and not being abashed (for drying up can happen to almost anyone) everything continued soon afterwards with the minimum of embarrassment.

'The greatest temptation is to try and get quick results. This is so important to remember. Our chief task is to help the people we are taking, not to show off oneself. Think what is really best for *them* and the balance of behaviour, pace of session, opportunity, discovery, pleasure and sometimes deep learning is more likely to arrive correctly. A well led group, particularly of those who may later guide others, is something to aim at through experience. The experience may ultimately affect many people. Although it may be fun or even at times a great joy, it is also serious fun; it is often a strain for with it goes a sense of deep responsibility.' Perhaps it is the depth of this feeling underneath the surface or behind the scene which turns an otherwise somewhat inconsequent happening, on almost any course, into a deep experience of spontaneity. To anyone who comes to me, this is what I try to give.

Where now?

Attitudes and conditions have changed a good deal in the last few years and even more in the last ten. It is over ten years now since an H.M.I. said: 'Of course, you know you are ten years before your time', and another one said 'Oh no, much more'. I laughed and answered, 'Oh dear, that sounds as if one came down and cooked an egg for someone's breakfast but they didn't turn up to eat it till its great-grandson had hatched out. I wouldn't really know, but it might explain why living has always seemed so difficult.'

But one has lived long enough to see youngsters who came as shy Junior children to Rea Street Centre begin to make relationships and come right through to become leading adult actors in the Theatre for Children performances; to see other established theatre companies doing splendid work for young and old alike; to see old opponents come to agree; to see imaginative work begin to percolate into colleges of education for teachers, with the dangerous words Child Drama included in the syllabus; to be accepted as a university examiner; to be invited by county medical officers to lecture at mental health courses; to discover Americans describing in their books what I mean; and to have had some small influence in the starting of the first University Diploma course for Drama in Education. In recent years it has been my pleasure to be a speaker at exciting university conferences on newer ways of teaching English; to see, with surprise, the diagram[1] of one of my last productions on a slide shown by a

---

[1] Diagram contained now also in *Secondary School Design* (*Drama and Music*), Department of Education and Science, Bulletin no. 30, page 23.

Department of Education lecturer at the Royal Institute of British Architects; to see and hear programmes of Child Drama on television and radio; and to receive news of organisations, based on my work, starting in other lands. A Unesco Conference has already stated: 'National governments should encourage the use of creative dramatics throughout all educational establishments.' Perhaps, therefore, the most personal pleasure for me was to be chosen as chairman for the Creative Dramatics section of the first International Conference on Theatre for Children, which took place in London in 1964 at the Commonwealth Institute. At this conference I could not help being deeply touched that representatives asked me to visit so many countries and that people came up to me with messages of goodwill from all over the world, thanking me for my writings and my work. One of the French group demanded quite angrily when my book was going to be translated into their language.

I had had a staff member of Warsaw University, who had made a special effort to see me when in England, but now a group from Russia came up to me with a message from a leading figure in Moscow. And an old Professor from Leningrad said, with tears in his eyes: 'and if that person thinks that your book is wonderful then I should read it too.' I was terribly moved. I felt, somehow, deeply humble. 'I will send you one,' I said, 'I'll send you both one.' The former rebel had come, as it were, in the context of this present book, from kitchen to conference table.

Finally, the Birmingham Education Committee has done me the honour to establish a Certificate Course in Child Drama under my direction.

For my own part, I am quite convinced that not only can spontaneous drama aid young individuals to evolve a balanced personality, but that a wider application of imaginative creative work amongst adults would aid them to adjust themselves socially to a group with greater ease and find thereby more brotherly contentment. Imaginative drama could play a considerable part in establishing understanding of other attitudes and peoples and sympathy amongst nations.

For ourselves, creative doing can work off the daily round and occasionally help us back to the joy of former days. Some of

us have missed our childhood, and can find it again in seriousness and fun. We can make up for childhood lost. We can refind
it again to help our children too. We forget so easily. So, although
this book was partly intended to give real but simple glimpses
of things actually created by adults and youth, descriptions of
children have been included too. Let no one mistake the recognition and admission of the child in us for babyishness. It produces such things as the British humour, which keeps us going
in the darkest hour and prompts us to treat a massive defeat as
our finest victory. Paradoxically, to say occasionally 'how d'you
do' to the child within us can lead to maturity. We need to find
ways of practising events in life before they occur, to blow off
steam, to lose self-consciousness and find the art of communication. It is hard to communicate: in the home, in the school, in
the office and on the factory floor. We are all apt to live our
lives at different levels and never really meet each other.

We are living in an age when greater leisure is expected, when
many old patterns of behaviour and society have gone. We see
vast sums beginning to be suggested for Children's Theatre and
the Arts, and a Minister advocating Arts Centres, large and
small, for the people to be gay—shades of Worcestershire and
Rea Street.

I hope this book may help students with the eternal problem
of their theses.

It will be noticed that the creations include a number of recurring symbols. Hero and heroine, boy–girl relationships, come into
almost every one. But that is as it should be, for we must take
people where and as they are. These symbols are, after all, basic
to all relationships, indeed there could be no society without
them. So of course they come into all primitive or polished
forms of creativity. It is how we treat them, treat each other,
that matters. We cannot pretend masculine and feminine do not
exist, even in an age of greater equality. These descriptions and
the simple histories at the end of the book, make fact and fantasy
combined, one being as important as the other; they are neither
concerned with pride nor assumed humility but only with the
truth. My attempt in thus describing is therefore based on honesty.

I hope, then, that the reader will forgive this rather personal account, but I believe it is important for mankind to clutch the Golden Hour, be grateful and savour it well. And I wanted to set it all down while my heart was still warm, in the hope that, with more leisure, people in future years might not forget nor be ashamed of happiness, lest social patterns, forced upon us by an overcrowded world, might stifle that most precious gift—our individuality.

Appendix 1

A Short History based upon a Report first produced on request for Birmingham Education Committee in 1957

One of my first experiences in 1947 in Birmingham was to be invited to meet the whole of the Ministry Drama Panel and establish what attitude I had to the work. There seemed to be great relief on the part of the Chairman and some others that it was not my intention to impose full scale theatre on young children and I was asked to develop my plans for the encouragement of dramatic play. The teachers themselves appeared to be in two sharply opposed camps. On one side were those who believed basically in dramatic play, but did not always know how to make it constructive. Some had been made aware of its existence in part by A. L. Stone's work at Steward Street Junior School and by the elaboration of it by K. R. Scott, his successor. On the other side were those who only thought in terms of formal theatre, but a few understood the meaning of dance drama.

Judging from work put on at the first Juvenile Dramatic Festival, the general attitude might be termed stiff and at times the content was quite unsuitable for the younger child. Speech was trite and unreal, and movement poor. The older children were better. But work I had seen in schools held more promise. Here and there were younger teachers trying to do imaginative work and valuable education, but as yet without a champion. Other experienced teachers and Heads were, in places, doing fine work.

In 1947 I was called to put forward certain principles on Drama in Education at National Level, as part of my work on the Advisory Committee of Theatre News Service. It was to have great repercussions on the work in Birmingham and some elsewhere. This Conference was held at the Y.M.C.A., London, and I understand it may be the one referred to at the beginning of the book *Leap to Life* by Alan Garrard and John Wiles. Garrard went away with the thoughts that I had been asked to put forward. Brian Way, Director of West of England Children's

[257]

Theatre met me then and joined forces. Members of the Ministry appeared concerned over the general lack of consideration for Child Values shown by many delegates and urged me to continue my efforts. Mr Way came up and talked things over at great length. Later he returned to work with me in Birmingham as being the centre of new ideas in the Children's Theatre World. Although he says he was greatly influenced by our work and training here, he brought valuable experience and many good ideas with him.

In 1948 came the historic Bonnington Conference in London at which, again, I was asked to put forward general ideas, but to suggest also a firm premise for Drama in Education as a whole. The National Committee of the Theatre News Service, London University and the Ministry were behind me in this, and most representatives from training colleges appeared to agree in general terms. But the suggestions were too revolutionary for theatre people as a whole. There was due respect on each side, but a complete split in opinion.[1] (The detail is now carefully set down in Coggin's *Drama and Education*.)

During my first year I had already had considerable contact with the Educational Drama Association in Birmingham, as it was in the terms of my appointment that I should do so. They had been running a Children's Theatre, but some members also had many views similar to my own on drama as a whole.

After the Bonnington Conference letters started to come in from all over the country, at first strongly critical, followed suddenly by more and more strongly supporting my general views and asking whether I would take some leadership as far as education was concerned. I did not really wish to do so, but pressure became so strong that I went up to consult with the Chairman of the Drama Panel and other members of the Ministry of Education. The feeling and advice at that time was that someone ought to do something and I was encouraged to go ahead. I was unsure whether to start some quite new Association or to try to work through one that already existed. In Birmingham the Educational Drama Association was very near what was needed. Considerable discussion followed. I was not entirely happy about some sides of this. Finally, I was invited to become their Director; I still hesitated but in the end, rightly or wrongly, deemed it more democratic to work with what existed, if that were possible, rather than to start something new. I accordingly amalgamated the Educational Drama Training Associa-

[1] Fortunately this has been almost entirely healed now, for, in recent years, many people have come to agree with me and much training and theatre presentation has changed.

[258]

tion (already under my direction) and the Birmingham Educational Drama Association, but because of the situation in the country as a whole, the Educational Drama Association rapidly became a national organisation because it could not help itself. But it is proud to have retained its headquarters and the main part of its research in Birmingham, and the National Committee is really the Birmingham Committee. Indeed, at the time of writing, the H.Q. is still in the same school at Rea Street that it used before my appointment. But since then the Drama Centre has evolved there, which, though humble in many aspects, has been visited by enthusiasts from all over the world.

At the Educational Drama Association Birthday Party that summer, Sir Peter Innes and Mr Lionel Russell[1] were amongst those present. Mr Russell in his speech stated that he was glad the Association now intended to give some lead in the matter of training.

In the same year (1948) a speech of mine was printed in full in *Theatre in Education* and later published by them in two forms of pamphlet. It was called *Acting in the Round* and was sent to every school in this City. This was rather shock tactics and it caused a considerable stir.

I had tried before this, several times, to run a course in Birmingham under the L.E.A. on Drama, but had been told on each occasion that the time was not appropriate. But the demand for one was rising. Remembering Mr Russell's words I accordingly decided that we could not wait for ever and made the experiment of running one through the Educational Drama Association. The result was 400 applications. We accepted the lot, and organised a series of talks, with all the teachers grouped in arena form in Rea Street School, as being the best way to begin explaining 'acting in the round'.

This was followed by numerous courses run at Rea Street. Some were under the L.E.A. 'in conjunction' with the Educational Drama Association, particularly the first courses for Tutors in Further Education. Some were entirely under the Voluntary Association. Most of these have been so successful that it has so far proved the best way of running courses for teachers and capturing their enthusiasm in a 'newish' subject. Many Drama advisers have found this, and in some places the voluntary pioneer work is continued to this day. London is working very closely with its Voluntary Associations too.

At this time I set about completing my research into what I was convinced to be the art of Child Drama, and encouraged various things which have in part affected education.

[1] Now Sir Lionel.

1. That elaborate stages were not necessary or correct for drama in junior schools, but that rostrum blocks aided Child Drama. (I wrote a report of this as part of my work on the Ministry National Working Party on Drama. When Ministry Building Bulletin No. 1 came out, a number of these ideas were in that too.)
2. That there should be some spotlights in junior schools, set up so as to be movable and to light 'polished' improvisations, flowing over the whole floor space, based on the great literary stories of the world. (A pamphlet was written on this too, and published by the Educational Drama Association.) So far as is known, this is the first serious attempt (a) to find a bridge between Child Drama and the Adult Theatre; (b) to provide proper equipment for the needs of older children in Junior schools. Some of the newer schools have this equipment and it is something which Birmingham started and which visitors ask to see.
3. That Senior Schools should not only have basic stage lighting equipment, but rostrum blocks or steps in front of the stage. There should also be spotlights in the body of the hall so that actors might flow out and away from the stage and still be lit. (See theory and detailed reports in *Child Drama*.) Alternatively, young actors might choose the arena form of acting and could now do so. I tried to provide for both traditional and 'new' forms of theatre. Again, I believe we were the first Authority to put this scheme forward, and although many of our schools are equipped with this lighting (sometimes individually controlled so that children can learn to control light themselves and work in a team) we are way behind in rostrum blocks. Other authorities have taken the ideas I put forward in 1932, 1937, 1945, 1947, and 1948 and developed them much better than we have.

CHILDREN'S THEATRE

4. My hope was to have an Amateur Children's Theatre Group in Birmingham run on the lines of my former professional companies. There were two groups that interested me. The Phoenix Players, a band of teachers from the Emergency Training College, who presented plays, but trained on improvisation methods; the Children's Theatre Players of the Educational Drama Association—who were acting plays in schools before I came. I offered to give them training in modern theatre methods and to explain the changes one might make in presentation, i.e. to present plays in the shapes that children use in their own play.

    Cinderella and *A Chinese Story* were the first two of their plays which

[260]

I had any influence over. Both these were produced so as to be presented in part, or wholly, in arena form. Cinderella was played amongst and between, the beds at the Children's Hospital.

A Shakespeare show was rehearsed, but withdrawn. Meanwhile, Mr Russell had taken a personal interest in my proposal to have a Drama Centre for children to play in and as a permanent Theatre Workshop. It was almost entirely due to him that we finally established the first Drama Centre of its kind at Rea Street (now Reaside) School, with special lighting arrangements in two halls to suit Child Drama or modern adult theatre. My first production here after the instalment of equipment and movable dimmer board was *A Midsummer Night's Dream*, since when I have run an almost permanent Theatre Course every Wednesday in every term for teachers to experience theatre. Subjects covered are: speech, poetry, movement, improvisation, acting, creative music, improvised dance, social drama and production. Subsequently, we have produced the following plays which have been presented to members of selected schools so as to further their particular programme in drama:

Cheapside by Parish (an intimate three-cornered production) in the small hall, selected for a report to Unesco. It was associated with a short talk on period furniture that I had brought for the play.

The Interlude of Youth, an old morality play (Avenue arena).

This Way to the Tomb, Duncan, lead taken by Brian Way (first known arena production).

Bonaventure (a half circle production in small hall).

What is Monarchy (Avenue arena, large hall). My feature programme written for the Coronation, about the common man's view of royalty from Henry IV to Elizabeth II (also subject of a Unesco report).

St Patrick, P. Slade (large arena).

The Shoemaker's Wife, Lorca (middle arena).

The Story of Katherine Parr (Avenue arena).

Strange Orchestra, R. Ackland (for adults only). The first known intimate diagonal arena production (small hall).

Since then, other plays have been produced and in intimate style: *The Old Ladies, After October, The Living Room, Private Lives, The Chalk Garden, Ring Round the Moon, Look Back in Anger*.

Lazybones and the Humbug Factory, an improvisation presented to juniors and infants in circular form and at times including all the audience as actors. (Many others have since been produced on these lines.)

[261]

As the general ideas of Child Drama expanded it was decided to start a Children's evening on Tuesday in term time at Rea Street. I obtained voluntary services for this and a staff has been present every Tuesday for the last six[1] years or so, accepting children from Infant to Youth Club age. At its height we had between 80 and 100 or more children attending every Tuesday. The idea was to have one place where children could come and play in their own manner, blow off steam and learn the elements of Theatre with sympathetic grown-ups. It would form a sort of pretraining to feed the adult group. Thus we could go right through from Juniors to young adulthood, all learning and training on the same set of basic principles. The idea is being enquired about from Lincolnshire, Canada, America, New Zealand, Australia, South Africa and London. There is already a 'Rea Street' in Abyssinia started by a member of the Educational Drama Association and visited by the Emperor.[2] Pictures and accounts have appeared in *Creative Drama*.

RESEARCH

At this Drama Centre there has been careful observation, not only of Child Drama, but study of emotional disturbance and quite a piece of research on delinquency. At one period we were dealing with a very violent lot. Reports on this work have been asked for, and sent to Unesco and details have been supplied on dramatherapy to the British Centre of the International Theatre Institute. Photographs of children acting in Birmingham Schools in their own manner have appeared in *World Theatre*, Children's Theatre Companies based on our Birmingham Centre Group have started in Western Australia, near Sydney, in New Zealand, and, nearer home, in Worcester and London. Brian Way's professional companies are now trained on similar methods to my own. Mention of Birmingham Drama Centre is also made in Coggin's *Drama and Education*, together with some results of research.

In 1954 the book *Child Drama* was finally published, and some individuals and organisations presented a special copy of it to the Queen, as being an outstanding piece of research technically finished in the year of Her Majesty's Coronation. The majority of, though not all, the reports in this book are on Birmingham Schools; most of the diagrams are of our work and nearly all the photographs are of our children.

Since this publication we have had visitors to Birmingham Schools, and particularly to the Drama Centre from all over the world, not only

[1] Many more years now.
[2] The person has now left.

teachers, but professors, actors, architects, psychologists, athletes, H.M.I.s, administrators and parents.[1]

SOME RESULTS OF THE WORK

(a) The Children's Evening has been taken up in various parts of the City and many 'out of school Drama Clubs' now exist in their own area, which was one of our hopes.

(b) The first attempt at an Adventure Playground in Birmingham was given to the Educational Drama Association to run for a trial period.

(c) A permanent outside playground is now at Reaside with special climbing pieces suitable for dramatic play.

(d) Some of the acting in the Juvenile Dramatic Festival, even in formal work, has improved and now each year there are several evenings of 'off the stage drama'. Although some of these items are frankly experimental still, the widespread interest in schools in newer ideas is reflected in these productions.

(e) As a result of all the above and of visits to schools by the Drama Adviser and the constant conferences and talks to staff members, drama has been introduced in Birmingham as a very wide form of education. Not only do we believe we have found the bridge between Child Drama and the Adult Theatre and developed the Art of Theatre in Schools, but drama has been used as a method of aiding backwardness, of enlivening other lessons such as Mathematics, English, History, Geography and Scripture, and of counteracting emotional disturbance. Particularly in secondary schools, I have instituted the beginnings of Social Drama, in which young people are taught to consider and practise simple everyday things like taking messages and using telephones, preparing for first interviews, also the elements of service and good manners and thought for others; personal appearance, cleanliness, team work, etc.

(f) Links have been made with the Home Office and there is regular training in Child Drama for intending parents of Cottage Homes. Remand Homes and Approved Schools have also been visited.

My own particular interest in recent years has been to continue research into Dramatherapy that I rather dropped after 1939, and quite a lot has been done in special schools, particularly at St Francis. My own work has been at this school and a little at the Birmingham University Clinic. Particular tests have been made with (i) general disturbance, (ii) brain damage, (iii) withdrawn children.

[1] Since this report, also regular visits from Courses wishing to observe.

Apart from the institution of regular national Summer Schools on the Arts in Education in which an almost totally Birmingham Staff has assisted me for the last six (coming seven) years,[1] I would say that, looking back, the main difference now is that throughout the schools our Children's work is much more human and much more imaginative. Drama in Birmingham is no longer just a minor subject, Specialists and Heads of Department have begun to be selected and the work is concerned no longer with Theatre only, but with the whole form of living.

The attitude and method of what we have tried to do in Birmingham in the last ten years was brought to a climax this Easter, 1957, when teachers who have trained with the Educational Drama Association gave an exhibition with older children, of Child Drama, at the big Conference on Education through the Arts, at the Festival Hall, London.

NOTES

Besides visits to schools by the Drama Adviser, to see work, advise on methods, aid productions and talk to teachers, there are regular visits from school to theatres other than the Drama Centre. Some visits are aided by the Foyle Trust, which has also assisted me in my speech research. But the L.E.A. assists visits each summer to selected Theatre by the John English Arena Theatre Company.[2]

A teacher's work in Child Drama methods, from Great Barr Comprehensive School, has already been televised. There are pieces of drama put on in the Town Hall too, but these are not part of the drama programme proper, but rather an adjunct to the music programme.

There has been intensive building of schools in Birmingham and one of the features of it has been some splendid halls from the theatre point of view. Although some of our halls are too big for intimate theatre, compromise on several for large numbers of children having to be made, others are of great interest. Examples are the charming Four Dwellings Senior Girls' School, with its movable apron stage, Great Barr Comprehensive, which is two theatres in one, and Bartley Green Girls' Grammar, where a simple Greek half-circle open air stage backs out into a courtyard from behind the normal proscenium stage of the Hall.

In all cases, though the primary concern has been to provide an environment and equipment suitable for the age of the children in any given school, the needs of Further Education groups have not been lost sight of. But this has been almost entirely in Secondary Schools, where the combined needs most nearly coincide.

[1] Now seventeen years (1967).
[2] His resident company is now at Midlands Arts Centre.

[264]

It has been a great pleasure trying to help with advice on this side of the work and it was my personal fortune to be Drama Adviser to the biggest city in the country, that actually had appointed an Adviser during all these years of reconstruction after the war.

Conferences and One Day Schools in Birmingham

Drama in Education
Drama and Religion
Drama, Art and Music
Drama and Art
Drama in the Infant School
Drama in the Junior School
Drama in the Senior School
Children out of School
The Arts and the Spirit
The Arts as Education
[1]Drama and the Disturbed Child
Children's Theatre

(These have been widely copied and there have since been many others.)

---

[1] Many others since, too numerous to mention.

Appendix 2

Diary Notes 1958-68

It would prove too vast, so far as this appendix is concerned, to write a continued history from this period onwards, things have developed too swiftly at times, too slow at others. No doubt a full history is needed, but apart from an average of visiting two to three schools a day as a normal part of the work in Birmingham as well as directing evening work at the Drama Centre, the following diary entries are included as being those which seem best to indicate expansion, or which seem to have some-what affected events. At least certain dates are pinpointed, which appear now to have been important to the work.

1958
22nd February: Art and Science Conference, London.
26th February: Own intimate theatre production of *The Living Room* at Birmingham.
March: Lectures to E.S.N. course, Birmingham University.
3rd March: Theatre in the Round at Theatre Centre, Birmingham. Directing course with Jack Beckett. 'Drama and Life', Warwickshire.
1st April: Mr John English comes to discuss plans and ask advice of Education Office, Birmingham.
13th–18th April: Giving course at Reading University.
8th May: Directing course for University of Liverpool.
8th July: Speak at Psychological Conference, Cambridge.
26th July: Directing Summer Course—Keele University.
4th September: Speaking Ministry of Education E.S.N. course.
22nd September: Alan Simpson, New Zealand—in Birmingham. (A meeting that was to prove so fruitful.)
22nd November: Dinner with C. J. Gill, H.M.I., Ruth Foster, H.M.I., and A. L. Stone to discuss policy and whole realm of Drama and Movement.

December: Discussions with Architects' Department on designs for play shapes in gardens of new flats in Birmingham.

Brian Way represented me in Canada this year. *Publication of 'Introduction to Child Drama' (U.L.P.).*

Self also President of Birmingham University Dramatic Society this year.

1959

2nd March: First night of *Old Ladies* at Birmingham. Own production.

7th March: Workers for Maladjusted Children Association Conference, London.

6th–7th April: Meeting of Representatives of Children's Theatre at Leicester. (Entered to hear Margaret Faulkes expounding my views.[1]) Out of this meeting the British Children's Theatre Association was born.

11th June: Speaking at Newman Association, Birmingham.

13th June: Speaking Manchester on E.S.N. children.

June: Speaking various parts of country on need for Adventure Playgrounds.

Early Summer: Speaking at Reading, for National Playing Fields Association. Became member of first National Committee of British Children's Theatre Association.

27th July—6th August: Asked to defend the Arts at Conference on 'Education in an age of Technology'. University of Birmingham at Worcester.

September: Birmingham University Department of Education initiated talks with Colleges on my work, at suggestion of Professor Jeffreys.

September: Myra Benson of Canada in Birmingham. Visited Rea St Centre and my herd of ponies.

8th–11th October: Direct Course. Somerset.

October: Own production of *Private Lives*, Birmingham.

Sent Brian Way again to represent me in Canada this year. Letter from Saskatchewan says 'We sold all your books we had in hand, plus a dozen more. Brian is a terrific missionary to send abroad to carry out your philosophy.' Self invited to New Zealand, America and South Africa.

1960

3rd February: A professional Children's Theatre comes to train under me for three weeks.

February: Discussions Gulbenkian.

[1] Shapes of presentation and difference between acting 'with' and acting 'at'.

2nd March: Speak Croydon Primary Club.

March: Discussions Nuffield.

April: Developing spontaneous work with Youth Department at Brighton.

Discussions Ministry of Education and speak at Conference (Psychology) Cambridge.

Discussions B.D.L.

18th May: Wolverhampton E.S.N.

20th May: Speaking at course on Dramatherapy at Uffculme Clinic.

June: Meeting with Group Captain Cheshire re. drama with physically handicapped.

31st June: Brian Way returns to lecture at Birmingham.

Whitsun: Brian Way goes to South Africa.

July: Brian Way's Theatre Company plays test performance in Birmingham.

Dance courses starting.

Became member of Committee of Association of Workers for Maladjusted Children.

5th August: Brian Way returns from South Africa.

On Committee of National Association of Drama Advisors discussing Drama Section—Duke of Edinburgh's Award. Drew up new syllabus.

29th September: Speak "Value of Child Drama in education". University of Leicester.

7th–8th October: Hertfordshire County Youth Course.

On Advisory Committee for Drama, Birmingham Diocesan Education Committee.

10th October: Speaking on Dramatherapy at Bristol.

11th October: Inspecting Old Vic Theatre School.

15th October: My lecture series starts at London University.

1st November: Peter Slade Studio established in London for people passing through Britain to meet me and later for foundation of Peter Slade Club for physically handicapped.

4th November: Own intimate theatre production of *Chalk Garden*, Birmingham.

Had received good wishes for New Year from Russia and had been invited to lecture in Canada, America, South Africa and Sweden this year.

1961

27th January: Discussions with John English about closer cooperation with Educational Drama Association and drama with young people. Speak at Religious Conference for Bishop of Worcester.

February: Speaking Leicester on Maladjusted Children.

13th February: At Television Studio, Aston. Selected for Midland Profile.

17th February: Speaking at Bolton.

February: Staff of National College for training Youth Leaders come to ask about and discuss whole realm of drama and personality training.

Speaking on Psychology, London.

7th March: Discussion with Charles Henry Foyle Trust.

18th March: Educational Drama Association Conference on Social Education.

25th March: Guest speaker at the London Discussion Group.

April: During Easter holiday, taking drama at clubs for physically handicapped, London; speaking at Conference on Maladjusted children, Nottingham University.

Speaking at Children's Theatre Conference, London.

Special Committee decided not to take hall in Kensington for Drama for Physically Handicapped which led to Peter Slade Club being started in Hampstead. In touch with Group Captain Cheshire and Sue Ryder all along.

28th April: Give special talk to Drama Panel of Ministry of Education at Leamington Office on 'Role of Drama as Emotional Training in Secondary Education'.

30th April: Arranged first of a series of conferences with staffs of Training Colleges for more constructive practical drama courses for students.

6th May: Lecturing on Dramatherapy, Bristol.

17th May: Speak at London Clinic.

27th May: Discuss with Dalcroze Society, London.

3rd June: One of many Children's Theatre National Committees.

6th June: Speak for National Playing Fields Association, Reading.

7th June: Speak at Council of Repertory Theatres, Northampton, on 'Relationships with the Public'.

13th–14th June: Newspapers taking photos at Rea Street Drama Centre, Birmingham.

16th June: Speak at Portsmouth.

18th June: Take spontaneous drama at Diocesan Course. 'Drama and Religion', Birmingham.

25th June: Speak Marlborough Day Hospital, staff and patients, London.

June–July: Further meetings of St David's Community at Rea Street Drama Centre, Birmingham.

[270]

13th July: Discussion with Ministry on possible development of Drama Centres.

28th July–4th August: Direct Summer Course at Keele University.

August: Discussion with H.M.I.s at Peter Slade Studio, London on possibility and shape of first Conference by Ministry on 'Drama and Education'.

9th September: Taking therapy group on dance, London.

22nd–30th September: Running courses at Bury for Cambridge University.

2nd October: Mrs Azmier of Canada in Birmingham. (Important meeting.)
    Direct Mime Courses, Birmingham, during month.

14th October: Speak Salisbury Training College where Social Drama had started under Miss Mogford.

20th October: Speak Ealing Technical College on Personality and Theatre.

21st October: Therapy group, London.

22nd October: Take session of Religious Drama, Birmingham.

27th October: Discussions on Educational gramophone recordings, London.

During November: Taking groups in own method of dance at weekends, London.

November–December: Starting special work at approved schools, Birmingham.
    Own production *After October* at Drama Centre, Birmingham.
    Invitations to lecture in America, Australia, Canada and Norway during year.

1962

January: Therapy groups in London at weekends.
    Committees. National Association Drama Advisers and British Children's Theatre Association.

February: Taking Personality Course for industry, Birmingham.

16th February: First discussions at Birmingham with Professor Hunt re possible development in drama at Manchester University.

22nd February: Miss Demmery flies to Guernsey to take course in my methods.

24th February: Press Conference at Y.W.C.A. Birmingham re my new Personality Courses for industry.

28th February: Birmingham papers full of photos and write up of the Personality Courses.

6th March: Lunch with Professor Jeffreys re Drama Centre and developing my work with University.

13th March: Television of my Personality Course.

15th March: Speak on 'Spontaneous Drama as an aid to backward children', Cambridge.

17th March: Invited to discussion with doctors in London on the techniques of using drama as therapy.

28th March: Mrs Dorothy Heathcote in Birmingham to discuss inclusion of Child Drama in a University Diploma course (then at Durham), the first for Drama in Education.

31st March: Conference at Birmingham Council House to launch Sparkbrook Adventure Playground. Will they accept my new salary rise to start them off?

8th April: A professional Children's Theatre Company comes for training at Rea Street Drama Centre, Birmingham.

14th April: Visiting clubs for handicapped, London and running dance group.

19th April: Write up of my Theatre for Children appears in the *Nursery World*.

During Easter holiday—attending Children's Theatre Association Conference and running course in Essex.

May: Personality course, Birmingham, starts again.

19th May: Programme of my Personality Course shown on television.

24th May: Mime and Dance Drama course starts at Birmingham.

1st June: Meeting about Midland Arts Centre. Cannon Hill Trust.

12th June: Taking own club for physically handicapped, London. Invited to first meeting, London, to introduce my methods for training of future secretaries.

14th June: Direct course at College of Education, Wimbledon.

Whitsun Holiday—Take own club for handicapped several times.

Lunch with Harley Street specialist re dramatherapy.

Invited discussion with College of Preceptors about a possible new centre to be built in London.

18th June: Visitors from America, South Africa and New Zealand to see me and discuss Child Drama.

Personality Course, Birmingham.

19th June: Present at opening Cannon Hill Midland Arts Centre.

22nd June: Lecture Central School, Embassy Theatre, London. Chairman, Alington.

Rush back to Birmingham to be on Television for discussion and programme on Theatre for Children.

28th June: Lecture at London Clinic.

During June—my method of drama being used to teach French in Birmingham Schools.

July: Students from London University in Birmingham to discuss theses, see work and take tape recordings of my answers to questions.

7th July: Taking own handicapped club.

14th July: Be present opening of Sparkbrook Adventure Playground, Birmingham. (Children's Theatre production by Tom Knowles.)

16th–17th July: Taking course at Attingham—Shropshire.

19th July: Attending as new member of an Advisory Committee for National Association Mental Health, London.

Taking a course in a psychological clinic that evening with patients.

22nd July: Invited to discuss whole realm of televising children's work, London.

27th July: Directing International course at Keele University.

26th August: Invited to Film Unit to advise on how to film children in various parts of Britain.

31st August: Speak at National Conference of Special Schools Association.

6th September: Starting new course in an Approved School, Birmingham. Miss Demmery as Tutor in Charge.

25th September: Give demonstration on own dance method at Stratford-upon-Avon.

29th September: Directing course, Liverpool.

Personality Course on still.

6th October: Directing course on Arena theatre, Leamington.

8th October: Mrs Polly Hill of Canadian Child Drama Association, here.

Visits to Remand Homes, Birmingham.

11th October: Speak on Drama and Athletics at Chelsea Physical Education College.

13th October: Take session at Religious Drama Course, Saltley College.

14th October: Mr Friend, Principal of Bretton Hall, Yorks, comes to visit me at Whitmore House for first discussion on development of work at Bretton Hall and possible outline of future one-year course.

15th October: Americans and Dutch arrive for long period of training.

19th October: Mrs Hill of Canada leaves.

25th October: Lecture on course, Essex.

During half-term: taking own club for handicapped and running general dance groups, London. Speaking Dartford College, Kent.

2nd November: Visit to Bournemouth to see work, see extract of my own play and to add plea for a Drama Centre (now established).

4th November: Rehearsing professional Children's Theatre Group, Rea Street, Birmingham.

6th November: Current Personality Course ends.

11th November: Conference with representatives of Religious Drama Society, Birmingham, to determine policy.

13th–14th November: Visit Bretton Hall for preliminary view of work.

15th November: Mime and Dance Drama course begins Birmingham, on own method.

Meetings of Committee of National Association Drama Advisers.

17th November: London Dance. St David's meetings.

18th November: First meeting? of selected national Leaders in own method at Peter Slade Studio, London.

29th November: Meeting of Peter Slade Leaders definite London. Policy re Drama and Arts Centres in Britain. Relationships with Colleges and Universities and discussion re certificate of Child Drama.

During Year: Invitations to speak in Africa, America, Canada and Israel.

1963

January: End of Christmas Holidays: Receive members of Ministry Drama Panel for tea at Peter Slade Studio, London, to discuss details of the Drama in Education Diploma, Newcastle University and also the advisability of Drama as examinable subject in Secondary Education.

Advisory Committe. National Association of Mental Health.

10th January: Made a courtesy member of Canadian Child Drama Association.

15th January: New Personality Course for industry starts, Birmingham.

9th February: British Children's Theatre Committee.

13th February: Home Office course starts, Birmingham.

19th February: Speak in House of Commons to a selected group of M.P.s interested in Education and problem of delinquency, about future national development of Child Drama.

Half-term: Mrs Dorothy Heathcote comes to Birmingham, to plan final details of Drama in Education Diploma at Newcastle University and my part in it.

26th February: Professor Stanley comes to Birmingham to

discuss and plan with me the Drama in Education Diploma and see Child Drama at Rea Street Centre.

Meetings of C. of E. Diocesan Advisory Committee on Drama.

9th February: Directing one Day School, Kesteven.

12th March: Speaking at Oxford Conference on Drama in Special Schools.

18th March: Direct course in Child Drama at West Ham and discuss possibility of a Drama Centre there with John Hudson.

31st March: Conferences of Tutors of Training Colleges at Rea Street Drama Centre.

2nd April: Lady Hampden visits my Personality Course for girls in Retail Trades.

11th April: Miss S. Demmery flies to represent me in Canada.

26th April: Research group starts to investigate creative faculty in Education and to compare parts of own work with findings of Piaget and others.

30th April: Took over new Cotswold house where my wife was to start a Girls' Club and Art Club.

4th May: Television Manchester.

8th May: Television comes to plan programme on my Social Drama in schools.

Professor Stanley visits me at Birmingham for further planning of Newcastle Diploma course, to see work at Rea Street Centre and the dance work.

10th–11th May: Directing course at Sheffield for Pegasus Theatre group.

15th May: Television of my Social Drama in schools.

25th May: Own handicapped Club and London dance group.

15th June (Saturday): Own handicapped Club. London Dance.

Rush back Birmingham meet Professor McIntyre of America at house of Professor and Mrs Mellers. Discuss whole approach to Creative Drama and differences between America and Britain in outlook and method.

22nd June: Direct course St Paul's College, Newbold Revel. Long article on Sylvia Demmery's trip to Canada in *Birmingham Post:* 'Child Drama proving unexpected export'.

25th–26th June: Examine Drama at Bretton Hall for Leeds University and plan the possible extra one-year course.

3rd July: Representative from Cannon Hill visits Rea Street Drama Centre.

4th July: Crowds of students from North of England to visit Rea Street Drama Centre and see schools.

First letters of inquiry re Drama and Children's Theatre from Russia answered and sent.

26th July for week: Directing E.D.A. international course at Keele University in own method.

22nd–24th August: Directing first special course for selected Peter Slade Leaders, Birmingham.

30th August–6th September: Directing Movement and Drama section of Seminar under National Association of Mental Health—Cheltenham.

11th September: Helping train and direct new children's theatre groups at Birmingham Training College.

This month serious talks on certificate in Child Drama at committees of National Association of Drama Advisers and with Leo Baker re possible development of Junior Section of A.D.B. examination.

28th September (Saturday): Discussion on Child Drama certificate with H.M.I.s at Peter Slade Studio, London.

7th October: Chief Representative on Drama of Egyptian Ministry of Education at Birmingham to study Child Drama and visit Rea Street.

11th October: Discussion with Leo Baker re Child Drama Certificate as definite part of A.D.B. examination.
Preparation of facts for Drama Board.

19th–20th October (Saturday and Sunday): Directing experimental weekend course, based on my Birmingham Course for Industry. First at High Wycombe, Bucks.

9th November: Further conference at National Council of Social Service, Bedford Square with Leo Baker to present case for Child Drama certificate to the Drama Board.

2nd December: Look Back in Anger production, Birmingham.

3rd December: Group of doctors at Rea Street Drama Centre to assess value of the work for disturbed children.

During Year: Invitations to speak in Australia, Egypt, Denmark and Holland.

1964

3rd–5th January: Be present at First Conference on Drama in Education, planned by Ministry of Education for invited Leaders, in London. (The one discussed earlier in Peter Slade Studio.)

13th January: Students on the new Diploma Course for Drama in Education of Newcastle University (formerly planned for Durham) arrive in Birmingham to study Child Drama.

14th January: New Personality Course starts Birmingham. Miss Demmery as Tutor-in-Charge.

25th January: Directing course at St Mary's College, Cheltenham.
   Look Back in Anger still running.

12th February: The Newcastle Diploma students present a piece of Children's Theatre at Rea Street Drama Centre.

20th February: Start course Birmingham on Drama in Junior Education.

26th February: Attend advisory committee at Crewe Training College for planning Drama syllabus to include Child Drama.

29th February–1st March (Sunday): Taking sessions in Personality Training, London.

7th March (Saturday): Directing Drama in Education—One Day Course at Wrexham.

8th March (Sunday): Speak on Modern Theatre at Conference at Avoncroft.

10th March: Ministry Inspection of my Birmingham Personality Course.

14th March (Saturday): Taking Personality Training at Salisbury.

16th March: Starting course on Shakespeare, Birmingham.
   Easter Holiday: Running Dance groups and Personality Training for Commerce.
   Planning final details of a film in London on children; at Peter Slade Studio.
   British Children's Theatre Committee; Personality Course; See John Allen.

15th April: Groups of students come to Birmingham to train in Child Drama.

17th April (Saturday): Directing course, Drama in Education, Newport, Monmouthshire.

21st–22nd April: Discussion with Ministry of Education on Personality courses in Day Release throughout the country.

23rd April: Groups of students and their tutor come to Birmingham for training in Child Drama.

24th April: Start new course on Drama, Birmingham. Leave to direct course at Rickmansworth 24th.

25th April: Attend committee on Mental Health, London.

25th–26th April: Go on to direct Personality Course at Brighton.

27th April, night: Rush back Birmingham for Conference with television on Education.

30th April: Invited to lunch at Keele University for special discussion on drama syllabus in Colleges of area and to investigate possibility of a cross section of professions course in Drama and Communication.

15th May: Attend First International Conference of Children's Theatre at Commonwealth Institute, London, opened by Sir Edward Boyle.

17th May: Self Chairman of Creative Drama Section of Conference. Introductory talk by Professor MacIntyre of America (already met at Professor Mellers', Birmingham).

28th May: First tentative approach to Ministry of Health on value of Drama.

30th May (Saturday): Directing one Day School on value of Child Drama, by special invitation of students at Trent Park College.

31st May: Speaking at Psychological Conference, London.

1st June: Receive groups of students to see Birmingham Schools and giving training in Child Drama.

Personality Course in Birmingham still running.

22nd June: Further contacts with Switzerland re Child Drama and visiting Birmingham. (They had given headlines in newspapers when my first book came out.)

25th–26th June: Examining at Bretton Hall. Considerable improvement noted.

28th June: Filming of Children trained on my methods in West Ham area.

5th July (Sunday): Speak at Conference of Incorporated Society of Musicians, London.

6th–8th July: Dorothy Heathcote and Gavin Bolton (of Diploma Course) in Birmingham to see Child Drama in schools and attend Drama Centre (Gavin Bolton attended a Summer Course at Keele with me also).

9th–10th July: Discussions about getting my personality training into Technical Colleges in Birmingham area.

11th July (Saturday): Another London Dance Group.

During month had been asked to send notes to Plowden Committee on Drama in Primary Education.

24th July: Direct usual International Drama Association Summer Course at Keele University.

8th–9th August: Continuation of filming takes place West Ham.

14th September: My Personality Course experiments now taken over by a Continuation College, but under my Assistant Tutor, Miss Demmery, for time being, who now directs course.

21st–25th September: Rehearsals of Children's Theatre groups at Birmingham College of Education.

26th September: Direct course at Leicester College of Education.

3rd October: Speak at Conference of English Association, Manchester University.

6th October: Attend Conference at Royal Institute of British Architects, London. Exhibition of Drama Spaces and Theatres. Slide of own production shown.

7th October: Conference of National Association of Drama Advisers at Missenden Abbey, Bucks, where a motion in favour of a certificate in Child Drama was passed, after much discussion, by a large majority.

11th October (Sunday): Speak at Conference of the Analytical Psychology Club, London.

14th October: University Induction Course for graduates. Take session.

17th October (Saturday): Direct sessions on Personality Training. Phillips House, Dinton.

During half-term break: taking dance groups, **and speaking at New College of Drama Hampstead, London, on 'Child Drama and Intimate Theatre'.**

9th November: Miss Demmery flies to represent me in Germany.

10th–11th November: Helping Birmingham College of Education with Children's Theatre.

14th November (Saturday): Taking Personality Course, Brighton.

18th November: Leif Kongsrud of Denmark returns for several days to Birmingham for discussion and confirmation of views.

23rd November: St David's community obtains own room, no longer needs to meet at Rea Street Centre. Has grown well.

26th November· Laying plans for personality training in a Birmingham Secondary School.

28th November (Saturday): Personality Training London.

2nd December: My Children's Theatre being filmed at Rea Street Centre, Birmingham.

5th December: Speak Youth Course. Windmill House, near Birmingham. Zoe Dawson representative for E.D.A. and takes dance with group from Rea Street Centre.

12th December (Saturday): Another committee. British Children's Theatre Association—and own Dance Group, London.

List of invitations to visit overseas resulting from Children's Theatre Conference too long to include.

1965

11th January: Newcastle Diploma Course comes again to Birmingham for training in Child Drama.

27th January: Take group of Secondary School lads at Rea Street Centre for 'photos to back up certain principles in Newsom Report.

30th January (Saturday): Conducting course at Northampton.

1st February: Start new course for Home Office, Birmingham.

3rd February: Film of Children's Theatre, Rea Street, Centre.

13th–14th February: Personality Training Y.W.C.A. London.

27th February: Speak on Drama at Birmingham College of Education.

February (Saturday): Personality Training for Industry, London.

11th March: Speak on 'History of Creative Drama in England', Manchester University.

13th March (Saturday): London Dance Group.

14th March (Sunday): Speak at Crescent Theatre, Birmingham on Arena Theatre.

19th March: H.M.I.s at Rea Street Centre, Birmingham to discuss whole realm of work in personality training and my views on emotional education for juniors.

Rush to Sheffield.

20th March: Speak Sheffield University on 'Symbols of myths and legends in Creative Drama'.

22nd March: Starting Oral English Course, Birmingham.

25th March: Lecture 'Drama in Education' at Luton.

26th March: At B.B.C. London for interview on radio: 'In Town Today' (angle on emotional training and general philosophy for mankind).

2nd April: Travel Bangor University to speak at first conference-course on Drama organised by Welsh Department of Education and Science. 'Child Drama and its value in Education.'

During Easter holiday: Be on hand to help cripples in London. Run Dance Session. Direct course at Padgate College of Education, Preston. Consider flying Scotland to open Conference on Child Drama and Drama Centres.

22nd April: Attend advisory committee re Bachelor of Education examination for Loughborough College at Nottingham University. Advise on preparation of syllabus and possible inclusion of Child Drama.

24th April (Saturday): Broadcast of the 'In Town Today' interview.

25th April (Sunday): Take sessions of Personality Training at Selly Oak, Birmingham.

26th April: Students from Crewe in Birmingham to study Child Drama.

1st and 2nd May (Saturday)[1] Personality Training with mixed course of Young Men and Women, Salisbury.

3rd–8th May: Visitors from Australia and B.B.C. in city seeing work in schools and attending Rea Street Centre.

10th–12th May: Judging at Juvenile Dramatic Festival, Birmingham. (Annual Event.)

11th May (Saturday): Directing course. Gloucester College of Education.

25th May: Full page spread of pictures in papers of proposed Birmingham development with **Drama Centre near Town Hall, to replace Rea Street.**

29th May (Saturday): Directing course Hereford College of Education.

June: Lecture 'Theatre for Children' Birmingham College of Education.

17th June: Be guest and staff Luncheon Speaker at Selly Oak Colleges.

18th June: Speak Derby. Midland Association for Teaching of English.

23rd, 24th, 25th June: Examining at Bretton Hall and Oastler Colleges.

27th June (Sunday): Film Children's Theatre.

20th July: Lecture on Personality Training at National Conference of Tutors in Technical Colleges and take session with Miss Demmery on team teaching. Huddersfield.

23rd–30th July: Direct usual International Summer Course for Educational Drama Association, at Keele University.

Twenty from Hawaii University this year.

First special course for Leaders in own method for staff of Colleges.

31st July: Attend special extra weekend course for Hawaiians.

August: Visit St David's as Trustee of Community.

7th September: Discuss Child Drama in relation to Selly Oak Colleges: re Teachers, Social Workers, course for Special Schools and present Home Office Course.

8th September: Meeting at Birmingham University to promote an interest in Birmingham Repertory Theatre. Put forward concise plan for relationships with public. Not taken up.

18th September (Saturday): London Dance group.

20th September: Miss Sylvia Demmery leaves to take up Drama appointment at Loughborough College.

21st September: Lunch with training staff of Tube Investments re Personality Training.

24th September: First inquiry from International Computers re Personality Training and sales promotion.

25th September: Taking Personality Training at Salisbury.

27th September: Conference with architects re new Drama Centre in middle of Birmingham for when Rea Street is pulled down.

28th September: New Personality Course. Birmingham.

1st and 2nd October: Directing Drama Course in East Suffolk.

9th October: Civic Reception given to Educational Drama Association and self at Council House, Birmingham. (Programme of Improvised Speech, own method of Dance and an excerpt of play given. Guests from all over Britain.

16th October (Saturday): Speak at Conference of Warwickshire County Teachers' Association to mark the appointment of County Music Organiser.

During half-term: visit Tube Investments Training Centre and advise on Personality Training (unfortunately missing invitation to be present at reception, Princess Margaret).

28th October: Dine with Sir Edward Boyle, Birmingham. First meeting new President of Educational Drama Association and discuss aims.

30th October (Saturday): Take Personality Training, London.

3rd November: Saltley students at regular Wednesday Movement Sessions, Rea Street Drama Centre, Birmingham.

7th November: Reception to meet Bishop of Coventry.

20th November: Direct course at C. F. Mott College.

24th November: News that my second book was to be made a talking book for the blind.

27th November: Attend Open Day at Arts Club for Children, Birmingham Museum.

30th November: Direct course on Nativity Plays, Birmingham.

7th December: Professor Siks of Washington comes to Rea Street, and to discuss terms used in describing Creative Drama from Scandinavia to South America.

'Introduction to Child Drama' translated in Dutch this year. Also news of some of my work being translated into Russian by the Association for Promotion of Literature and Art for Children.

Renewed acquaintance with Stephen Joseph from Manchester

University. Arts Council had invited me to send report on a new Drama Centre, my scheme for training teachers and a team of actors. In correspondence also with Minister (Jennie Lee).

1966

10th January: Start new Home Office course.

25th and 26th January: Groups of students and tutors seeing schools and Drama Centre.

1st February: Self made approach to Birmingham Repertory with a scheme for schools.

12th February (Saturday): Meeting of tutors for Religious Drama Society (Sesame), London.

24th February: Mrs Mellers at Rea Street Centre. Discuss developing Arts Centre for children in York.

10th March: Visitors from Brazil.

14th March: Own production of *Blithe Spirit,* Rea Street Drama Centre, Birmingham.

30th March: Representatives of Hornsey College at Rea Street Centre to discuss creativity.

9th April: London Dance Session.

13th–16th April: Easter holiday: attend British Children's Theatre Conference, Embassy Theatre, London. Discussed creative work with Professor Mellers of York afterwards.

25th April: Newcastle University Diploma Course arrives.

9th May: Entered hospital for emergency operation.

13th May: Miss P. Lutley takes over my talk at Bangor University. Leads to other talks for her.

24th and 25th May: John Hudson takes over my course on Movement for Sesame at Coventry. Leads to others.

8th–9th June: John Hudson again takes Movement course at Coventry for me.

22nd–29th July: Determined to be ready to direct International course for Educational Drama Association and take Leaders course again at Keele University. Must not let them down (Sixteenth Annual Summer Course).

5th September: Investigation into results of courses in improvised drama on radio and television in Birmingham schools.

1st October: Attend British Children's Theatre Committee, London re arrangements for conference in Birmingham 1967 and production at Rea Street Centre.

7th October: Talk to staff of English as Second Language

Centre on Child Drama for Immigrant children and how it can help. (My discussion with other teachers on this already published in *Creative Drama*, vol. 3, no 8, 1966).

25th October: Discussion re Birmingham University running a Child Drama Certificate course.

29th October: Attend conference at Stratford Theatre on taking plays to schools.

5th November: Another long discussion Stratford. Just myself this time and members of Royal Shakespeare Theatre Company on whole concept of building a bridge between Child Drama and Theatre, the in-between stages and some plan for consolidating the work nationally.

9th November: B.B.C. Television representative to discuss programme on deprived and special children.

12th November: Directing course, Hereford College of Education.

16th November: Lecture and give course at York University.

17th November: Publication by Cassells of Drama Course, (A chance for Everyone)—Hudson and Slade.

22nd November: Start course on Nativity Plays, Birmingham.

24th November: Inspected work on Delacato method at Clinic in St Francis School, Birmingham, with view to working out relationship with Child Drama for neurologically abnormal children.

8th December: Lunch Selly Oak Colleges to discuss possible development of course there.

12th December: Production by Michael Hall of *The Long Goodbye* at Rea Street Drama Centre, Birmingham.

14th December: Professor Oscar Quero of Mexico visited to discuss personality training and dramatherapy.

During year: Felt a little out of things because of being in hospital. But there had been discussions at Loughborough re further development of training in Child Drama; aspects of Child Drama had come into a report prepared by a special committee for the Standing Conference of Drama Associations. There had been a proposal from Denmark for founding an Educational Drama Association based on my work and affiliated to our Association. *St Patrick* and my speech 'The value of Child Drama in education' had been prepared for publication by our Educational Drama Association.

Invitations to visit America, Denmark, Africa and New Zealand. Scheme for Child Drama Certificate at Birmingham backed by N.U.T.

1967

10th January: Course for Home Office starts.

8th February: Start Course on improvisation, Birmingham.

11th February: Direct Youth Course at Ingestre Hall.

20th February: Lunch at Sussex University.

22nd February: Urgent request to visit Mexico.

26th February: Organisation based on my work founded in Denmark: The Society for Educational Drama.

7th March: Publication of my play St Patrick.

8th March: Visitors from London University.

15th March: Start Course for Special Schools.

20th March: Newcastle Diploma Course arrives.

29th March: Bought St David's House, Moreton-in-Marsh as possible Centre.

1st April: On panel at Questors Theatre, London, to end up British Childrens Theatre Association Conference.

7th April: Saw nephew Francis Slade's production of Pinter's 'The Room' at Madeley College, Staffs.

23rd April: Important discussions with Drama Adviser for county of Gloucestershire. Tea in Cotswolds.

26th April: Speak to group of Probation Officers.

28th April: Speak University of Leicester.

29th April: Recording in London.

6th May: St David's Council meeting, Self speak.

13th May: Speak at Central Training in Child-care course, Knuston Hall, Wellingborough.

18th May: Judge Juvenile Dramatic Festival, Birmingham.

23rd May: Discussion re Theatre-go-Round of Royal Shakespeare Festival Company at Birmingham.

31st May: Speak University of Sussex.

5th June: Speak Loughborough College.

9th–10th June: Lecture Selly Oak Colleges.

14th June: Attended Centre. Re Child Drama Certificate.

15th June: Speak Wakefield N.A.T.E.

16th–17th June: Lecture Selly Oak Colleges, Birmingham.

21st June: Own Theatre for Children production starts at Drama Centre.

1st July: Give Course on Dance Drama, Birmingham.

3rd July: Birmingham Education Committee decides to start Certificate Course under my direction with two assistants.

8th July: Recording in London.

[285]

14th July: Discussion with Sir Alfred Owen.

21st–28th July: Direct usual International Summer School at Keele University. Leaders from Denmark on course. Also visit and speak at course for Teachers of handicapped children, Madeley College.

30th July: Sylvia Demmery leaves to represent me in America (Rhode Island University).

12th August: Visit St David's as trustee.

16th September: Attend Standing Conference of Drama Associations.

23rd September: Invited be Chairman of National Association Drama Advisers. Declined, but spoke on Child Drama Certificate Course, Bristol. Discussion Michael Mac Owen re work at L.A.M.D.A.

2nd October: First publicity over Child Drama Certificate Course. Three times over applied for in first 48 hours.

6th–7th October: Direct Course, Gloucestershire.

12th October: Discussions re Child Drama and A.D.B. Exam.

13th October: Direct Course Devizes.

4th November: Direct Gloucestershire Course.

9th November: Lecture Durham and Newcastle University Courses.

21st November: Television of Dance and Child Drama with Four Dwellings School, Birmingham.

16th December: Visit Theatre Centre, London.

During year: Invitations to visit Denmark, America, Norway and Mexico.
　　1968 Chief events to date:

　　Making recordings for Canada; starting work with autistic children; news of my *Introduction to Child Drama* being translated into Danish; speaking at Bournemouth Drama Centre; speaking on Drama and Religion for a conference of the Department of Education and Science for Wales; producing a play for the British Children's Theatre Conference.

ESTABLISHMENT BY BIRMINGHAM EDUCATION COMMITTEE OF A CERTIFICATE COURSE IN CHILD DRAMA UNDER MY DIRECTION.

Appendix 3

What we ought to be Doing in Education about Creative Arts

Birmingham University Summer School, Worcester, 1959, 4 August

In this technological age there is a danger that the creative arts may be squeezed into a position where they are fighting with their backs to the wall. It is important that wise thinking should save them from final annihilation. But if they are to be saved, those responsible for them have got to consider whether they are being used to the utmost advantage, or whether we are just reclining on a bed of trust that the arts are important in themselves. We are living in a highly competitive age and it may be necessary to prove the value of our wares. It is no good just relying on the hope that a few people in authority will always have some sentimental whim that a spot of culture keeps us all up with the Jones family. Those folk will die and the day may come when most people see through this. Cold-blooded selection and the high pace of living in a world of perpetual tension may take their effect. I have long felt that the attitude towards the arts in education and the method of their application was years behind the times. In many instances one could say that the whole teaching of such subjects is in an archaic rut, and a completely new form of thinking is now needed.

The attitude necessary for some forms of science has things in common with that of the artist, and to my mind the arts, on their side, would not suffer at all by being applied in a more scientific manner. Painting, drawing and modelling have had something of a revolution in application since the first pioneering days of Professor Cizek and are now more widely used in a constructive manner, which at least takes into consideration the needs of the individual and his rate of maturation. But there is much still to be done in balancing the relationship between art and drama so that the passive and the active inspirations may be used to the best advantage in each person. The drama itself is far too often confined to the production of stage plays and far too many would-be producers are applying theatre at the wrong age to the wrong people in the wrong way. What defence can we make for this to a penetrating scientific mind? Such a mind might well wish to scrap the lot.

Most producers in schools today are still using an over-directed method of dominating production, developing exterior forms of acting which began to go out of fashion in the theatre some twenty to thirty years ago. We should be using forms of individual encouragement that develop into strong group associations, passing an energetic message through interior forms of acting, much more in touch with our time. The teaching of music and speech is probably more behind the times than any of the arts. Music is still largely taught with a view to hurrying children on to 'appreciate' adult music, mostly of a former age, and to read a notation which half of them will never use. Speech training, where taught at all, still suffers from a rigid approach, is seldom of great joy to those who learn, and is not always lastingly successful, whereas both speech and music teaching should be firmly based upon a love of sound, and careful ear-training, drawing out a deep interest in exploration of rhythm, use of phrase and full development of the imagination; extension of vocabulary and the ability to produce our personal message with efficiency and joy (incidentally such training could be of value in aircraft spotting and in judging engine defects too).

Professor Vick, speaking at my own Summer School at North Staffordshire University recently asked—Why do children finally stop asking questions about the wonders of nature? Why indeed. And we might ask why young children have a deep love of sound when they go into school and not when they come out, and a deep feeling for poetic expression when young and seldom any deep poetic sense left when they have been 'taught' poetry—particularly through choral speech. Now I do not mean to say these things in a destructive, critical attitude. But it is vital that we should take stock of ourselves from time to time in a very honest way. In my own area, and no doubt in others, there is a lot of fine teaching, but I am talking about the position in education as a whole and the unwise risks to the arts that are being run.

What ought we to do in education about the creative arts?—the subject upon which I was asked to speak. Their main general purpose should be as an enrichment to the total personality of each individual, achieved by grouping of other subjects and by thoughtful integration with them. We should replace formal instruction as soon as possible by opportunity for personal experiences which develop imagination and promote personal rather than class discipline. Discipline must be your own before you leave school. There are too many signs that for many young people this is not so. They are still relying on regulation, and directly the atmosphere of ordering is removed, they become ships without a rudder. We cannot afford this type of 'ship' in a technological age. I have had to deal with numbers of them at my Centre. Their full energies should be harnessable at once. Their personalities should be balanced and reasonably mature for their age. This is partly what I mean by a more scientific approach to the arts. We should consider much more carefully what is the nature of young people and consider what the arts *do to a person* when well taught—not just suffer what persons do to the arts so often. There should be far less public performance and far more honest arts education in school. First of all we must consider that Man's activity is divided into two main parts:

(*a*) The passive form where he infuses his mind into objects, symbols and cyphers outside himself and brings them to life. I have called this elsewhere Projected Activity. This is the realm of organisation, government of others, the three Rs, crafts, painting and technical accomplishment.

(*b*) The active form where Man takes on the personal responsibility of doing something, of being someone, indulging in accurate communication, playing a role in special situations of authority and generally using the whole body in an active, physical sense. It is discovered in acting and in dance. I have called this Personal Activity.

When these two main functions are properly recognised, it will be possible to develop a curriculum which offers the necessary balance to each child. They all need some of both. In formal education they get far too much Projected Activity and suffer unnecessary tiredness of enthusiasm. (Grammar School children often suffer a complete lack of development of one side of their nature.) In loosely arranged Activity Method, children get far too little stretching in Projected Activity and often fail to reach as high an academic standard as the training was intended to achieve. Somewhere in the middle is a form of education which will develop the dynamic response which brings *cooperation* in learning. This is partly achieved by the process of balancing the personality needs in Projected and Personal Play, and partly by the fact that any such approach necessitates a vastly improved personal relationship between teacher and child. This happy relationship is the basis for all successful and swift teaching, and the arts have a tremendous contribution to make in this realm, particularly the drama, if used in a wide imaginative way. It is possible, for instance, to improve such things as the Projected Activity of Arithmetic by giving certain types of experience in Personal Play (drama). During these experiences the subject may have been felt and understood, and a return to Arithmetic often shows an understanding and bringing to life of these curious signs we call numbers. This appears to be the basis of the Ministry's latest pamphlet on the subject. I am quite convinced that there is a clear connection with the realm of Physics too.

Through drama of a spontaneous but guided nature, one could precondition the mind on imaginative lines when young, so that for the mature adult to come, when faced with a mass of collected figures and data, the 'illumination' period would be likely to come sooner. Forms of 'playing out' during the early years help to free the mind from unconscious anxiety and other mounds of rubbish too, so that mental energy is released and intuitive perception for the types of premise needing an act of faith in modern science can be arrived at more swiftly. It is urgent that we should start consciously preparing minds for 'the imaginative theoretical concept' now. It is these unprovable premises based on faith, arrived at by imagination, though backed by a wealth of likelihood, to be followed by flashes of further disciplined imagination in order to extract truth from the accumulated mass of facts, for which we have got to find a completely new education. Drama could be harnessed for this, and for ten to fifteen years now I have been developing a method which trains minds to dive deep to the truth of a situation and become one with it—first in the realm of emotion and then in the capacity for marshalling facts, and—most important—perceiving their significance. I wish some vital department of a university or research unit would work closely with me at depth to make use of these discoveries, for I am not clever enough to develop them alone, only to perceive the general lines upon which they should and do run. It is for wiser minds to make them useful in their several applications at higher specialist levels.

Might I now turn fully to my own subject of Drama? I feel it is the most important of all the arts (because it includes all the others) and is the only one which contains both Projected and Personal Play, and is the only one which carries the meaning 'doing' and 'struggling' in its own name. In this wide context it can be developed as the whole of the doing of Man. Children use it naturally in this way, and if we had the sense, we should all harness what is natural to Man to develop what is inside him. Briefly my method is this: at infant stage, to develop individuality, a love of sound, and then awareness of the group; to foster spontaneous speech, movement and observable leadership. At 7–9 years to canalise the cooperative energies of the gang during play, which will later help the adult to work in a team under strict discipline. The process of catharsis appears to come at its deepest during these years too, by the themes chosen during Child Drama, which we can endure, share and guide to other more constructive channels, thus contributing to the 'hope' process, so necessary for balancing the psychic banking account. From 9–11 years comes the first slow building of the bridge between Child Drama and the adult world in discovery of more truth about character, situation and plot, when age-old stories and legends may be turned into pageants. During these years one intentionally develops the tremendous qualities (*a*) of absorption in the task done (necessary for all study), and (*b*) of deep sincerity in the manner of doing it, arising out of the child's innocence. One notices that this leads to permanent traits of honesty in the personality, and no doubt to the perceptions of truth affecting who knows what realms in the future. By frequent discussion I try to develop the understanding that wisdom is discovered and built *together* between adult and child. I foster, through building of stories, the ability to marshal and present facts, and at all turns try to keep alive, and continually developing, an *inquiring mind* in children. This is necessary in any good education, but vital for the scientific age of the future.

With twelve-year-olds I try to safeguard the climax of childhood so that maturity is deep and unhurried. This is very difficult to do under our present system, and needs unusual cooperation from Heads, if it is to be effective. From thirteen-years onwards drama training should develop in three separate spearheads:

1. Imaginative training for all.
2. Social Drama for most (preparation for life, interviews, cultural behaviour and situations of responsibility. Personal problem plays. Service to others, etc.).
3. Theatre for some (final emergence from spontaneous speech, via group play making, into the disciplines of the adult art).

These three categories round off a very carefully planned emotional training, based not upon any traditional attitude or presupposition, but upon a scientific observation of the actual behaviour of human beings. During this training, it is hardly necessary to say, there are many links with the other arts and other subjects, such as English, History, Geography, Scripture, bringing them alive by making them interesting for young people instead of a penance. Sound is used in special ways to bring quietness and peace. Inner peace is hard to find, but its discovery can be trained to some extent. Peace is necessary for all mature and deep thinking.

Where adult education is concerned, there is much to be done by helping grown-ups to relive some of the education they should have had when young, but presented at a different intellectual level. This can be done in all the arts and often has a profound effect upon unexpected people. In drama there are particular ways of developing individuality and confidence and of further adjustment to a group, so that team spirit begins to take the place of selfish personal advertisement, and a higher form of poetic understanding and living can be discovered through dance.

For years our dictators of education once subordinated drama, the doing of *all life*, to English literature, which is only one child thereof. What curious lack of perception! Apart from the fact that they are worthy in themselves, I would say that the arts, properly used, produce emotional balance and promote just that confidence which is necessary for mental adventure. Finally, they are of the spirit, and if we are to avoid the tempting materialism inherent in a scientific and technological environment, we may use the arts for an approach to God. The arts touch our deepest selves and help to keep us sane. If Man should ever banish them, he will do so at his peril.

P.S.

Appendix 4

Childrens' Needs: Answer to a Letter

29th November 1966

Dear Mr Doll,

Thank you for your most interesting letter of November the 13th. Your query is a wide one and I have had to think carefully about the different parts of it. Might I make an attempt at answering your second paragraph first and then give more particular consideration to the half on television.

I would feel that it was tremendously important to develop imagination in children, partly because this is a natural thing and it is no good preventing it, they have got imagination and we might as well get used to the fact that they have. By imagination children discover, experience and prove events; this is where imagination is associated with dramatic play. Imagination properly guided does not drive children purely into a fantasy world. But, with sympathetic discussion, helps them to perceive the truth between dream and reality. It also helps them to develop sympathy by perceiving another person's attitude, situation, and feelings, by role playing; confidence arising out of ability to express both with the body and with the development of language flow is also concerned here, and the quality of absorption in the task and sincerity over the way of going about it are qualities which I have tried to describe in Child Drama. Absorption in the task is what is needed for all learning; and sincerity of doing can become a permanent part of the personality, developing such things as honesty of attitude, integrity and true feelings. For these reasons alone, apart from artistic achievement, I would feel that imagination being such a strong element in human nature can be of considerable importance. It should be fostered, encouraged, guided and developed, rather than feared, avoided, or positively denounced.

[293]

In my own investigation into children's needs, I felt I had discovered that they divided sound into time beat, rhythm and climax, in a very logical way. But we must add to their experience, declimax (an intentional bringing down to quietness, not the same as anticlimax), for children seem to love elementary sounds and primitive noises; and when they come into school they love sound, but I am not sure they always love it when they come out of school. I therefore often use elementary sounds as a simple inspiration for creative and imaginative work, particularly in creative drama, which brings us to your first paragraph and the particular consideration of television. Television of course has a strong effect upon the minds of young people and the characters seen will affect the play and attitudes chosen as role testing by youngsters. After the experience it is possible for them to get into a rut of role playing because of what they have seen. And this is one of the reasons for the need for guiding, in order to help them play out quite freely with true character, so that by discovering slowly who they are not, they find more truly who they really are. I think that the use of abstract music is valuable and can arise out of creative child-made music, which itself is an advance from elementary noise-making, such as tapping, knocking and whistling. Often one sees children doing this all together and group noise-making soon follows. Out of group noise-making clever guides can form some more cohesive, recognisable music. Without too much imposition from the adult mind, a genuine creation can arise which begins to bridge the gap between the younger and older ways of life. I should think abstract music would come after this; and that is the way I use it. Certainly Child Drama and improvised dance are often greatly enriched by abstract music.

As to 'Chamber Theatre' type of programmes, I am not absolutely sure whether we are talking in the same terms here, but if you mean intimate theatre, say, in the corner of a small room, then I have the greatest regard for the value of this sort of creation, for I think it brings a close-up feeling of intense believability to a young mind. And theatre of this kind, which I have been creating for about ten years now, seems to me to link the art of film and television with living theatre. It allows room for aesthetic fantasy but employs a terrific load of reality. It is this combination which proves such a vital factor. Quite a lot of drama created partly by the child, partly polished and guided by adults, has been creeping into our television programmes lately, and it is interesting to see that the public find that there is an interest for them in a subject that is often considered to be unimportant. It is the old reasoning about the difference between childishness and childlike and traditional use of such remarks as 'child's play'. The time is passing when play was considered unimportant, but the attitude dies hard.

If you have had time or opportunity to follow my main theory on the difference between personal and projected play, which is an added factor of importance, it will be seen that we are really dealing with the deepest parts of emotional education, and if we are to proceed in a world so often concerned with civilisation, in its broadest sense, we must take account in a much more scientific way of all forms of manifested and primitive behaviour for the benefit of up and coming people and up and coming nations, so that the task of building confidence, giving enlightenment and strengthening personalities unto the realm in which they can take proper responsibility, may be achieved.

I hope that these few considerations may be of some value to your study.

Every good wish

Yours sincerely,
PETER SLADE
Drama Adviser

Mr P. Doll,
Teaching Assistant,
600 North Park Street—room 101
Madison,
Wisconsin 53706,
U.S.A.

Further Reading

By PETER SLADE
the Author of this book:

CHILD DRAMA, University of London Press, 1954. (Presents the whole philosophy of an art form, of education through drama, its value in and out of school and how it should affect presentation of theatre for children. *Many Illustrations.*)

INTRODUCTION TO CHILD DRAMA, University of London Press, 1958. (Shortened version of the above with a little additional suggestion on Social Drama in Secondary Education. Also includes some illustrations of drama and dance drama as above.)

DRAMATHERAPY AS AN AID TO BECOMING A PERSON, Guild of Pastoral Psychology, 1959. Mailborough Court, 109 Lancaster Gate, London W.2. (Short outline of the approach with ten direct examples of case work.)

EEN INLEIDUNG TOT KINDERTONEENSPEL. Introduction to Child Drama, translated into Dutch by J. Van der Ster, Muusses, 1965.

CHILD DRAMA AND ITS VALUE IN EDUCATION, Educational Drama Association, 1967. (Talk at first Conference Course on Drama organised by Welsh Department for Education and Science at the University, Bangor. *Obtainable c/o Education Office, Birmingham, England.*)

ST PATRICK, Educational Drama Association, 1967. (A play based on a radio version, broadcast before the war but now rearranged for arena theatre presentation, with notes and suggestions, comic and serious and suitable large or small cast for older children and adults. *Obtainable c/o Education Office, Birmingham, England.*)

Contributions to Creative Drama, Magazine of the Educational Drama Association. (Many articles and discussions from 1949 onwards on children's play, therapy, Adventure Playgrounds, dance drama, Drama Centres, Theatre for Children, personality training and experimental adult theatre. *Obtainable from Charles Marshall, 68 Dalbury Road, Hall Green, Birmingham.*)

BY OTHER AUTHORS

The following are concerned with the same subject or closely connected ones, and, amongst much other valuable information, give reference to the work outlined in this book.

COGGIN, PHILIP. *Drama and Education,* Thames & Hudson, 1956. (A valuable history of uses and views on drama from ancient times to our own, which includes detailed description of the Educational Drama Association and considerable generous analysis of the philosophy of Child Drama, with numerous quotations from the book.)

MCFARLAND, H. F. N. *Psychology and Teaching,* Harrap, 1958. (Draws attention to psychological aspects, analyses In-Flow and Out-Flow as described in Child Drama and commends the discipline within a free method.)

SIKS, GERALDINE BRAIN. *Creative Dramatics, An art for children,* New York, Harper, 1958. (Amongst much useful information, with illustrations, has a section on work in other countries and mentions international recognition of work at Rea Street Centre, Birmingham, England, and includes illustrations of a children's group and of the Children's Theatre in action there.)

ORJASAETER, TORDIS. *Med Barn i Teater,* Oslo, Gyldendal Norsk, 1959. (Research in Theatre for Children and audience reaction based on 'report of film investigations, Slade and Child Psychology particularly Gessells' character traits'. Published in Norwegian but with most useful summary in English.)

BATCHELDER, M. and COMER, V. L. *Puppets and Plays (a creative approach).* Faber, 1959. (Analyses and contributes to description of Personal and

[298]

Projected Play as outlined in Child Drama. Much other useful information.)

TANSLEY, A. E. and GULLIFORD, R. *The Education of Slow Learning Children*, Routledge & Kegan Paul, 1960. (A useful short book on a general approach to the subject. Includes short description of the contribution of Child Drama in this field.)

BURGESS, C. V. *Discovering the Theatre*, University of London Press, 1960. (One of a series of 'discovering'. A most useful short guide for young people. Mentions Slade as leading a movement for improvisation in schools and invites the reader to find out more about his work.)

TUCKER, KENNETH. 'Active Learning and Personality', *Special Education*, vol. 49, no 4, Special Schools Association, 1960. (Clear description of Personal development with valuable assessment of Child Drama as an aid in Special Schools. Illustrations of Children at Rea Street Centre.)

FISHMAN, MORRIS. *The Actor in Training*, Herbert Jenkins, 1961. (Useful handbook for amateurs. Speaks briefly of Child Drama as therapy but also as potential for training actors.)

COURTNEY, RICHARD. *Drama and Education*, Cassell, 1965. (Amongst other valuable descriptions of work and suggestions, includes generous recognition of the contribution of 'Child Drama' as a psychological approach to education.)

WILKINSON, ANDREW. *Spoken English*, Educational Review, Occasional Publication no 2, University of Birmingham, 1965. (Many useful views. Contains reservations and somewhat unsupported statements but admits Child Drama as being a contribution to education.)

HUDSON, JOHN. *A Chance for Everyone* (a progressive drama course for Secondary Schools) Book I, Cassell, 1966. (Assisted by the author of *Child Drama*, this series is based on that philosophy and therefore brings out the three main elements of imaginative drama, social drama and theatre. Each pupil's book is accompanied by a teacher's book where simple advice is offered for young teachers on guiding creations of those in their charge. A short gramophone record of children creating drama with John Hudson is included with the teacher's book.)

BOOK II 1968
H.M.S.O. 1968 Education Survey 2. Drama. Some interesting information. Mentions the historic role of Rea Street Centre and admits of the Educational Drama Association, as having made a great contribution to the teaching of drama.

The following books appear to be in sympathy. Some of them use the technical terms of Child Drama and its approach.

WILES, J. and GARRARD, A. *Leap to Life*, Chatto & Windus, 1957. (Many people have found this a useful book. Deals with an approach to Movement for Youth.)

SEALEY, L. G. W. and GIBBON, V. *Communication and Learning in the Primary School*, Blackwell, 1962. (A delightful and interesting book on a varied approach.)

PEMBERTON-BILLING, R. N. and CLEGG, J. D. *Teaching Drama*, University of London Press, 1965. (Gives many useful suggestions. A very practical book for secondary work.)

HODGSON, J. and RICHARDS, E. *Improvisation*, Methuen, 1966. (An approach to the subject closely connected with theatre).

WAY, B. Development through Drama, Longmans, 1967 (Expoundsfurther the philosophy of social drama. Many valuable suggestions.)

Now almost classics:
NEWTON, ROBERT G. *Acting Improvised*, Nelson, 1937.
Story of a School, H.M.S.O.
HUGHES, MEARNS. *Creative Power*, rev. edn, Constable, 1958.

For those wishing to undertake much wider research or investigation, it might be of interest to compare the simple self-found philosophy of this book, Experience of Spontaneity, with Jung, Stanislavsky, Moreno and Piaget for psychology, theatre, sociodynamics and education.